MARINA POLVAY is an internationally known cuisine consultant, food stylist, radio and television personality, writer, lecturer, teacher of gourmet cooking, and author of several other best-selling cookbooks. She was born in Siberia, the daughter of Prince Scherbatoff, and lived in many countries, including Russia, Austria, and Hungary, before settling in Florida. She continues to travel and teach cooking all over the world. Her many articles have appeared in such magazines as *Bon Appetit, Town and Country, Gourmet, Tropic, Travel Holiday,* and *Palm Beach Life.*

THE CREATIVE COOKING SERIES
Every recipe in each of our cookbooks
has been kitchen tested by the author.

BOOKS IN THE CREATIVE COOKING SERIES

All Along the Danube: Classic Cookery from the Great Cuisines of Eastern Europe, Marina Polvay

Authentic Mexican Cooking, Betty A. Blue

The Bread Baker's Manual: The How's and Why's of Creative Bread Making, Rosalie Cheney Fiske and Joanne Koch Potee

In Grandmother's Day: A Legacy of Recipes, Remedies, and Country Wisdom from 100 Years Ago, Jean Cross

Just Desserts: Fast But Fancy, Susan Katz

The Return to Natural Foods Cookery, Kathleen LaCore

The Orient Express Chinese Cookbook, Iris Friedlander and Marge Lin

Two Burners and an Ice Chest: The Art of Relaxed Cooking in a Boat or a Camper or under the Stars, Phyllis Bultmann

The World of Cooking: Recipes, Techniques, and Secrets of the Kitchen, Mary Owens Wyckoff

THE ENERGY SAVER'S COOK BOOK

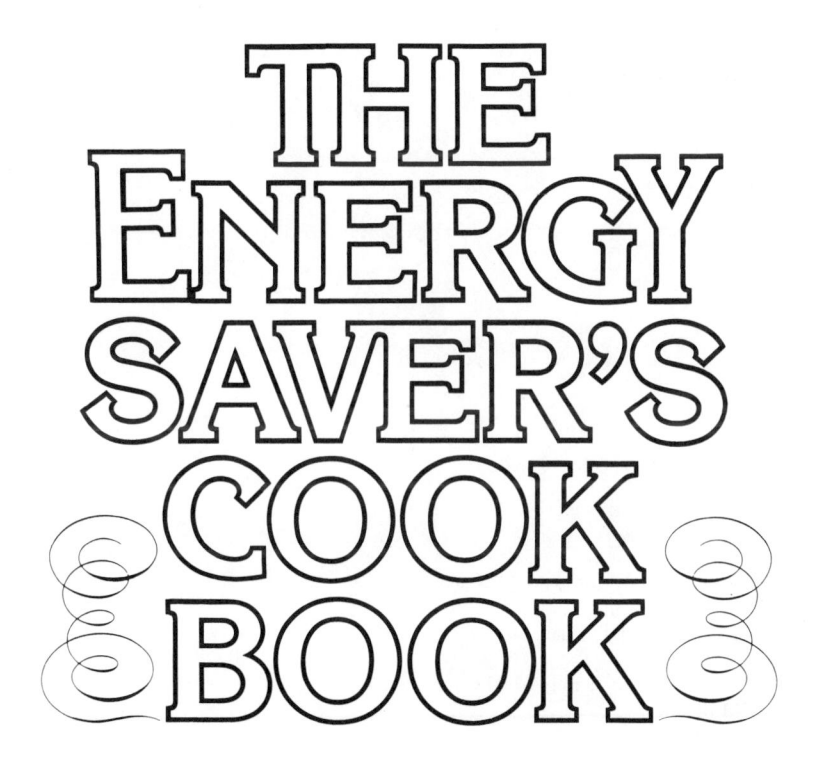

MARINA POLVAY

A SPECTRUM BOOK

PRENTICE-HALL, INC., Englewood Cliffs, New Jersey 07632

Library of Congress Cataloging in Publication Data

POLVAY, MARINA,
    The energy saver's cookbook.

    (The Creative Cooking Series) (A Spectrum Book)
    Includes Index.
    1. Cookery. 2. Energy conservation. I. Title. II. Series: Creative cooking series.
TX652.P65   641.5'8   80-15239
ISBN 0-13-277616-2
ISBN 0-13-277608-1 (pbk.)

Production supervision by Heath Lynn Silberfeld
Cover design by Irving Freeman
Manufacturing buyer: Cathie Lenard

© 1980 by Prentice-Hall, Inc., Englewood Cliffs, New Jersey 07632
A SPECTRUM BOOK

All rights reserved. No part of this book
may be reproduced in any form or by any
means without permission in writing from the publisher.
A Chelsea House Book

10 9 8 7 6 5 4 3 2 1

Printed in the United States of America

PRENTICE-HALL INTERNATIONAL, INC., *London*
PRENTICE-HALL OF AUSTRALIA PTY. LIMITED, *Sydney*
PRENTICE-HALL OF CANADA, LTD., *Toronto*
PRENTICE-HALL OF INDIA PRIVATE LIMITED, *New Delhi*
PRENTICE-HALL OF JAPAN, INC., *Tokyo*
PRENTICE-HALL OF SOUTHEAST ASIA PTE. LTD., *Singapore*
WHITEHALL BOOKS LIMITED, WELLINGTON, *New Zealand*

Contents

PREFACE, vii

1
Fireplaces and Franklin Stoves, 1
APPETIZERS, 11
SOUPS, 14
EGG DISHES, 18
FISH AND SEAFOOD, 22
POULTRY, 28
MEATS, 39
STEWS, 49
VEGETABLES, 61
PASTA, GRAINS AND RICE, 66
BREADS, 73
DESSERTS, 79

2
Outdoor-Indoor Grills, 91
FISH AND SEAFOOD, 97
POULTRY, 106
MEATS, 112
VEGETABLES, 126
DESSERTS, 133

3
Wood- or Coal-Burning Range, 135

APPETIZERS, 137
SOUPS, 141
SALADS, 146
FISH, 149
POULTRY, 159
MEATS, 163
STEWS, 169
VEGETABLES, 175
PASTA, GRAINS AND RICE, 181
BREADS, 186
DESSERTS, 190

4
Saving Energy in the Modern Kitchen: Conventional Stoves and Small Appliances, 201

APPETIZERS, 205
FISH, 210
POULTRY, 213
MEATS, 219
VEGETABLES, 228
BREADS, 231
DESSERTS, 234

5
Little-or-No-Cook Recipes, 241

APPETIZERS, 243
SALADS AND VEGETABLES, 247
DESSERTS, 256

6
Holiday Favorites, 269

APPENDIX: ENERGY SAVER'S DIRECTORY, 289
INDEX, 297

Preface

Not long ago, when our vocabulary suddenly became permeated with phrases such as "energy shortage," "fuel saving," "conservation of resources," a nation of somewhat wasteful people began to learn a new set of rules. About that time I had my own television show, "Cooking with Elegance," and suddenly my fan mail was inundated with letters from viewers asking how to save energy and beat the "crunch," how to cook over the grill and prepare food over an open hearth, instead of the usual how to peel hard-boiled eggs or bake crispy quiche. I received letters from northern visitors asking how to cook in a fireplace or on an old-fashioned wood-burning stove, and there were even requests to do research about grandma's kitchen and come up with some energy-saving techniques.

Luckily, I didn't have to dig deep to come up with some conservation-conscious cures for the impending crisis. I grew up in Budapest, Hungary, and lived in Salzburg, Austria, following World War II. In Budapest, the kitchen of our large rambling villa was ruled with a firm hand by our family cook, Brigitta. As a little girl I used to sneak down to the kitchen, and seated on a high chair with my elbows propped up on the white, scrubbed kitchen table, I would watch Brigitta perform her particular brand of culinary magic for hours. Our kitchen contained what for the early thirties was quite a modern gas stove and oven, but Brigitta preferred a relic of old-time cookery, a blackened wood burner with mysterious shelves, a gaping cavity of an oven and rings on top of the iron cooking surface. This greedy monster was stoked with logs by a perennially complaining scullery maid, who could in no way comprehend Brigitta's strange attachment to the obsolete iron workhorse.

Brigitta came to my grandmother's household as a young kitchen helper, later was sent to several cooking schools and became an accomplished chef. Her culinary indoctrination took place on a wood-burning stove, and when she reigned over my mother's kitchen and ultimately taught me everything she knew about cooking, it was too late for her to learn a new set of rules on how to use the "newfangled" gas stove.

By the time I was 12, the dear old soul would allow me to stoke the ancient iron marvel and help her prepare intricate gastronomic creations. In spite of mother's protests and scolding from ever-changing governesses, my adoration of Brigitta and fascination with culinary accomplishments prevailed, and the wood-burning stove was, from that time forth, no stranger to me.

Each summer our entire household moved to the great house at Lake Balaton in Hungary, where Brigitta presided over the so-called summer kitchen, a large, airy room with floor-to-ceiling windows on all sides to catch the cool breezes from the lake. There was a wood-burning stove here as well and an open hearth with all kinds of intricate attachments—pulleys, grates, tripods. Skillets with long handles, cauldrons, black kettles and other utensils—all suitable for open-hearth cookery—hung on walls around the fireplace. I was not allowed too close to the hearth, but could watch from a few feet away as Brigitta, with the help of two kitchen girls, suspended the black kettle from a specially notched bracket in the fireplace to cook a true country *gulyas*, which in Hungary is a thick, hearty soup and not a stew at all. Suckling pigs, 4 or 5 pullets or ducks strung out on a spit were roasted over the fire, which imparted to them incomparable outdoor flavor. Fish fresh from the lake were clamped between two wire grates, and Brigitta would toss just picked aromatic herbs onto the fire before roasting the fish. She also made authentic Hungarian *halaszle*, "fish soup," in a black kettle and even baked featherlight *pogacsa*, the most delectable rolls made with lard. Steamed puddings, stews and soups were cooked over the hearth. In early summer there were berries, mushrooms, tiny potatoes, baby carrots and sugar-sweet green peas to be preserved; in fall, juicy fruits, corn, tomatoes, peppers, cucumbers and cabbages. Village girls examined each fruit and vegetable, gently placing the good ones into flat baskets and neatly placing the blemished produce on the grass. Brigitta supervised this entire operation, as well as the peeling, chopping and slicing. The berries and fruits were made into jams, marmalades and preserves in huge black kettles over a wood fire, while Brigitta marched between the cauldrons like some sorceress of old, tasting and savoring the glorious results. The vegetables were put into jars, and all the fresh preserves, jams, compotes, fruit butters and pickles were stored away in the ice cellar.

When we fled Budapest during the last few months of World War II, my knowledge of over-the-fire cookery certainly came in handy. After a long march we landed in a refugee camp near Salzburg where, in spite of my youth, I became a kind of local heroine thanks to my ability to cook on an iron stove, in a hearth and even on a potbellied stove. And that is why when questions come up about energy saving, I answer them with a bit of nostalgia for Brigitta, who taught me so many things I thought I would never have a chance to use.

Recently, I had a daily radio show, and once again my mailbag was filled with questions about energy-saving tips and cooking on a grill, in a fireplace, Franklin

PREFACE

stove or on an old-fashioned iron stove. As a result of answering these queries, with my first-hand knowledge and some research into modernized ways with ancient cooking techniques, I became really involved with energy saving from a cuisinière's point of view—how to cook with the "newfangled gadgets," how to prepare all kinds of delicious dishes on an outdoor grill and how to adapt a good old-fashioned fireplace to modern cookery. I also discovered that in many parts of this country—especially because of the severity of recent winters—people are buying and installing wood-burning stoves as well as adapting their fireplaces for cooking purposes, and they're stocking up on all kinds of modernized counterparts of early American accessories. The most popular old-new cooking appliance seems to be the Franklin stove, which can be readily installed anyplace where a ventilation pipe can be run through a wall or window or even placed into an existing fireplace. I also discovered there are many utensils, brackets, grills, pots and pans that can be attached to a fireplace or Franklin stove for a true old-fashioned cooking experience. The foundries, which for many years were relegated to manufacturing primarily decorative items for fireplaces, are now going full blast producing iron cooking stoves with all kinds of modern improvements including thermometers, water heaters and warming drawers.

I began adapting recipes for cooking outdoors and indoors on hibachis, braziers, Mongolian hotpots, and outdoors on charcoal barbecues and gas grills with independent gas tanks. I soon discovered that people need not forsake their favorite foods when electricity fails, gas is shut off or the energy shortage drives us to use alternative types of fuel. With a bit of ingenuity, patience, and pioneering spirit, a completely new culinary vista is yours!

1
Fireplaces and Franklin Stoves

There's nothing like the aromatic scent of a wood fire and the comforting sound of a slow-simmering kettle to warm the atmosphere of the home. For those of you fortunate enough to have a wood-burning fireplace, it is relatively easy, with a touch of adventurous spirit, to convert the hearth or adjust it for heating and for cooking over an open fire.

Many of today's houses have built-in fireplaces, but not all are functioning at full capacity. The opening may be too large or the flue too small. Be sure your fireplace is properly adjusted and maintained to maximize its efficiency and heat retention. Check out the flow of air, the ventilation and the flue. Investigate the best way to rig up your hearth for easy, old-fashioned cooking.

Cleaning the Chimney

If you haven't used your fireplace recently, have the chimney cleaned, or clean it yourself. It's a bit messy, but really not too difficult. First of all, line the bottom of the fireplace and the surrounding floor area with lots of newspaper. Cover your hair, wear sunglasses to protect your eyes and, if you wish, use a gauze mask over your mouth to prevent inhalation of dust and soot.

Using a long-handled broom wrapped in a soft rag or old towel or sheet, reach up the walls of the fireplace as far as you can, pulling down the dirt and debris with the broom. Then if you're still game, climb up on the roof and brush out the chimney and upper portion of the fireplace, pushing down the soot along the walls. You may need a longer pole for this chore. A heavy-bristled brush attached to a pole or rope may do the trick. Be sure when cleaning your chimney that the flue is wide open.

If all this seems a bit much, call a fireplace store or installation center and ask for a fireplace cleaner or old-fashioned chimney sweep complete with top hat, black frock coat, pewter buttons and tools of his trade.

Buying a Fireplace

If your home lacks a hearth, you can take your pick of decorative models from early American types with brass trim to modern freestanding models with baked-on enamel finishes. Precast, freestanding fireplaces may hang on the wall, be suspended from the ceiling or stand alone. Some are cone-shaped or even circular in design and are mounted on legs or on a base of brick or stone.

Installing a Fireplace

All fireplaces must be connected to a chimney and vented to the outside, which requires cutting a hole in the ceiling and roof or through the wall. Fire stops must be placed at intermittent levels, and there should be a rain cap on top of the protruding chimney. Be sure that the installation complies with your local fire codes; an improperly insulated fireplace or chimney can be a dangerous hazard.

The side walls of the fireplace should be constructed in such a manner as to project heat into the room, and the back wall should slant forward just a bit. The chimney must be high enough to provide a good draft. Chimney and pipe must be clean inside to avoid blockage and backup of smoke and soot.

As soon as your fireplace is installed, carefully read any accompanying instruction booklets to find out everything you need to know about the draft, flue and damper. Fireplaces draw air and have drafts that must be adjusted to burn properly.

An existing fireplace that is not functioning well can be improved by reshaping the inner walls or by installing one of the new devices available on the market that retain and circulate the heat produced by a fire.

Fireplace Grates

Modern, warm-air grates are a good investment because they direct heat into the room and distribute warmth where needed. Most fireplaces roast you on one side while you're chilled with a cold draft on the other. Uneven heating not only wastes fuel, but also smokes up cooking utensils and may even burn your food in the skillet.

A regular cast-iron grate placed into the fireplace to hold the logs allows air to circulate around the wood. Today special warm-air grates are manufactured that are made of open pipes and a blower; they not only hold the logs, but draw in cold air and blow it out warmed into the room.

Other devices may be attached to the water-heating system to increase heat in radiators, thereby reducing the load on the boiler and saving precious fuel. There are also ducts that may be installed to ventilate the fireplace without losing heat, and all kinds of heat-exchange devices, shields, and glass screens.

Wire screens and other protective, often decorative implements are a "must" for any fireplace.

Buying Fuel: Wood and Charcoal

A good hot fire for cooking can be made with either wood or charcoal. Wood catches fire easily and burns with a clean, high flame, which varies with the draft and type of wood used.

Hard woods, such as oak, maple, apple and birch burn the longest, and are the most desirable. It is economical and convenient to buy wood in cords—stacks 4' high × 4' wide × 8' long—or half cords if you're short on storage space. The length of the logs depends on the size of your fireplace and grate. Be sure you buy to fit.

To burn well, wood for fireplaces, Franklin stoves or iron wood-burning stoves should be seasoned, that is completely dry. Green, or unseasoned wood, however, is often indistinguishable to the novice, so be cautious. Green wood will sputter, smoke and burn poorly. It's always a good idea to leave some of last year's logs around. That way you can use those up while any newly purchased, unseasoned wood is drying out.

Don't forget to order kindling for starting a fire when you buy your wood. It's relatively inexpensive and is usually sold in sacks or bundles. Pine kindling, which is most popular, should be used sparingly. Too much burning of pine coats your chimney with creosote, which is a major cause of chimney fires. One of the best kindlings is made of rolled newspapers: take six or seven sheets and roll them crosswise; secure the roll with a wire. Place three or four rolls into the fireplace and light with a match. When they begin to blacken but still don't emit any flames, place a little split kindling on top, and you're ready to add your logs.

If you prefer to use charcoal, hardwood briquettes are best. Place them securely, not too close to the edge of the fireplace, so they will not spill out. Be especially sure, when burning charcoal indoors, that your fireplace is drawing properly and you have adequate ventilation. Otherwise the fumes can be dangerous to your health. Never use lighter fluid to start a charcoal fire in your fireplace; it can spill over onto the floor and cause a fire.

Accessories and Utensils for Fireplace Cooking

Although an open fire may seem intimidating at first, today convenient attachments, grills, brackets, tripods, pots and pans are available that can make fireplace cooking almost as comfortable as the familiar backyard barbecue. Many fireplace shops and foundries carry cooking accessories for both fireplaces and Franklin stoves. The most versatile is a solid cast-iron grill with permanent brackets that attach to the wall of the fireplace or to the grate. The brackets have notches so that the grill can be adjusted to different cooking heights. You can cook by placing your pot on the grill or barbecue food directly on the grill. Another handy attachment is an adjustable bracket with a swing-out arm on which to suspend a large pot or kettle. A third option is a large tripod that fits right over the grate. However, this is not adjustable and makes temperature adjustment a bit trickier.

The proper cookware also simplifies open-fire cooking as well as maximizes heat retention, economizing on fuel. Stainless steel pots and pans with copper bottoms, heavy cast aluminum and copper pots lined with tin, cast-iron lined with enamel, and non-stick cookware are totally unsuitable for open-fire cookery. The best utensils are heavy, black cast-iron pots and pans. Choose from the large assortment available to best suit your needs.

Aside from various sized saucepans and skillets, there are several specialized utensils that are especially useful. A large, cast-iron skillet with high sides, similar to a chicken fryer, will serve well in preparing meat, chicken and fish recipes. It's worth investing in a cast-iron Dutch oven with a special rimmed lid onto which hot coals are placed to provide heat from above. It's indispensable for baking, and marvelous for soups, stews, all kinds of casseroles and vegetable and bean dishes, as well as for deep frying and steaming. A 9" cast-iron frying pan with lid is excellent for sautéing or frying seafood, meat and eggs, and you may also use it for baking some of the over-the-fire breads. A good quality cast-iron wok is ideal for stir-frying, steaming and many other uses, and a griddle with a grease drain works well over the fire for a variety of uses.

For baking, you will also need a round 2½" to 3" high cake pan; and a metal trivet or two or three flan rings in assorted sizes. Depending on your needs, you may also want a good cast-iron loaf pan or muffin pan.

You'll also want to equip your modern, old-fashioned kitchen with a hinged wire basket or rack for broiling hamburgers and fish over the coals and an assortment of kitchen implements, such as a fork, tongs, pancake turner and spoon—all with long, insulated handles. Use a large paint brush with handle as a baster, invest in asbestos potholders or mitts and have plenty of heavy-duty aluminum foil on hand.

Many modern recipes may be easily converted to cooking in a fireplace when using cast-iron utensils, which maintain steady, evenly distributed heat, but remember, the temperature cannot be adjusted at will. Equip yourself with a meat thermometer, a high-quality oven thermometer and a candy or deep-frying thermometer to help. Through trial and error, you will learn the tricks of adding a log when necessary or pushing away some hot coals, or perhaps adjusting the level of your grill.

How to Season and Care for Your Iron Pots

It is difficult to prevent iron pots and pans, as well as woks, from blackening or burning when one is cooking over an open fire. Rub the outside of the pots and pans or wok with a little detergent before cooking. You will discover that the job of cleaning is much easier.

Most pots, pans and woks are sold with seasoning instructions, which should be followed carefully, even if they have been "preseasoned." "Preseasoning" usually means that there is

FIREPLACES AND FRANKLIN STOVES

no protective coating to be removed and applies to plain iron, not the polished utensils, which come with their own instructions. Some iron pots are sold completely preseasoned and ready to cook, but these are not readily available. However, it's worth inquiring where you can obtain them.

To season most utensils, place on a low fire, add 2 Tbs. lard, shortening or oil, and spread the melted grease evenly over the entire surface using a pastry brush or wooden spoon. Remove from heat and, with a paper towel, continue rubbing in the grease all over the inside surface. Then, using another paper towel, wipe off excess fat. If the towel shows too much black, scrub the pot with a mild detergent and a bit of salt. Wipe dry, then repeat the greasing process. You must rub quite a lot of grease into the surface of the pot to prevent sticking.

After each use, wash the pots with mild detergent. Never scrub with abrasive powders or iron pads. When the pot is dry, coat the inside lightly with oil, then wipe clean. If your pots, pans or wok show rust spots, you may have scrubbed too hard or the liquids have run over and you have forgotten to wipe the outside. In this case you may use steel wool to scour the pan inside and outside, then coat the inside with oil, heat on low flame, wipe clean and coat the outside with detergent again.

Building a Fire

To start a fire easily, purchase a "fire-starter brick," if available, in a fireplace or mantel shop. Place your wood kindling or rolled-up newspaper on top of the small brick and ignite it with a long match. When it catches, add your logs in a pyramid formation, being careful not to smother the fire. Once the logs are burning well, spread them out to the cooking surface you desire.

Following is some helpful information about fires and fireplaces courtesy of the Atlanta Stove Works, Inc.

TO BUILD A FIRE

Warning: "Never use gasoline or a lighting fluid."

1. *Open the damper.*

2. *Place the paper and/or kindling in the grate basket.*

3. *You can get a better chimney draft with a warm flue. Hold a lighted roll of paper in the opening as near as you can to the flue opening inside the fireplace.*

4. *Then light the fuel in the grate. Add fuel, carefully at first to avoid smothering the fire. When the fire is going well, fuel may be added in the amount desired. (By fuel we mean kindling or newspapers.)*

5. *You can control the rate of burning by moving the damper or closing the front doors in a Franklin stove. Never close the doors when a large fire is burning.*

6. *Always use a firescreen to prevent sparks from entering the room.*

IF FIREPLACE SMOKES, CHECK THE FOLLOWING:

Incorrect Chimney
1. Chimney should extend at least 3 feet above the highest point where it passes through the roof. It should also be at least 2 feet higher than any portion of the building within 10 feet.
2. The fireplace chimney should have no other appliances attached to it. All unused openings and the clean-out door at the chimney base should be sealed.
3. The draft or "drawing" of the fireplace is fully dependent on the chimney. A chimney must be high enough and warm enough to provide draft. Adding chimney height should improve draft.

Air Supply
1. A tightly constructed home with well-fitting windows, weather stripping and storm sash has little air infiltration. No air will move up a chimney unless air enters the room containing the fireplace. A tight house should have a fresh air intake at least as large as the fireplace flue area. If there is no air intake in the room with the fireplace, air must be provided through open windows and doors when the fireplace is operating.
2. Ventilating fans move large volumes of air. If normal air infiltration is not great enough to satisfy the needs of a fireplace and ventilating fan, air will be drawn down the chimney creating a smoking condition. The fresh air intake must provide enough for both.
3. A furnace or boiler also requires an air supply for proper burning. This air must be provided in addition to the fireplace and other needs.

Helpful Hints
1. Starting a fire in a cold room tends to produce smoke while the chimney is cold. When the chimney warms up, the smoking should stop.
2. Fires should be built to the rear of the unit.
3. When adding fuel make sure that the damper is open.
4. The use of the grate basket promotes a better fire and minimizes smoke.

Other Conditions That May Cause Problems
1. Pipe inserted too far into chimney opening.
2. Pipe obstructed with soot.

The Franklin Stove

Benjamin Franklin wrote, "a penny saved is a penny earned" and, perhaps to prove his words, invented this stove in 1740.

As an alternative to the open fireplace, the modern Franklin stove combines the comfort of a heating unit with the old-fashioned charm of a hearth. It saves energy by providing heat and serves as an excellent means of cooking as well. The Franklin is usually made from solid, durable cast iron and is equally attractive with casual or more formal decor.

A Franklin stove may be installed into an existing fireplace by either adding a metal panel to the fireplace opening or by inserting a stovepipe directly up into the area of the chimney flue. A fireplace that is poorly vented or that leaks when in use can be readily altered by the installation of a Franklin stove with a metal chimney and proper flue.

If you don't own a fireplace, or prefer a freestanding look, your stove can be hooked up to an existing masonry chimney as long as a proper chimney connector is fitted and sealed with a fireproof substance such as asbestos or furnace cement. Stoves may be hooked up to prefabricated chimneys installed through the ceiling, wall or window. Stovepipe is available in a number of materials, the most popular being galvanized or heavy sheet metal. The heavier sheet metal is recommended as being less likely to collect soot and creosote or to burn out quickly. Although it may be more expensive initially, it will be more economical in the long run because of its durability.

According to specifications, the top of your chimney should be at least two feet above the rooftop and, according to the eminent Mr. Franklin, a "chimney should be put on the south side of the house where it is warmed by the sun and shielded from the chilling north winds."

Your Franklin stove can be vented from the top or back to make installation simpler, and a cast-iron basket-type grate is usually included, which can burn either wood or coal. Franklin's fire may be readily controlled by an easy-to-reach damper on the vent pipes.

A very important accessory for the Franklin stove is a fire screen, and there is one made to fit every size of this stove. A heat shield kit is also available for all models. This includes a rear firebox heat shield plus insulation and an additional heat shield for the bottom of the firebox.

Pots, pans and other cooking equipment for the Franklin stove are the same as for a fireplace.

How to Cook Over an Open Fire

As soon as the logs are burned through and the flames have died down, you may start to cook. To boil or deep fry, use a hot fire—glowing logs with a very low flame still visible. To sauté or bake, use a medium fire—red-hot embers with no flame visible. To simmer, wait for the embers to turn gray—a low fire. Food will simmer slowly for a long time over a good bed of embers. However, there is really no way to regulate the fire exactly; you will learn from trial, error and experience. To raise heat, add a log or move pot closer to the fire. To lower heat, push a log or two off the fire, adjust distance of pot or wait a little while until the fire cools down. Don't be discouraged at first. Once you catch on to the art of open-fire cookery, you'll feel confident and eager to explore its possibilities.

There will be a few disappointments —soufflés are out; so are featherlight cakes and pastries. But a whole vista of interesting, new dishes will evolve from this modernized approach to ancient cookery with our up-to-date ingredients, utensils and improved techniques.

Our recipes may appear similar to recipes used for cooking with conventional energy and, in fact, most of them may be cooked on a conventional gas or electric stove, but they have been especially created and tested for cooking over an open fire. They are most appropriate for heavy, cast-iron pots and will come out even better, with all their old-fashioned charm intact, when served bubbling from a black kettle.

As a beginning fireside cook, you cannot expect to attach your Dutch oven or bean pot to the armature or to place a skillet on the grill over the fire and just walk away. You must stay with your pot most of the time, watch for flare-ups and have a pail of water handy as well as a flare-up quencher, which could be a water pistol or a straw whisk. A portable fire extinguisher is always good safety insurance when kept out of the food area and in easy reach of the cook.

Baking Instructions
Baking over an open fire is a bit tricky, so here are some pointers.

Use a cast-iron Dutch oven or high-sided pot which has a special rimmed lid* for hot coals by placing it onto an adjustable grate that is attached to a notched bracket of a fireplace or Franklin stove, or suspending it from a swingout arm that is also attached to the bracket. The same utensils may be used for baking by placing them onto a hibachi or barbecue grill.

To bake: Preheat your largest iron Dutch oven or pot with a cover over low heat for about 15 minutes. To test for heat, hold hand in center of pot about 3 inches above the bottom and count to 3. If you feel high heat on the palm of your hand you are ready to bake, and the temperature should be about 350°–375°. If you wish to be more accurate and double-check the temperature, get an oven thermometer, place it into the pot, cover and wait until the thermometer reaches the desired temperature.

Place an inverted pie pan or the rim of a springform or flan ring with a rack on top of it into the center of your pot

---

*If your pot does not have a lid, use double foil to cover.

to serve as a liner. Depending on your recipe, place loaf pan with bread or cake, small baking sheet with biscuits or cookies, muffin tin or round cake pan on top of one of the liners. Cover the pot, and if your pot cover has a special rim for coals place 6 to 8 hot embers or briquettes onto the cover. This will provide heat from above and equalize the baking temperature. It will also brown whatever you are baking evenly from the top. Do not lift the cover for the first 15 minutes of baking a cake or bread and carefully follow recipe instructions for other baked goods.

If cake, bread or other baked goods are browning too rapidly on the bottom, move a few coals away from the pot or push a flaming log aside to reduce heat and prevent burning. If the temperature on top is too high and cake or bread is browning too fast, remove a few coals from the cover using tongs.

If, when baking time is up, your bread or biscuits have not browned sufficiently on top because you do not have a rimmed cover, or possibly because the coals are too cold, cool the bread or biscuits for a few minutes, remove from baking pan and place top side down into the pot on an elevated ring covered with a grate for 3–6 minutes. Be sure the pot has cooled down, and in a few minutes your creation will be deliciously brown on top.

Read the recipes carefully when baking more delicate cakes. These may call for a bit of water in the bottom of the Dutch oven, which will evaporate quickly without actually steaming your cake. For steamed puddings, custards and flan, use a slightly different technique. Preheat your Dutch oven as directed above, place the liner into the pot and then pour in enough water to reach the top of the liner. Place the pan with pudding, flan or custard on top of the liner. Cover, but do not use coals on top of the rim. Look into the pot several times; the water should never boil but should simmer gently. If necessary, push a few coals or logs aside under the pot to cool down the heat, or you may have to add a few coals or stoke your fire if it is necessary to generate more heat.

The adage "practice makes perfect" certainly applies to Dutch oven over-the-coal or log-fire baking. Do try it, and don't deprive yourself of marvelous baked goods. Once you've developed the knack for this particular technique, you'll be happy that you took time to learn to bake without an oven, and you'll be delighted with the results as well!

Other Tips

Several recipes in this chapter call for rice as an accompaniment or cooked rice as an ingredient. The recipe on page 255 is quick and easy to do over the fire. Also, in recipes where macaroni, noodles or other cooked vegetables, eggs or sautéed ingredients are called for, they may be cooked in your usual manner but in a heavy pot over the fire. You may have to move logs around to generate more heat or reduce heat. To keep a cooked dish warm, wrap pot in foil and set on side of grill away from heat. All these techniques are learned by trial and error, but they do work—just have patience!

A number of foods—potatoes, vegetables, corn and fish among them—are excellent when wrapped in well-greased foil and baked right in the coals. After cooking open-hearth style for awhile, you may just come up with some inventive ideas of your own, as you step back in time to become a newfangled, old-fashioned fireside cook.

APPETIZERS

SWEET PEPPERS WITH GARLIC AND ANCHOVY SAUCE

8 green peppers
½ cup butter
¼ cup olive oil

4 cloves garlic, crushed
8 anchovy fillets, minced

Serves 6 to 8

Wash the peppers. Drop into a pot of boiling water suspended over a hot fire, reduce heat and simmer for 2 to 3 minutes. Take off fire and let stand in water for 10 minutes.

Cut peppers in half. Peel off skin, remove seeds and fibers and cut into narrow strips.

In a skillet on a grill over a low fire, heat butter and oil together, add garlic and sauté carefully without letting it brown.

Remove skillet from heat and add anchovies. Beat and stir with a wooden spoon. Return to grill over low fire and continue stirring and beating until the mixture is smooth and pastelike.

Place peppers into a serving dish and pour hot anchovy sauce over them. Cool and refrigerate. Serve with Italian bread or bread sticks.

NOTE: The sauce may be served hot in a fondue dish, over sterno heat. Sliced peppers, celery, mushrooms, cauliflower or bread cubes may be dipped into the sauce.

CHICKEN LIVER PÂTÉ

2 medium onions, chopped
2 Tbs. butter
1 Tbs. paprika
2 lbs. fresh chicken livers (do not use frozen livers)
½ tsp. salt
¼ cup dry white wine
¼ tsp. freshly ground black pepper

2 Tbs. melted butter
3 hard-boiled eggs, chopped
1 Tbs. chopped scallions
3 slices white bread with crust removed
¾ cup milk
1½ pkgs. plain gelatin
Pimientos, scallions, parsley and capers for garnish

Serves 6 to 8

In a large cast-iron skillet on a grill over a medium fire, sauté onions in butter until golden brown. Add paprika. Add livers and mix well (the livers should be coated completely with the paprika and onions). Cook livers for about 7 minutes. Add salt and wine and cook for another 3 to 4 minutes.

Cool livers slightly, place into a blender or food processor and purée, adding enough liquid from the skillet to make a smooth paste.*

Add the pepper, melted butter, chopped eggs, scallions and salt to taste; mix well. Soak bread in milk and press out slightly; add to liver.

Sprinkle gelatin over water in a small pot. Heat on a grill over a low fire until gelatin is melted. Add to livers. Pour into a bowl and refrigerate for at least 3 hours.

Serve on toasted rye bread, decorated with pimientos, scallions, parsley and capers.

*If blender or processor is not available, mince liver as fine as possible on a cutting board, using a cleaver or sharp knife.

SALMON MOUSSE

Poached Salmon
- ½ cup water
- ½ cup pale dry sherry
- 2 sprigs parsley
- 2 cloves
- 1 clove garlic
- 1 bay leaf
- 3 or 4 peppercorns
- 1 small onion, quartered
- 2 lbs. salmon steaks

Serves 6

To poach salmon, bring water and sherry to a boil in a skillet on a grill over a medium fire. Add remaining ingredients except salmon and simmer for 2 to 3 minutes.

Wrap each salmon steak in cheesecloth and place into the liquid. Simmer for 10 to 15 minutes, or until fish flakes easily. Push a few logs away to lower heat if liquid begins to boil. Remove fish from liquid and cool.

Flake cooked salmon with a fork.

Mousse
- Flaked poached salmon (above)
- ½ cup mayonnaise
- 1 Tbs. lemon juice
- 2 Tbs. minced scallions
- 2 Tbs. minced fresh dill or
  - 1 tsp. dried dill weed
- Salt and white pepper to taste
- 1 pkg. plain gelatin
- ¼ cup cold water
- ½ cup boiling water
- ½ cup unsweetened whipped cream
- 2 egg whites, beaten until stiff
- ½ lb. small cooked shrimp

Place salmon, mayonnaise, lemon juice, scallions, dill and salt and pepper into blender and purée until smooth.* You may have to blend small amounts at a time.

Soften gelatin in cold water; mix with boiling water and add to salmon mixture. Fold in whipped cream and beaten egg whites.

Oil well a fish mold or any mold you choose. You may use small individual molds if you wish. Place shrimp in bottom of mold. Pour salmon mousse on top and refrigerate overnight.

*If blender is not available, mince salmon as fine as possible or press through a sieve; then place in a bowl with other ingredients and beat with a whisk.

SOUPS

BROCCOLI AND MACARONI SOUP

¼ lb. salt pork, finely chopped
2 Tbs. olive oil
3 cloves garlic, minced
4 Tbs. tomato paste
7 cups chicken broth
½ tsp. salt
½ tsp. basil

¼ tsp. black pepper
⅛ tsp. fennel seeds
3 cups broccoli flowerets (or 2 pkgs. (10 oz. each) frozen broccoli flowerets)
2 cups short macaroni, cooked*
½ cup grated Parmesan cheese

Serves 6

Brown salt pork in a large pot on a grill or suspended over a medium fire. Add olive oil, garlic, tomato paste, chicken broth, salt, basil, pepper and fennel seeds. Bring to a boil, then push away a few logs to cook over low heat for 20 minutes.

Add broccoli, cover and cook for 5 minutes. Mix in macaroni and cook for 5 minutes longer. Serve with grated cheese.

*See Other Tips, page 9.

CREAM OF CELERY SOUP

3 cups finely chopped celery hearts
8 Tbs. butter
1 cup hot water
4 cups chicken broth
3 Tbs. flour
1½ cups heavy cream
2 egg yolks
Salt and pepper
1½ cups bread croutons

Serves 6

Place celery and 4 Tbs. butter into a large cast-iron pot with cover on a grill over a medium fire. Cook, stirring often, for about 5 minutes. Add hot water and cook until celery is very soft. Purée in a blender or press through a fine sieve into a bowl. Pour purée back into the pot. Add chicken broth and set aside.

In saucepan, melt remaining 4 Tbs. butter, add flour and stir well until smooth and bubbly. Add cream and cook, stirring continuously, until slightly thickened. Remove from heat and beat in egg yolks. Keep beating until very smooth. Add to pot and mix well. Season with salt and pepper to taste. Simmer over a low fire to heat thoroughly, but do not let soup boil. Serve in soup cups or bowls with croutons.

CHICKEN SOUP

- 4 quarts water
- 4 carrots, scraped and cut into 1½″ pieces
- 2 large onions, quartered
- 2 green peppers, cut in half
- 4 stalks celery, cut into 3″ pieces
- 3 sprigs parsley
- 4 scallions
- 3 sprigs fresh dill (optional)
- 3 cloves garlic, crushed
- 6 peppercorns
- 1 crushed bay leaf
- ½ tsp. rosemary
- Salt to taste
- 2 broiling chickens, cut into serving pieces
- 2 pkgs. (10 oz. each) baby lima beans
- 2 pkgs. (10 oz. each) green peas
- ½ lb. medium egg noodles, cooked as directed on package and drained*

Serves 6

Bring water to boil in a large cast-iron pot on a grill or suspended over a hot fire. Add carrots, onions, peppers, and celery.

Tie parsley, scallions and dill with a string and add to pot. Tie into a cheese-cloth garlic, peppercorns, bay leaf and rosemary and add to pot. Season with salt. Bring to a boil and simmer for 15 minutes. Add chickens to pot, cover tightly and simmer for 1 hour, skimming off foam periodically.

With a slotted spoon remove onions, green peppers, celery and seasoning bundles. Take out chicken and remove bones. Cut chicken into large chunks; return to the pot. Add lima beans. Cook for 10 minutes. Add peas and cook for 5 to 6 minutes longer, or until lima beans and peas are tender.

Adjust seasoning, adding more salt and pepper if desired. Serve in soup plates with chicken pieces, vegetables and about ½ cup noodles to each plate.

*See Other Tips, page 9.

MEATBALL SOUP WITH PISTOU

1 lb. ground beef
2 slices white bread, crumbled and with crust removed
1 egg
1 tsp. salt
¼ tsp. pepper
½ cup water
3 to 4 cups beef broth

3 cups cooked navy beans
2 onions, chopped
10-oz. pkg. frozen peas and carrots
9-oz. pkg. frozen cut green beans
1 cup tubetti macaroni
Pistou (*below*)

Serves 6 to 8

In a bowl mix beef, bread, egg, salt, pepper and water. Roll mixture into ¾" balls; set aside.

In a large kettle or Dutch oven on a grill or suspended over a medium fire combine beef broth, beans and onions. Simmer, covered, for 30 minutes. Add frozen peas and carrots, green beans and macaroni. When mixture simmers drop in meatballs a few at a time. Soup should not stop simmering. Simmer, covered, for 15 minutes, or until all vegetables are tender.

Add Pistou to the soup. Stir and heat until soup is very hot but not boiling. Serve with toasted slices of French bread.

Pistou

6-oz. can tomato paste
½ cup olive oil
5 cloves garlic, crushed
½ cup grated Parmesan cheese

½ cup chopped parsley
2 Tbs. fresh basil or 1 Tbs. dried basil
1 tsp. salt

In a small bowl blend all ingredients to a smooth paste.

EGG DISHES

EGGS FLORENTINE

5 Tbs. butter
3 lbs. fresh spinach, chopped
1½ cups light cream
¼ tsp. nutmeg
2 cloves garlic, crushed

Salt and pepper to taste
6 eggs
1 cup heavy cream
1 cup grated cheddar cheese
Dash of cayenne pepper

Serves 6

In a large cast-iron skillet with cover melt butter on a grill over a low fire. Add spinach, light cream, nutmeg, garlic, salt and pepper. Simmer, stirring often, over a low fire until the spinach is just tender.

Smooth the top of the spinach with a wooden spatula. With a large spoon make 6 indentations in the spinach. Carefully break eggs into the indentations, cover and cook over a medium fire for 3 minutes, or until a film forms over eggs. Move grill to a lower notch on bracket or add a log if necessary to raise heat.

In a saucepan heat the cream. Add grated cheese and pepper and stir until cheese is melted. Pour about 3 Tbs. of cheese sauce over each egg. Cover and heat the sauce for a minute or two. Serve immediately with remaining cheese sauce on the side.

EGGS BERCY

4 Tbs. butter
6 large eggs
Salt and pepper to taste

6 precooked breakfast sausage links
1 cup tomato sauce
½ cup minced parsley

Serves 6

In a large skillet on a grill over a low fire, melt the butter. One at a time, break eggs onto a small plate, and slide into skillet. Sprinkle with salt and pepper. Place sausages between eggs. Cover and cook for 10 to 15 minutes, or until eggs are cooked. Watch eggs carefully, they burn easily.

While eggs are cooking, heat tomato sauce. Pour hot tomato sauce around cooked eggs. Sprinkle with parsley and serve immediately with buttered toast or toasted English muffins which you have toasted high above the fire on a grill.

EGGS EN COCOTTE

2 to 3 Tbs. butter, softened
6 eggs
Salt and pepper to taste

6 Tbs. heavy cream, warmed
6 Tbs. finely grated Gruyère cheese

Serves 6

Butter well 6 small ramekins or cocotte pans. Break an egg into each pan. Place ramekins into a large cast-iron skillet. Pour hot water into skillet to create a *bain-marie*, being careful water does not spill into ramekins. Do not allow water to boil; it should just simmer gently. Cover skillet and cook on a grill over a low fire for 3 to 4 minutes.

Sprinkle eggs with salt and pepper and pour 1 Tbs. cream over each egg. Cover and cook until whites are set but yolks are still creamy, about 2 to 3 minutes.

Sprinkle 1 Tbs. cheese over each egg. Cover and cook for another 2 to 3 minutes, or until cheese is melted.

LLAPINGACHOS (ECUADORIAN POTATO PANCAKES WITH POACHED EGGS)

2 lbs. boiling potatoes, peeled (or use 3 cups ready-made mashed potatoes. Follow cooking directions on package)
¼ lb. butter
1 raw egg, slightly beaten
1 cup grated cheddar cheese
½ cup flour

Salt and pepper to taste
3 Tbs. peanut oil
1 large onion, chopped
3 large tomatoes, diced
1 chili pepper, minced (or less to taste)
6 eggs, poached or fried sunnyside-up on a griddle*

Serves 6

Cook potatoes in boiling salted water to cover in a cast-iron pot with cover on a grill over a hot fire until tender. Drain and mash in a bowl until smooth. Add 3 Tbs. of the butter, the raw egg, cheese, flour and salt and pepper.

Place a heavy iron skillet on the grill and heat the oil over hot fire. Sauté onion until just tender. Add tomatoes, chili pepper and salt to taste. Stir and cook until a thick sauce has formed; set aside.

In another iron skillet heat the remaining butter, drop the potato mixture by spoonfuls into the skillet and spread with a wooden spoon into the shape of pancakes. Brown pancakes on both sides.

Place on a heated platter. Spread some of the sauce on each pancake and top with poached or fried eggs. Serve immediately.

*Cook over medium fire regulating heat as necessary by adjusting height of griddle or moving logs around. Watch carefully.

FISH AND SEAFOOD

CACCIUCCO (ITALIAN FISH STEW)

4 lbs. assorted salt-water fish fillets or steaks, cut into 3" pieces	1 cup dry red wine
12 clams	1½ tsp. salt
30 shrimp, shelled and deveined	½ tsp. sweet basil
½ cup olive oil	½ tsp. red pepper flakes
1 cup onion, chopped	¼ tsp. oregano
3 cloves garlic, minced	2 Tbs. minced parsley
16-oz. can whole tomatoes, drained and chopped	3 Tbs. minced scallions
	Salt and pepper to taste
	Italian garlic bread

Serves 6

Wash and dry fish. Scrub clams under cold running water. Shell and devein shrimp.

In a large cast-iron pot on a grill over a medium fire, heat olive oil; add onion and sauté until tender. Add garlic, tomatoes, wine, salt, basil, red pepper flakes and oregano. Cook for 10 minutes.

Add fish, clams and shrimp. Cook for 10 to 15 minutes, or until fish and shrimp are tender. Add parsley and scallions. Stir gently but do not boil. Adjust seasoning.

Serve in soup plates with hot garlic bread which you have toasted on a grill high above fire. Bread burns easily so watch carefully.

SAUTÉED FILLETS OF SOLE

6 sole fillets, about ½ lb. each
1 tsp. salt or to taste
¼ tsp. white pepper
1 cup milk
1 cup flour

1 tsp. paprika
10 Tbs. butter
Juice of 1 lemon
1 lemon, thinly sliced

Serves 6

Sprinkle fillets with salt and pepper. Pour milk into a shallow pan. Place fillets into pan and turn a few times.

Combine flour and paprika and dredge fillets in flour.

Melt 6 Tbs. of the butter in a large cast-iron skillet on a grill over a hot fire until just golden brown. Brown fillets in butter on both sides. Remove to a heated platter.

Add remaining 4 Tbs. butter and the lemon juice to the skillet and cook for 1 to 2 minutes; pour over fish. Serve immediately garnished with lemon slices.

SHAD PROVENÇALE

6 shad fillets, cut into 4" pieces
Salt and pepper to taste
⅓ cup olive oil
3 cloves garlic, crushed
1 tsp. crushed fennel seed
1 Tbs. minced parsley

½ cup cognac
1 lemon, thinly sliced
1 lb. spinach with stems removed—washed, drained and chopped

Serves 6

Sprinkle fillets with salt and pepper.

In a bowl combine oil, garlic, fennel seed, parsley and cognac; beat with a whisk. Pour ½ of the mixture into a large cast-iron skillet. Place ½ the lemon slices into the skillet; arrange the shad fillets over the lemon. Spread spinach over the fish, sprinkle with salt and pepper and pour the remaining seasoned oil mixture over the spinach.

Cover tightly, place on a grill over a low fire and cook for about 1½ hours.* Add a little water if needed and scrape with a wooden spatula under the fish to prevent sticking.

Test fish for doneness often. When it flakes easily it is done. Cooking time may be more or less than the estimated 1½ hours.

Serve garnished with remaining lemon slices.

*If you wish, bake the fish in an au gratin pan in a 350° oven covered with foil for 1 hour.

SHRIMP BOILED IN BEER

2 lbs. medium shrimp
2 bottles or cans (12 oz. each) beer
1 clove garlic, peeled
2 tsp. salt
½ tsp. thyme
2 bay leaves
1 tsp. celery seed
1 Tbs. chopped parsley
⅛ tsp. cayenne pepper
Juice of ½ lemon
Melted butter, lemon juice and Tabasco sauce to taste

Serves 4

Wash shrimp but do not remove shells.

In a large pot on a grill or suspended over a hot fire combine beer with garlic, seasonings and juice of ½ a lemon. Bring to a boil and add the shrimp. Return to a boil and simmer, uncovered, for 2 to 5 minutes, depending on the size of the shrimp.

Drain and serve hot with plenty of melted butter seasoned with lemon juice and Tabasco sauce; or cold with mayonnaise or shrimp sauce. The shrimp may be shelled and deveined before serving, if you wish.

SHRIMP CREOLE

24 to 30 large shrimp, shelled and deveined
½ tsp. salt
½ cup olive oil
3 cloves garlic, mashed
1 cup heavy cream
½ tsp. oregano
¼ tsp. white pepper

½ cup dry white wine
½ cup tomato sauce
1 Tbs. butter
1 Tbs. flour
3 tomatoes, finely chopped
Red pepper flakes to taste
¼ cup minced scallions

Serves 6

Split shrimp down the back and sprinkle with salt.

Heat oil in a large heavy iron skillet on a grill over a hot fire. Add garlic and cook for 1 to 2 minutes. Add shrimp and cook for 5 minutes. Add cream and cook, stirring constantly, until cream has almost cooked down. Add oregano, pepper, wine and tomato sauce.

Knead together flour and butter until smooth. Add to shrimp and stir well until sauce thickens slightly.

Add tomatoes, red pepper and scallions. Cook 10 minutes longer. Serve hot with white rice.*

*See Other Tips, page 9.

DEEP-FRIED STUFFED SHRIMP

16 large shrimp—shelled, deveined and butterflied, with tails left on
½ cup pale dry sherry
¼ tsp. salt
6 scallions, minced
2 Tbs. minced fresh ginger root
¼ lb. pork, sliced into julienne strips
¼ tsp. salt
2 tsp. cornstarch
¼ cup peanut oil

2 oz. black Chinese mushrooms* soaked in hot water, drained and sliced into strips
¼ lb. bamboo shoots,* cut into thin strips
1 cup Chinese cabbage,* thinly sliced
2 eggs, beaten
¾ cup flour
1½ cups peanut oil

Serves 4

Place shrimp into a shallow dish. Add 2 Tbs. of the sherry, the salt, scallions and ginger. Stir to coat shrimp with the ingredients and let stand for an hour.

In another dish marinate pork in the remaining sherry. Sprinkle with salt and cornstarch and let stand for 10 minutes.

In a wok or large, heavy skillet on a grill over a hot fire heat ¼ cup of the peanut oil. Sauté the pork, black mushrooms, bamboo shoots and cabbage for 2 to 3 minutes, stirring continuously. Cool completely and stuff butterflied shrimp with the pork mixture, pinching the sides together.

Mix eggs and flour into a medium-stiff dough. Roll out dough until very thin and cut into squares to fit shrimp. Wrap each shrimp in dough, leaving the tails exposed.

Heat remaining oil in the wok until it begins to smoke. Deep fry shrimp until golden brown. Drain on paper towels and serve hot.

*Available in most specialty or Chinese grocery stores.

POULTRY

BONED STUFFED CHICKEN

½ lb. lean ground chuck
1 egg
½ cup bread crumbs
½ cup evaporated milk
¼ cup minced onion sautéed in
    1 Tbs. butter*
½ tsp. salt
¼ tsp. pepper
¼ tsp. oregano
¼ tsp. basil

2 Tbs. brandy
1 clove garlic, crushed
1 large roasting chicken, boned
    (have butcher bone chicken or
    bone it yourself)
Lemon juice, salt and pepper to
    taste
¼ cup roasted pignoli (pine nuts)
½ cup dry white wine
1 tsp. paprika

Serves 4 or 5

Place the ground chuck into a bowl; add egg, bread crumbs and milk. Blend well, using your hand. Add onion, salt, pepper, oregano, basil, brandy and garlic. Blend well.

Spread boned chicken skin side down on a board. Sprinkle with lemon juice, salt and pepper. Place ½ the stuffing in the center of the chicken; sprinkle with pignoli. Spread remaining stuffing over the nuts. Roll up chicken into a cylinder. Wrap in double foil, but just before sealing pour wine over chicken; then seal foil.

Place wrapped chicken into a large cast-iron skillet on a grill over a hot fire. Cover and bake for 1½ hours or longer.

To test for doneness, open foil and slice a small piece of chicken. When chicken tastes tender, it is done. Sprinkle with paprika and bake opened for an additional 5 to 6 minutes, or until top is lightly browned. Cool for 5 to 10 minutes before slicing.

*See Other Tips, page 9.

CHICKEN WITH CHAMPAGNE

3- to 4-lb. whole broiling chicken
½ cup flour
Salt and pepper to taste
4 Tbs. butter
5 shallots, minced
2 carrots, grated
2 stalks celery, minced
½ lb. mushrooms, minced

3 cups champagne (leftover may be used)
¼ tsp. thyme
½ cup heavy cream
2 cups cooked sliced carrots*
12 to 14 mushroom caps,* sautéed in 2 Tbs. butter
2 cups cooked green peas*

Serves 4

Dust chicken with flour mixed with salt and pepper. Cook chicken in butter in a large iron pot with cover on a grill over a low fire, turning occasionally until tender but not browned, about 20 to 25 minutes.

Add shallots, carrots and celery. Cook until vegetables are very tender, about 15 minutes. Add mushrooms and cook until mushrooms are tender, about 10 minutes.

Pour champagne over chicken, cover and cook until chicken is very tender, another 10 to 15 minutes. Add thyme, cream and salt and pepper to taste. Simmer for 5 minutes but do not boil.

Serve garnished with additional carrots and sautéed mushroom caps, green peas and the sauce that forms around the chicken.

*See Other Tips, page 9.

CHICKEN IN THE POT

2- to 3-lb. broiling chicken, cut in ½
½ tsp. salt or to taste
3 onions, diced
6 Tbs. butter
1 lb. mushrooms, sliced

3 cups diced peeled potatoes
½ cup chicken broth
½ tsp. pepper
½ tsp. tarragon
3 Tbs. minced parsley
3 Tbs. minced scallions

Serves 6

Salt the chicken and set aside.

Place onions in a large Dutch oven or heavy pot. Place pot onto a grill or suspend it over a hot fire. Add butter and cook until onions are slightly browned.

Remove onions with slotted spoon. Add chicken and cook until barely tender, about 30 minutes. Return onions to pot and add mushrooms, potatoes, chicken broth, pepper and tarragon. Cover and cook for 1½ hours, or until chicken is very tender. Serve sprinkled with parsley and scallions.

BAKED CHICKEN

1 cup flour
1 tsp. salt
½ tsp. pepper
1 Tbs. tarragon
1 tsp. thyme
1 tsp. coriander

2 Tbs. minced scallions
2 broiling chickens, quartered
⅔ cup melted butter
Juice of 1 lemon
½ cup dry white wine
3 Tbs. minced parsley

Serves 8

Mix together flour, salt, pepper, ½ Tbs. tarragon, ½ tsp. thyme, ½ tsp. coriander and 1 tsp. minced scallions. Coat chicken quarters with flour mixture.

Pour ⅓ cup melted butter into a large cast-iron skillet or Dutch oven. Place chicken skin side down into the skillet or pot.

Cover and bake tightly covered on a grill over a medium fire for about ½ hour. In a small bowl mix together the remaining seasonings, scallions, melted butter, lemon juice and wine.

Pour ¼ of the butter mixture over the chicken. Cover and cook for ½ hour longer. If the pieces have browned on the skin side, turn them over; if they are still pale, cook for about 15 to 20 minutes longer, or until browned.

Turn chicken over and pour on remaining butter mixture. Cook for an additional ½ hour, or until chicken is very tender and underside has browned.

Place chicken on a heated platter, sprinkle with parsley and serve with pan juices.

CHICKEN À LA VICEROY

1 broiling chicken, skinned and boned
½ tsp. salt
5 Tbs. soy sauce
½ cup cornstarch
1 egg, well beaten
¼ cup peanut oil

1 small chili pepper, chopped
¼ cup fresh ginger root, minced
4 cloves garlic, minced
2 Tbs. vinegar (if available, use rice vinegar)
1 Tbs. sesame oil

Serves 4

Cut chicken into 2" pieces. Sprinkle with salt. Place in a bowl and add 3 Tbs. of the soy sauce. Set aside for 10 minutes.

Remove chicken from bowl and pat dry with paper towels. Dredge in cornstarch and coat with beaten egg.

In a wok or heavy skillet on a grill over a hot fire, heat peanut oil until it begins to smoke. Add chili pepper, ginger root and garlic. Cook for about 10 to 15 seconds, stirring continuously. Add chicken pieces and stir-fry for 5 minutes.

Add remaining 2 Tbs. soy sauce, vinegar and the sesame oil. Toss together and cook for 2 minutes. Serve immediately.

CHICKEN PROVENÇALE

3 boned chicken breasts
6 chicken thighs, with bone left in
2 cloves garlic, crushed
2 Tbs. olive oil or vegetable oil
½ tsp. ground fennel seed

2 Tbs. lemon juice
½ tsp. basil
½ tsp. salt
¼ tsp. white pepper
Sauce (*page 34*)
*½ cup clarified butter

Serves 6

Cut each chicken breast in ½ and remove skin from breasts and thighs.

Using a mortar and pestle or a small bowl and wooden spoon, crush together garlic, olive oil, fennel seed, lemon juice, basil, salt and pepper.

With a large pastry brush or your hands, brush chicken with seasoning mixture, place into foil and refrigerate for at least 2 hours. While chicken is in the refrigerator prepare Sauce.

In a chicken fryer or skillet with a cover on a grill over a medium fire, heat the clarified butter. Pat chicken dry with a paper towel, place into skillet and brown well on one side. Turn chicken over, cover and cook until very tender, about 20 to 25 minutes. Pour Sauce over chicken in skillet. Cover with foil and seal on all sides. Simmer on low heat for 25 to 30 minutes.

This dish may be frozen and heated right out of the freezer. To freeze, take out of skillet and wrap chicken and Sauce into heavy-duty double foil. To reheat, wrap another sheet of foil around chicken, place on a grill over a low fire and cook for 35 to 45 minutes. Serve with Rice Venetian Style, page 183.

*To clarify butter or margarine, melt in a small pot. Let stand for 10 minutes, remove the white sediment on top and pour off the golden liquid. Throw away white residue on the bottom.

Sauce

- ½ cup olive oil or vegetable oil
- 2 large onions, minced
- 2 green peppers, minced
- 2 cloves garlic, minced
- 1 cup minced parsley
- 1 cup minced fresh mushrooms, about 12 to 15 whole mushrooms
- 3 Tbs. minced capers
- ½ tsp. oregano
- ½ tsp. basil
- ¼ tsp. salt or to taste
- ¼ tsp. pepper
- 16-oz. can plain tomato sauce

Place oil, onions and peppers into a saucepan on a grill over a medium fire; cook until just limp, about 5 minutes. Add all the other ingredients except the tomato sauce and cook for 7 to 10 minutes. Add tomato sauce and cook for 10 minutes. Taste for seasoning.

CHICKEN ED DZONG

4 boned chicken breasts, cut into 1½" pieces
5 Tbs. peanut oil
Salt to taste
¼ lb. ground pork
1½ cups tiny cooked shrimp*
2 Tbs. cornstarch
2 Tbs. soy sauce
1 tsp. salt
¼ cup pale dry sherry
1 tsp. ground ginger
3 Tbs. chopped scallion
2 cloves garlic, minced
1 Tbs. sugar
2 Tbs. wine vinegar
2 eggs, well beaten
¾ cup chicken broth
1½ cups bean sprouts

Serves 6

In a wok on a grill over a hot fire, brown chicken on all sides in 2 Tbs. of the oil. Sprinkle with salt, reduce heat and cook until tender, about 25 minutes. Remove from wok and set aside.

In the same wok heat the remaining oil, add pork and brown thoroughly, stirring constantly to avoid lumps. Add shrimp and simmer for 2 minutes.

To prepare sauce, in a bowl combine cornstarch, soy sauce, salt and sherry. Mix into a smooth paste. Add ginger, scallion, garlic, sugar and vinegar; blend well. Add beaten eggs and ½ cup of the chicken broth.

In a separate pot heat the bean sprouts in the remaining chicken broth.

To assemble, add chicken pieces to pork and shrimp and toss together; heat. Reduce heat by raising pot away from fire or pushing a log aside, pour sauce over the chicken and stir. This must be done fast or the sauce will curdle and thicken. If the sauce is thickening too fast, add a bit more chicken broth or sherry. The sauce should have the consistency of buttermilk.

With a slotted spoon scoop out the bean sprouts and sprinkle over the chicken dish. Serve immediately.

Serve with white rice or fried rice or fried Chinese noodles.** You may prepare everything in advance and then assemble the chicken just before serving.

*You may buy these shrimp frozen and shelled. Defrost and they're ready to use.
**See Other Tips, page 9.

WALNUT CHICKEN

2 tsp. cornstarch	2 Tbs. Canadian whiskey
2 Tbs. pale dry sherry	1 tsp. sugar
1 egg white, slightly beaten	6 Tbs. oil
3 large whole chicken breasts, skinned, boned and cut into 1½" cubes	5 scallions, cut into 1" pieces
	½" fresh ginger root, minced
	2 garlic cloves, crushed
¼ cup soy sauce	1 cup coarsely chopped walnuts

Serves 6

In a bowl combine cornstarch, sherry and egg white. Add chicken and toss until well coated.

In a small bowl combine soy sauce, whiskey and sugar.

Heat an iron wok on a grill over a hot fire. Add 3 Tbs. of the oil. Stir-fry chicken for about 4 to 5 minutes, tossing and stirring with wok utensils or 2 forks. Remove from wok and place on a heated platter.

Add remaining oil to wok and stir-fry scallions, ginger and garlic for 1 minute. Return chicken to wok and continue cooking for 2 minutes. Add soy-whiskey mixture and cook quickly until sauce has thickened. Add walnuts. Serve with rice.*

*See Other Tips, page 9.

ROAST DUCKLING

4- to 5-lb. duck, quartered
3 Tbs. minced scallions
1 tsp. minced fresh ginger root
1 tsp. salt
3 pieces star anise,* crushed

2 Tbs. rice wine or pale dry sherry
1½ cups peanut oil
Po-ping (*below*)

Serves 4

If duck is frozen, defrost in refrigerator for 36 hours. Place duck into a bowl and add scallions, ginger root, salt, star anise and wine. Rub duck with the seasonings inside and out. Set aside for 2 hours.

Place duck pieces on a well-buttered wire trivet in a Dutch oven with rimmed lid. Cover and place a few hot coals onto the cover. Bake on a grill over a medium fire for 2 to 2½ hours, or until duck is very tender. Look into the pot to make sure the duck is cooking and browning properly, not burning. You may have to push some logs aside to reduce heat or add logs for hotter fire.

In a wok or large pot, heat oil and fry cooked duck until very crisp and dark brown in color. Remove from pot and slice before serving. Serve with Po-ping (Mandarin Pancakes).

*Available in specialty or Chinese grocery stores.

Po-ping (Mandarin Pancakes)
2½ cups unbleached all-purpose flour
1 cup boiling water
3 Tbs. sesame seed oil

Place flour into a bowl. Make a well in the center of the flour and pour boiling water into the well. With a wooden spoon, quickly mix flour and water into a soft dough.

Place dough onto a floured board. Knead gently for about 10 minutes until dough is smooth and elastic. Cover with a damp cloth and let rest for 20 minutes.

On a lightly floured board, roll dough to about ¼" thickness. Cut with a 3" cookie cutter into circles. Leftover dough should be rolled out again and cut into circles.

Place circles side by side on a board. Brush one half of the circles with sesame seed oil. Place unoiled circles on top of the oiled ones. Press firmly together. Roll each double circle into an even 6"-round disk, turning once while rolling.

Heat 1 or 2 ungreased, heavy 8″ to 9″ skillets or a griddle over a hot fire for 30 seconds and cook pancakes, turning them over as they puff up. Bake about 1 minute on each side, or until pancakes are speckled with brown on both sides.

MEATS

RIBS À LA BURGUNDY

4 quarts water
1 Tbs. salt
10 whole peppercorns
1 medium onion
4 whole cloves
4 cloves garlic
5 lbs. baby pork spareribs
2 cups red Burgundy wine
½ cup honey
½ cup apricot preserves

2 cloves garlic, crushed
1 small onion, grated
⅛ tsp. nutmeg
⅛ tsp. allspice
Salt to taste
¼ tsp. pepper
3 Tbs. wine vinegar
3 Tbs. brown sugar
1 tsp. cornstarch
1 Tbs. red Burgundy wine

Serves 6 to 8

Pour water into a large pot; add 1 Tbs. salt, peppercorns, whole onion stuck with cloves and 4 cloves garlic. Place on a grill over a hot fire and bring water to a boil. Add pork ribs. Bring to boil again, reduce heat by raising pot away from fire and simmer for 15 minutes. While ribs are cooking, prepare sauce.

In a saucepan combine 2 cups wine, the honey, apricot preserves, crushed garlic, grated onion, nutmeg, allspice, salt, pepper, vinegar and brown sugar. Bring to a boil, reduce heat and simmer for about 20 minutes, or until the liquid has been reduced to about 1½ cups. Taste for seasoning, adding more salt, pepper or vinegar as needed.

Mix cornstarch with 1 Tbs. wine. Add to the sauce and simmer for 2 to 3 minutes, or until slightly thickened.

When ribs are through simmering, drain well. Place ribs on a grill over a medium fire. Start with the underside down, baste with sauce and cook until brown; turn and continue basting and grilling until ribs are brown and tender.

NOTE: If using an oven, place a rack into a large baking pan. Place ribs with underside up onto the rack and baste generously with the sauce. Place under the broiler about 6" away from the heat and broil, basting often, until browned. Turn, and continue broiling, basting often until ribs are browned and tender.
Optional: Just before serving, in a small pot or ladle, heat about ⅓ cup brandy until lukewarm, ignite and pour over the ribs.

CUBED STEAKS

3 onions, diced
¼ lb. margarine or butter
2 lbs. cube steak, cut into 2" squares

1 cup flour
1½ cups water
½ tsp. salt
½ tsp. pepper

Serves 6

In a large cast-iron skillet with cover, sauté onions in ½ of the margarine on a grill over a low fire until slightly limp and glazed. Remove onions to a platter.

Dredge steak in flour on both sides. Heat remaining margarine and sear steak on both sides until lightly browned. Add more margarine if necessary.

Cover steak with onions. Add water, salt and pepper. Cover and cook over low fire for 2 hours.

GREEN PEPPER STEAK

1½ lbs. flank steak, trimmed of fat
1 Tbs. pale dry sherry
3 Tbs. soy sauce
1 tsp. sugar
2 tsp. cornstarch
¼ cup peanut oil

2 large bell peppers, seeded and cut into 2" long strips, ¼" wide
2 onions, cut into long strips, ¼" wide
4 slices fresh ginger root, about ⅛" thick
Sauce (*below*)

Serves 6

With a Chinese cleaver or sharp large knife cut flank steak lengthwise into strips 2" wide; then cut strips crosswise into ½" slices.

In a large bowl mix sherry, soy sauce, sugar and cornstarch. Add steak slices and toss to coat meat thoroughly. Marinate for 3 hours in the refrigerator.

Set a large cast-iron wok on a grill over a hot fire for about 1 minute. Pour in 1 Tbs. of the oil and swirl around in wok for 30 seconds, or until oil just starts to smoke. Immediately add peppers and onions and stir-fry for about 2 to 3 minutes, until tender but still crisp. Remove vegetables with a slotted spoon; set aside.

Add 3 Tbs. oil to wok and heat until almost smoking. Add ginger root and stir-fry for a few seconds. Add steak with marinade. Stir-fry over high heat for about 3 minutes, or until meat shows no sign of pink. Discard the ginger.

Return pepper and onion to wok and cook for 1 minute, stirring and tossing. Place steak and vegetables on a platter.

Pour Pepper Steak Sauce into wok. Cook, stirring continuously, for 1 to 2 minutes, or until thickened. Pour sauce over steak and vegetables on platter. Serve with rice* on the side.

*See Other Tips, page 9.

Pepper Steak Sauce
2 cups chicken broth
¼ cup soy sauce
1 Tbs. cornstarch

2 Tbs. sugar
½ cup pale dry sherry
Salt to taste

Combine chicken broth and soy sauce in a small saucepan and bring to a boil. Dissolve cornstarch and sugar in sherry and add to saucepan.

PEPPERY BEEF ROLLADES

6 thin slices top round or sirloin of beef, about 3" × 6" each
5 Tbs. peanut oil
2 to 3 tsp. coarsely crushed peppercorns
1 to 2 tsp. coarsely crushed coriander
1 large onion
1⅔ cup dry red wine
Salt and pepper
Filling (*below*)
1 egg, beaten
3 Tbs. peanut oil
1 cup tomato sauce

Serves 6

Pound meat with a mallet until paper thin. Brush generously with oil on both sides. Places slices side by side on foil.

Sprinkle meat generously with peppercorns and coriander. Hit with the mallet once or twice to push peppercorns and coriander into meat.

Slice onion into thin rings and spread over meat. Pour ⅔ cup of the wine over the meat, seal foil and refrigerate for 36 hours. Remove from foil and scrape off pepper and coriander. Sprinkle meat with salt and pepper to taste.

Place about 1 to 2 Tbs. Filling on the edge of each strip of meat and roll up tightly; secure with a toothpick.

Heat oil in large iron skillet with a cover on a grill over a hot fire. Dip open ends of rollades into beaten egg and sauté in oil until browned on all sides.

Pour remaining 1 cup wine over meat and simmer for ½ hour, pushing away a log if necessary to lower heat. Add tomato sauce and simmer for 20 to 25 minutes, or until meat is very tender.

Filling

⅔ cup minced cooked ham
½ cup bread crumbs
3 scallions, minced
½ cup minced parsley
1 egg
½ cup minced green pepper
⅓ cup dry red wine
1 tsp. allspice
Salt and pepper to taste

In a bowl combine all the ingredients and blend well.

MEATBALLS GÖTTEBORG

1 cup oatmeal
1 cup evaporated milk
1 lb. very lean ground chuck
1 lb. very lean ground pork
2 eggs
½ cup minced onion sautéed in 1½ Tbs. butter*
1 Tbs. Worcestershire sauce

Salt and pepper to taste
¼ tsp. basil
¼ tsp. thyme
⅛ tsp. nutmeg
2 cups sour cream
1 cup bread crumbs
4 Tbs. butter
2 Tbs. minced fresh dill

Serves 6 to 8

In a large bowl soak oatmeal in milk for 2 to 3 minutes. Add chuck, pork and eggs and blend well. Use your hands for best results. Add onion, Worcestershire, salt, pepper, basil, thyme and nutmeg and blend well.

Make medium-sized meatballs. Roll meatballs in a little sour cream, about 1 Tbs. per meatball, then in bread crumbs. Flatten the meatballs into patties about 1" thick.

Melt butter in a skillet with a cover on a grill over a hot fire and fry meatballs on both sides until nice and brown.

Five minutes before serving, top each meatball with about 2 Tbs. of sour cream. Cover and simmer over a low fire for 5 minutes. Sprinkle with dill and serve immediately.

*See Other Tips, page 9.

PICADILLO

1 medium onion, minced
1 green pepper, minced
¼ cup plus 2 Tbs. olive oil
2 lbs. ground beef
1 large tomato—peeled, seeded and chopped
1 clove garlic, minced
½ tsp. oregano
Salt and pepper to taste
⅔ cup chopped pitted green olives
½ cup chopped pimientos
¼ cup drained capers
⅓ cup dry white wine
A few drops of Tabasco sauce

Serves 6

In a large cast-iron skillet with cover sauté onions and pepper in ¼ cup olive oil on a grill over a hot fire until just limp. Remove with a slotted spoon and set aside.

Add 2 Tbs. oil to the skillet, add ground beef and cook, stirring constantly, until all the red disappears. Add tomato, sautéed onion and pepper, the garlic, oregano, salt and pepper. Simmer for 4 to 5 minutes.

Add olives, pimientos, capers, wine and Tabasco. Stir well and simmer for 5 to 7 minutes. Serve with white rice.*

*See Other Tips, page 9.

VEONA'S VEAL AND PINEAPPLES

4 Tbs. butter
6 center-cut veal chops, ¾" thick
Salt and pepper to taste
½ cup honey
1 cup tawny port

⅛ tsp. nutmeg
⅛ tsp. thyme
2 cups drained pineapple chunks
Fresh lemon juice

Serves 6

Heat butter in a Dutch oven on a grill over a hot fire. Brown veal chops on both sides. Sprinkle with salt and pepper.

In a bowl whisk together honey, port, nutmeg and thyme; pour over the chops. Cover and simmer for 4 to 5 minutes.

Add pineapple chunks to pot. Stir and mix until pineapple is coated with sauce. Sprinkle with salt and pepper to taste, cover and simmer, stirring occasionally, until the sauce has reduced and thickened slightly. If sauce thickens too much or caramelizes too fast, add more port and stir well.

Sprinkle chops and pineapple with fresh lemon juice. Simmer for 2 to 3 minutes and serve.

STUFFED PORK SHOULDER

1 fresh pork shoulder, boned
Salt and garlic powder to taste
½ lb. sliced bacon, finely diced
2 cups chopped onion
1 cup chopped green pepper
2 pkgs. (10 oz. each) cornbread stuffing, prepared as directed and cooled*

1 cup chopped parsley
3 eggs, well beaten
2 tsp. salt
1 tsp. poultry seasoning
½ tsp. pepper
Cherry tomatoes and parsley for garnish

Serves 6

Pull firm outer skin off pork. Trim surface fat to ¼". Cut a deep pocket in the meat. Rub all surfaces well with garlic powder and salt.

In a large skillet on a grill over a medium fire, fry bacon until crisp. Add onion and green pepper. Sauté until vegetables are tender, 7 to 10 minutes. Remove from heat.

Crumble cornbread. Add to skillet along with parsley, eggs, salt, poultry seasoning and pepper. Stir.

Pack stuffing firmly into cavity of pork. Place pork in a Dutch oven with a few hot coals on the cover and roast meat over medium fire for 2 hours, or until pork is completely cooked and tender.

Place pork on serving platter. Garnish with cherry tomatoes and parsley sprigs.

*See Other Tips, page 9.

SLICED PORK AND CABBAGE WITH HOT SAUCE, SZECHUAN STYLE

1 lb. boneless lean pork
1 scallion, cut into 2" lengths
¼ cup vegetable oil
2 cloves garlic, sliced
40 square pieces Chinese cabbage, about 2" × 2"*
2 green peppers, cut into 12 wedges

3 Tbs. soy sauce
2 tsp. sugar
1 tsp. Tabasco sauce or ½ tsp. red pepper flakes
1 tsp. cornstarch mixed with 1 Tbs. water

Serves 4 or 5

Cook pork and scallion in a saucepan in enough water to cover for 15 minutes; drain. Cut pork into 12 slices and reserve along with scallion.

Heat oil in a heavy iron wok on a grill over a hot fire until oil begins to smoke. Add garlic, pork, scallion, Chinese cabbage and green peppers. Sauté for 1 or 2 minutes over high heat.

Add soy sauce, sugar and Tabasco and cook for another 1 or 2 minutes. Add cornstarch mixture and stir until thickened. Serve hot.

*About 2 bunches Chinese cabbage.

SWEET & SOUR SPARERIBS

4 lbs. pork spareribs, preferably baby ribs
2 Tbs. soy sauce
1½ cups flour
1 tsp. salt
¼ tsp. pepper
1 tsp. garlic powder
5 to 6 Tbs. shortening
1 cup light brown sugar
3 Tbs. finely chopped fresh ginger root
¾ cup vinegar
1 cup water
1 cup pineapple juice
2 cups drained pineapple chunks, or crushed pineapple
1 Tbs. cornstarch

Serves 10

Separate spareribs into individual pieces. Sprinkle with soy sauce.

In a shallow dish, combine flour, salt, pepper and garlic powder. Dredge spareribs in the seasoned flour.

In a large cast-iron pot with cover on a grill over a medium fire, heat shortening and brown spareribs on both sides. Add brown sugar, ginger root, vinegar, water and ¾ cup of the pineapple juice and cook for about 45 minutes to an hour, or until spareribs are very tender.

Add pineapple chunks and stir well. Mix cornstarch with remaining pineapple juice and stir into pot. Simmer for about 5 minutes, or until sauce is slightly thickened. Taste for seasoning.

STEWS

PAELLA RUSTICA

1 tsp. oregano
2 tsp. pepper
2 cloves garlic, minced
2 tsp. salt
1 cup olive oil
2½- to 3-lb. chicken, cut up into serving pieces
¼ lb. baked or boiled ham, cut into small pieces
2 strips bacon, cut into small pieces
2 onions, chopped
2 green peppers, chopped
2½ cups rice, washed and drained
4½ cups boiling chicken broth (powder or cubes dissolved in boiling water may be used)
½ tsp. ground coriander
¼ tsp. ground fennel seed
1 Tbs. capers, chopped
½ cup tomato sauce
½ to 1 tsp. saffron threads
24 raw shrimp, shelled and deveined
1 lb. cooked lobster meat cut into pieces (rock or Florida lobster may be used)
10-oz. pkg. frozen peas
24 small clams or mussels
8 raw shrimp in shells, washed well
1 jar pimientos, heated in their liquid and sliced

Serves 6

In a small bowl combine oregano, pepper, garlic, 1 tsp. of the salt and 2 Tbs. of the olive oil. Crush with a wooden spoon and blend well. Rub mixture into chicken. Let chicken stand for at least ½ hour before cooking.

Brown chicken on both sides in 6 Tbs. of the olive oil in a preheated paella pan on a grill over a medium fire. Cook for about 10 minutes on low heat. Add remaining ½ cup olive oil, the ham, bacon, onions and green peppers. Cover with foil and cook for 10 minutes.

Add rice to chicken and simmer for 5 minutes. Add hot chicken broth, remaining 1 tsp. salt, the coriander, fennel seed, capers, tomato sauce and saffron. Cook for another 5 minutes.

Stir chicken and rice from top to bottom. Add shelled shrimp, cover and cook for about 20 minutes, or until liquid has been absorbed and rice is tender. Add more salt if necessary.

Add lobster and peas and cook for another 7 minutes, or until peas are tender.

Wash and debeard clams and steam them with remaining shrimp in a little water over a hot fire until clam shells open.

Add sliced pimientos to the paella. Place unshelled shrimp and clams on top. Decorate with more pimientos and serve piping hot.

KIDNEY BEAN CHILI

4 slices bacon, chopped
2 lbs. lean stewing beef, cut into ½" cubes
2 large onions, finely chopped
2 green peppers, finely chopped
3 cloves garlic, minced
2 Tbs. flour
2 cans (16 oz. each) stewed tomatoes
2 Tbs. chili powder, to taste
Salt
4 cups canned kidney beans

Serves 8 to 10

In a cast-iron kettle on a grill or suspended over a medium fire, cook bacon until crisp. Add beef cubes and cook, stirring often, until browned on all sides.

Add onions, green peppers and garlic; sauté with meat until peppers are just tender. Sprinkle with flour and stir well. Add tomatoes, chili powder and salt to taste; stir well. You may have to push aside a log or two to reduce heat. Simmer, stirring often, for about 1½ hours.

Add beans with their liquid. Cook for 1½ hours longer, until meat is so tender that it falls apart when touched with a fork.

BAYOU JAMBALAYA

3-lb. frying chicken
Salt and pepper to taste
2 Tbs. shortening
2 Tbs. flour
1 lb. smoked sausage, sliced and boiled in water for 5 minutes
2 medium onions, minced
1 large bell pepper, minced
3 cups peeled and diced tomatoes
1 clove garlic, crushed
1 lb. shelled shrimp, cut in half
3 cups water
1½ tsp. salt
½ tsp. thyme
½ tsp. Tabasco sauce
½ tsp. black pepper
2 cups raw rice
¼ cup minced parsley
½ cup minced shallots

Serves 8

Cut chicken into serving pieces. Season with salt and pepper. Melt shortening in a heavy iron pot on a grill or suspended over a medium fire. Fry chicken until brown; remove from pot, set aside.

Make a roux by adding flour to drippings and stirring until light brown. Add sausage, which has been parboiled and drained. Then add cooked chicken, onions, bell pepper, tomatoes, garlic and shrimp. Cook, stirring constantly, for about 10 minutes.

Add water, salt, thyme, Tabasco and black pepper. When water boils, add raw rice. Let mixture come to a boil again, then stir thoroughly to combine all ingredients. Cover and simmer for 30 to 45 minutes, or until rice is tender. Add parsley and shallots and stir lightly with a fork to mix. Cover and cook for 5 minutes. Serve hot.

FILÉ GUMBO

3-lb. frying chicken
Salt and pepper to taste
2 Tbs. butter
½ lb. lean ham, diced
1 bay leaf
3 sprigs parsley, chopped
1 tsp. thyme
1 large onion, chopped
2 quarts boiling water

2 quarts clam broth or oyster water
½ a red pepper (jalapeno or chili), seeded and cut in 2
Salt, black pepper and cayenne pepper to taste
3 dozen shucked fresh oysters
3 Tbs. filé powder*

Serves 4 to 5

Cut up chicken into small pieces. Sprinkle with salt and black pepper to taste. Put butter into a large iron soup kettle on a grill or suspended over a medium fire and when it is hot but not brown add ham and chicken. Cover and cook for about 5 to 10 minutes.

Add bay leaf, parsley, thyme and onion, stirring occasionally to prevent burning. When chicken is nicely browned, add boiling water, clam broth, red pepper, salt, pepper, and cayenne pepper. Simmer gumbo for about 1 hour.

When nearly ready to serve and while gumbo is boiling, add oysters. Let gumbo remain on stove for about 3 minutes longer, then remove pot from fire.

Have a large tureen ready, set in a *bain-marie*, or hot water bath, for once filé powder is added, the gumbo must never be warmed over or it will congeal. Gradually add filé to pot of boiling hot gumbo, stirring slowly to mix thoroughly; pour into a large tureen and serve with boiled rice.**

*Filé powder, an authentic Creole seasoning, is available in most specialty and gourmet stores.
**See Other Tips, page 9.

GUMBO LA BELLE MARIE

5 strips bacon, cut into small pieces
2 Tbs. olive oil
1 large onion, thinly sliced
4 stalks celery, sliced
2 green peppers, diced
2 cloves garlic, crushed
6 chicken thighs
6 chicken drumsticks
2 Tbs. Worcestershire sauce
1 tsp. thyme
1 tsp. salt or to taste
⅛ tsp. red pepper flakes or to taste
¼ tsp. crushed bay leaves
2 cans (16 oz. each) peeled tomatoes, cut up (reserve liquid)
1½ lbs. fish fillet (your choice), cut into 2" pieces
1 lb. medium shrimp, cleaned and deveined (fresh frozen may be used)
6 oz. king crabmeat (optional)
1 cup chicken broth
3 cups cut-up okra, or 2 pkgs. (10 oz. each) frozen okra

Serves 8 to 10

Place bacon into a very large heavy pot on a grill or suspended over a medium fire and cook for 5 minutes, stirring occasionally. Add oil, onion, celery, peppers and garlic. Cook until the vegetables are just limp.

Add chicken. Stir well, cover and cook, stirring occasionally, for 25 minutes.

Add Worcestershire, thyme, salt, red pepper and bay leaves. Add tomatoes and their liquid to chicken. Bring to a boil. Remove from fire and add fish, shrimp, crabmeat, chicken broth and okra.

Return to fire, bring to a boil, cover, reduce heat and simmer for 20 minutes. Taste for seasoning. Serve with crusty French bread.

STUFFED CABBAGE À LA CEVENNES

1 medium cabbage
3 Tbs. minced scallion sautéed in 2 Tbs. butter*
1½ cups cooked chicken,** ground
¾ cup cooked rice*
½ tsp. salt
¼ tsp. pepper
¼ tsp. oregano
1 clove garlic, crushed
1 egg, beaten
4 strips bacon
2 cups tomato sauce

Serves 4

Remove outer leaves from cabbage. Put into a large pot or Dutch oven with boiling salted water to cover; place on a grill over a medium fire and boil for 10 minutes. Remove cabbage and plunge into cold water; drain well. Reserve 4 to 6 leaves for decoration.

Prepare stuffing by mixing together scallion, chicken, rice, salt, pepper, oregano, garlic and egg.

With a sharp knife cut out a 3" to 4" piece from the center of the cabbage, leaving about 2" at bottom. Place stuffing into opening in cabbage.

Using white string, tie cabbage together. Place bacon criss-cross on top and wrap cabbage in well-buttered double foil. Just before sealing the foil, pour tomato sauce over the cabbage; then seal foil. Place cabbage right onto the grill and cook for 1 hour over a low fire. Be sure coals are gray and heat is low. Push away a log if necessary to lower fire.

After an hour turn foil package on one side for ½ hour, then on the other side for ½ hour. Make sure foil does not leak. If necessary, wrap in additional foil.

If you prefer baking the cabbage in a cast-iron pot or Dutch oven suspended over the fire, place a trivet or a skillet grill into the pot and you do not need the foil. Just pour in tomato sauce, place cabbage into the pot on top of the trivet and bake for 2 to 2½ hours, adding more tomato sauce or water as needed.

*See Other Tips, page 9.
**Such as leftover Chicken In The Pot, page 30.

CHOUCROUTE WITH SAUSAGE

24 small whole potatoes
½ lb. bacon, diced
½ cup chopped onions
2 bags (16 oz. each) sauerkraut

1 cup dry white wine
1 Tbs. caraway seeds
1 Tbs. paprika
1 lb. knockwurst

Serves 6

Boil potatoes in water to cover over hot fire until tender. Peel and reserve.

In a large heavy skillet on a grill over a medium fire, fry bacon until crisp. Add onions; fry until wilted.

Drain sauerkraut and rinse under cold water. Squeeze out excess water. Add sauerkraut, potatoes, wine, caraway seeds and paprika to skillet. Stir to blend well.

Cut knockwurst lengthwise and then cut each half crosswise. Add to skillet. Cover and simmer for 20 to 25 minutes, or until knockwurst are easily pierced. Stir occasionally.

PORK AND VEGETABLES

½ cup butter or margarine
2 lbs. boneless lean pork, cut into thin strips
10-oz. pkg. frozen whole baby onions
2 pkgs. (10-oz. each) frozen whole baby carrots

2 pkgs. (10 oz. each) frozen peas
2 cups apple juice
1 cup heavy cream
½ cup flour
Salt and pepper to taste

Serves 8 to 10

Melt butter in a large skillet on a grill over a medium fire. Add pork strips and brown well. Add frozen onions, carrots and peas. Pour on apple juice, cover and simmer for 20 minutes, or until vegetables are tender.

In a small bowl blend cream with flour until smooth; stir into pork and vegetables. Stir constantly over low fire until sauce bubbles and thickens. Add salt and pepper. Serve with broad noodles.*

*See Other Tips, page 9.

PORK PILAU

4 lbs. pork, cut into 1" cubes
5 strips bacon, cut into pieces
2 cans (16 oz. each) tomatoes, drained and chopped
3 onions, chopped
1 tsp. sugar
2 green peppers, sliced
1 hot pepper (jalapeno or chili)
2 cups uncooked rice
3 cups water
Salt

Serves 8

Place pork and bacon in a large heavy pot on a grill over a medium fire. Brown pork on all sides, stirring often. Pour off ½ the fat.

Add tomatoes and onions. Cook for about 10 minutes, stirring occasionally. Add sugar, green peppers, hot pepper, rice, water and salt to taste; stir well. Cook, stirring occasionally, for 20 to 25 minutes, or until rice is done and liquid has cooked down.

A HEARTY THICK STEW

6 Tbs. shortening
2 very large onions, thinly sliced
4 carrots, thinly sliced
4 stalks celery, thinly sliced
2 lbs. baby pork spareribs, cut into 2" pieces
2 lbs. very lean pork (shoulder or butt), cut into 1½" cubes

Salt to taste
¼ tsp. coarsely ground black pepper
½ lb. thinly sliced Polish sausage
1 lb. fresh green beans, sliced
3 large green peppers, sliced
4 tomatoes, thinly sliced
½ cup beef broth

Serves 6

Melt shortening in a heavy cast-iron pot suspended over a medium fire. Add onions, carrots and celery. Cook until just limp.

Place spareribs and pork into the pot and stir until meat is coated with vegetables. Sprinkle with salt and pepper. Cook for 1 hour, stirring frequently and adding a little water if needed.

Add sausage. Cook 25 minutes longer.

Add green beans, green peppers, tomatoes and beef broth. Adjust seasoning. Cook until the beans and peppers are tender, about 10 to 15 minutes. Serve with buttered noodles or white rice.*

*See Other Tips, page 9.

ALASKAN BEANPOT

5 strips bacon, cut into small pieces
1 large onion, chopped
16-oz. can sliced carrots, drained
2 cans (16 oz. each) whole peeled tomatoes, drained and cut up
½ tsp. salt
¼ tsp. pepper
¼ tsp. tarragon
¼ tsp. crushed bay leaves
1 cooked rabbit,* cut up
1 cooked wild duck,* cut up
1½ lbs. sausage, cut into 1" slices (use any sausage of your choice)
½ lb. ham cut into 2" slices (in Alaska, bear hams are used)
3 cans (16 oz. each) Great Northern or navy beans
½ cup pale dry sherry

Serves 6

Place bacon into an iron bean pot or Dutch oven on a grill or suspended over a medium fire. Cook until just beginning to crisp. Add onion and cook until limp but not browned. Add carrots, tomatoes, salt, pepper, tarragon and bay leaves; stir well. Add rabbit, duck, sausage and ham; cook for 30 minutes, stirring occasionally.

Drain beans well and add to pot. Stir well and cook for 1 hour, stirring occasionally. Add sherry, stir and cook for 15 minutes.

Bean pot is now ready to be served, but usually tastes better reheated the following day.

*Chicken and domestic duck may be used instead of rabbit and wild duck. Precook as in Chicken In The Pot, page 30.

VEGETABLES

ASPARAGUS WITH HOT BUTTER AND PARMESAN CHEESE

2 lbs. fresh asparagus
¼ lb. butter or margarine

½ cup grated Parmesan cheese

Serves 4

Wash asparagus and cut off white part of stalk. Cook in boiling water in a heavy pot on a grill over a hot fire for 10 to 12 minutes, or until just tender. Drain and arrange on a large platter. Coat asparagus with melted butter and sprinkle generously with grated Parmesan cheese.

NOTE: This dish can also be served as an entrée with two fried eggs for each serving.

OLD-FASHIONED BAKED BEANS

28-oz. can brick oven baked beans
3 Tbs. dark molasses
3 Tbs. finely chopped onion
2 tsp. dry mustard
4 slices bacon, crisply fried and crumbled

Serves 6

Combine all ingredients in a 2- to 3-quart iron bean pot. Cover and suspend over a low fire. Cook for 40 to 45 minutes, moving pot once in a while to a cooler part of the fire.

FRIED POTATO CAKE

2 lbs. potatoes
6 Tbs. butter

Salt to taste
3 Tbs. hot water

Serves 4 or 5

In a heavy iron saucepan with a cover on a grill over a medium fire, boil potatoes in their skins until tender; cool. Peel and grate coarsely.

Heat butter in a large skillet. Slowly add potatoes and salt. Cook over low heat, turning frequently with a spatula, until the potatoes are soft and yellow.

Press down with a spatula to form a flat cake. Sprinkle with the hot water. Cover and cook over low heat until potatoes are crusty and golden at the bottom, about 10 to 15 minutes. Shake the pan frequently to prevent sticking or scorching. If needed, add a little more butter to prevent sticking.

Turn into a hot serving platter crusty side up and serve immediately.

Bernese Rosti
Cook 4 slices diced bacon with 1 medium minced onion until the onion is light golden. Add to the potatoes, then cook as directed above, using lard instead of butter.

HASH BROWN POTATOES

3½ cups* peeled, cooked
    potatoes, coarsely grated**
2 Tbs. flour
½ tsp. salt
⅛ tsp. pepper

½ cup minced onions, sautéed
    in 2 Tbs. butter**
½ cup light cream
6 Tbs. butter, or more as needed

Serves 6

In a large bowl combine potatoes, flour, salt, pepper, onions and cream; toss lightly with 2 forks.

In a 9" or 10" iron skillet on a grill over a hot fire, heat 3 Tbs. of the butter until it stops foaming. Spread potatoes evenly in the skillet and cook slowly, lifting occasionally off the fire to prevent burning. Check from time to time to see how well bottom is browning. If the potatoes stick to skillet, add more butter, lifting potatoes with spatula.

When potatoes are browned underneath, loosen potatoes all over with spatula and invert onto a platter. Add remaining butter to skillet. Slide potatoes back into skillet browned side up and cook until underside is browned, about 10 to 15 minutes. Check by lifting gently with a spatula. Serve immediately right from skillet or slide onto a heated serving platter.

*About 4 large boiling potatoes.
**See Other Tips, page 9.

BAKED SWEET POTATOES OR YAMS

6 large sweet potatoes, well scrubbed and wrapped in foil
6 Tbs. butter, softened
1 cup crushed, drained pineapple

½ cup honey
¼ tsp. nutmeg
Salt and pepper

Serves 6

Wrap sweet potatoes in foil and bake on a grill over a hot fire until soft to the touch, about 35 to 45 minutes.

Mix butter with pineapple, honey and nutmeg. Cut a slit into each potato, scoop out some of the inside and mix with butter-pineapple mixture. Season with salt and pepper to taste.

Fill potatoes with the mixture. Wrap securely in foil and heat for about 15 minutes right on the grill.

PASTA, GRAINS AND RICE

PASTA E FAGIOLI (PASTA AND BEANS)

1 lb. navy beans
2 quarts beef bouillon
1 lb. ham hock
1 ham bone
1 large onion, diced
3 stalks celery, diced
1 carrot, diced

3 cloves garlic, minced
Salt and pepper to taste
½ tsp. basil
½ tsp. oregano
1 lb. small macaroni (about ¼" long), cooked as directed on package*

Serves 8

Soak beans overnight in water to cover. Drain and discard water. Place beans into a large heavy pot on a grill over a hot fire. Add beef bouillon, ham hock, ham bone, onion, celery, carrot, garlic and seasonings. Cover and cook, stirring occasionally, for 1 to 1½ hours, or until beans are tender. Remove ham hock and bone and discard.

Take 3 cups of beans out of the pot, cool slightly and purée in blender.** Return purée to the pot. Add macaroni and mix well. Season if needed with salt and freshly ground pepper. Serve as a main dish with green salad or as a side dish with a hearty stew.

*See Other Tips, page 9.
**Or use a hand-operated food mill.

NOTE: You may have to add more bouillon or water to the beans and macaroni if the mixture seems dry, or before adding macaroni you may have to drain off some liquid if beans have not absorbed all the liquid.

ROMAN PASTA

3 Tbs. olive oil
3 cloves garlic, crushed
1 lb. fresh mushrooms, thinly sliced
3 anchovy fillets, minced
3 Tbs. butter, softened
½ tsp. oregano
½ tsp. rosemary
Salt and pepper to taste
1 lb. fettuccine, cooked as directed on the package and drained*
½ cup grated Romano cheese

Serves 6

In a large cast-iron skillet combine oil and garlic, stirring well. Place on a grill over a medium fire. Heat oil and as soon as haze appears, add mushrooms and toss lightly. Cook mushrooms for about 5 to 6 minutes, stirring occasionally.

In a small bowl cream together anchovies and butter; add to mushrooms. Stir gently until butter melts and is well distributed. Add seasonings and stir.

Toss fettuccine with mushroom sauce in a large heated serving platter. Sprinkle with Romano cheese and serve immediately.

*See Other Tips, page 9.

FETTUCCINE WITH NUT SAUCE

½ lb. unsalted butter, melted*
⅓ cup Italian bread crumbs
2½ cups light cream, scalded*
2 cloves garlic, mashed
1 cup coarsely chopped walnuts, sautéed in butter for 2 to 3 minutes
½ tsp. Italian seasoning
Salt to taste
1½ cups toasted pignoli (pine nuts), coarsely chopped
1 lb. fettuccine
1 cup grated Gruyère cheese
1 cup heavy cream
Black pepper to taste

Serves 6

In a saucepan on a grill over a low fire, combine 12 Tbs. of the melted butter, the bread crumbs and light cream. Heat together, beating continuously; then cool. Place into a blender,** add garlic and walnuts and purée into a smooth paste. Pour back into saucepan, add Italian seasoning, salt and pignoli. Heat but do not boil.

Cook fettuccine according to directions on package over a hot fire; drain well. On a large heated serving platter toss fettuccine with remaining melted butter, Gruyère cheese and heavy cream. Pour on nut sauce and toss again. Serve with freshly ground black pepper.

*Prepare in your usual manner, but in a heavy pot or pan over the fire.
**Or use a hand-operated food mill.

CORNMEAL DUMPLINGS FOR STEWS

1 cup unbleached all-purpose flour
1 cup yellow cornmeal
¼ cup double-acting baking powder
1 tsp. salt
⅛ tsp. pepper
2 Tbs. sour cream
1 egg, well beaten
About ⅓ cup buttermilk
2 Tbs. minced parsley

Makes about 10 to 12 dumplings

In a bowl combine flour, cornmeal, baking powder, salt and pepper. Beat together sour cream and egg, add to flour and toss lightly with 2 forks.

Add ⅓ cup buttermilk and gently toss with the cornmeal mixture. Add a little more buttermilk if necessary to make a medium-soft dough. Add parsley and toss lightly again.

Drop dough by tablespoonfuls into a barely simmering stew. Cover and simmer for 15 to 18 minutes, without uncovering pot. Serve with the stew.

STEW DUMPLINGS

3 cups all-purpose flour
4½ tsp. double-acting baking powder
1 tsp. salt
2 tsp. butter
2 tsp. lard or vegetable shortening
About 1 cup milk

Makes about 12 dumplings

In a bowl combine flour, baking powder and salt. Cut in the butter and lard with a pastry blender or 2 knives. Add just enough milk to moisten flour.

To form dumplings you may scoop up the dough with a tablespoon dipped in water. Or you can turn the dough out onto a lightly floured board and roll it out with a rolling pin to ½" thickness. Cut with a 2½" cookie cutter.

Drop dumpling into boiling stew. Cover and boil for 10 to 12 minutes. Remove dumplings to a serving platter and serve with stew.

FRIED RICE WITH CRABMEAT AND GREEN PEAS

2 eggs
¼ cup vegetable oil
4 cups cooked rice,* cooled
1 tsp. salt
1 cup frozen crabmeat, defrosted and well drained

½ cup chopped scallions
½ cup cooked green peas*
Cucumber, sliced diagonally for garnish

Serves 6

Beat eggs, adding a dash of salt. In a wok on a grill over a hot fire, heat oil and fry eggs for 1 minute. Add rice and salt. Sauté, mixing well, for 3 or 4 minutes.

Remove cartilage from crabmeat. Add crabmeat and scallions to wok. Stir-fry for 1 minute. Then add green peas.

Serve on a heated platter decorated with cucumber slices.

*See Other Tips, page 9.

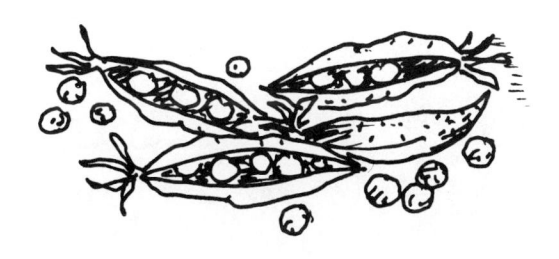

RISOTTO WITH MUSHROOMS

1 large onion, diced
2 Tbs. olive oil
¼ cup pale dry sherry
4 Tbs. butter
1 cup converted rice

2 cups thinly sliced fresh mushrooms
2½ cups hot chicken broth
½ tsp. salt
½ cup grated Parmesan cheese
½ cup minced parsley

Serves 6

In a large cast-iron skillet combine onion and olive oil and cook on a grill over a medium fire until the onions are just soft but not browned.

Add sherry and cook until ½ the liquid has evaporated.

Add butter and rice and cook stirring continuously, until the rice begins to turn yellow, about 5 minutes.

Add mushrooms, chicken broth and salt. Stir once, cover and cook without stirring for about 15 minutes, or until all liquid has been absorbed by rice. Sprinkle with Parmesan cheese and parsley. Serve immediately.

BREADS*

CAJUN CORN BREAD

½ lb. butter or margarine
1 cup sugar
2 cups yellow cornmeal
4 eggs
2 cups flour

4 tsp. baking powder
½ tsp. salt
¼ tsp. nutmeg
2¼ cups lukewarm milk

Makes 1 loaf

Cream butter until fluffy. Add sugar and cream for 1 to 2 minutes longer. Add ½ cup of the cornmeal, mix well and then add the eggs one at a time, beating well after each addition. Add remaining cornmeal and blend well.

Sift together flour, baking powder, salt and nutmeg; add to cornmeal mixture. Add milk and blend well.

Butter well a 9" × 5" loaf pan and sprinkle with cornmeal. Pour batter into loaf pan. Place a trivet or inverted pie pan into a preheated Dutch oven with rimmed lid big enough to accommodate the bread pan. Place bread pan onto the pie pan, cover the Dutch oven, place hot coals on the lid and place on a grill over a medium fire. Bake for about 50 to 55 minutes or until a cake tester comes out clean.

*Be sure to read Baking Instructions, page 8.

STEAMED BROWN BREAD

1 cup yellow cornmeal
2 cups whole wheat flour
1 tsp. baking soda
1 tsp. baking powder
1 tsp. salt
⅔ cup crushed walnuts

2 eggs
¾ cup light molasses
¼ cup honey
2 cups buttermilk
1 cup dark raisins

Makes 3 loaves

Butter well three 1-lb. coffee cans and set aside.

In a bowl combine cornmeal, flour, baking soda, baking powder, salt and walnuts.

In another bowl beat eggs until thick and light in color. Add molasses and honey and blend well. Add buttermilk and raisins and blend. Combine the dry ingredients with the molasses mixture and beat with a wooden spoon for 30 seconds.

Fill buttered coffee cans ⅔ full. Cover with wax paper, then foil, and tie with a string. Place into a kettle suspended over a medium fire. Pour in enough water to cover ½ the can. Cover tightly and let simmer for 3 hours.

If your kettle is too shallow for the cans and you are unable to use the cover, cover with double thickness of foil and mold the foil around the rim of the pot.

DUTCH OVEN DILL BREAD

1 envelope yeast
¼ cup lukewarm water
1 cup creamed cottage cheese, at room temperature
2 Tbs. sugar
2 Tbs. melted butter
1 Tbs. dill seed

1 Tbs. fresh dill (optional)
1 tsp. salt
¼ tsp. baking powder
2 eggs, beaten
2¼ to 2½ cups flour
Soft butter

Makes 1 round loaf

Dissolve yeast in water in a large bowl. Let stand for 3 minutes.

Add cottage cheese, sugar, melted butter, dill seed, fresh dill, salt and baking powder. Beat together until blended.

Add eggs and enough flour to make a stiff dough. Knead for about 1 minute until dough is smooth. Cover and let rise in a warm place until doubled in bulk, about 1 hour.

Punch dough down and place into a well-buttered, 8" or 9" round baking pan. Cover and let rise for 35 minutes.

Preheat a Dutch oven with rimmed lid for 5 to 10 minutes over a hot fire. Place an inverted pie pan or metal trivet into the Dutch oven. Place pan with dough onto inverted pan. Cover tightly with rimmed lid. Place a few hot coals on the lid and bake for about 45 to 50 minutes on a grill over a medium fire until a cake tester comes out clean.

If bottom of bread is browning too fast, push a few coals aside or roll away a burning log. You may also want a more browned top. Five minutes before bread is baked, loosen with a knife and flip over for 5 minutes to brown top.

To unmold bread remove from Dutch oven, cool for 5 minutes and invert onto a plate. Brush top with soft butter. Serve hot or cooled.

THE ENERGY SAVER'S COOKBOOK
ALL-DAY BISCUITS

2 cups unsifted all-purpose flour
½ lb. unsalted butter or margarine
4 tsp. baking powder
¾ cup buttermilk
½ tsp. salt

Makes 12 to 14 biscuits

Place flour into a bowl; add butter and crumble with your hands or 2 knives until it resembles a coarse meal. Add baking powder, buttermilk and salt. Mix well, very quickly; speed is essential.

Turn out dough onto a lightly floured board, press down and flatten with your hands. Fold over and flatten out again to ½" thickness. Cut into biscuits with a 2" floured biscuit cutter or small glass and place on an ungreased cookie sheet or baking pan that will fit into your Dutch oven. (Bake 2 batches if necessary.)

Preheat a Dutch oven with a rimmed cover to 350°*. Place an inverted pie pan or metal trivet into the Dutch oven. Place baking pan on pie pan. Cover and place hot coals on the cover of the Dutch oven.

Bake biscuits on a grill over a medium fire for 15 to 20 minutes, or until barely golden. Do not overbake.

*See Baking Instructions, page 8.

CURRANT OR RAISIN MUFFINS

1½ cups sifted flour
3 Tbs. sugar
1 tsp. baking powder
½ tsp. salt
2 eggs plus 1 egg yolk

¾ cup buttermilk
3 Tbs. melted butter or margarine
½ cup black currants or raisins

Makes 12 muffins

Grease two 6-muffin pans well and sprinkle generously with flour.

In a bowl combine flour, sugar, baking powder and salt.

In another bowl beat eggs and yolk, then add buttermilk and melted butter. Add liquid ingredients to the dry mixture and toss lightly with 2 forks until just moistened. Fold in currants. Fill muffin pans to about ⅔.

Preheat Dutch oven until oven thermometer reaches 350°. Place an inverted pie pan or metal trivet inside Dutch oven. Place muffin pans onto pie pan. Cover, place some coals on the lid and bake on a grill over a medium fire for about 25 to 30 minutes, or until a cake tester comes out clean.

HONEY "DIPPERS"

2 egg yolks
1 cup milk
1 tsp. baking powder
1 cup sifted all-purpose flour
½ tsp. salt

¼ tsp. nutmeg
2 egg whites
Butter
1 cup honey

*Makes 8 muffins**

Beat egg yolks until thick. Add milk and beat for 30 seconds. Add baking powder, flour, salt and nutmeg. Beat again for 1 minute.

Whip egg whites until stiff but not dry. Fold into yolk mixture.

Butter well an 8-muffin baking tin. Pour 1 tsp. honey into each tin. Fill each tin ⅓ with batter.

Preheat a Dutch oven with rimmed lid to 350°. Place an inverted pie pan or metal trivet inside the Dutch oven. Place muffin tin on pie pan and cover Dutch oven. Put some hot coals on the lid and bake on a grill over a medium fire for 20 to 25 minutes, or until cake tester comes out clean.

Remove from oven and immediately remove from baking tin onto a serving platter. Pour 1 tsp. honey over each muffin and serve hot.

*You may have to bake them in two batches if the 8-muffin tin does not fit into the Dutch oven.

DESSERTS*

BANANA CAKE

4 Tbs. unsalted butter or margarine
2 Tbs. melted butter
1½ cups light brown sugar
2 eggs
1¼ cups sifted all-purpose flour
½ tsp. allspice
2 Tbs. dark rum
1 tsp. grated lemon rind

2 medium bananas, peeled and mashed
¾ cup coarsely chopped walnuts
3 tsp. double-acting baking powder
Syrup (*page 80*)
Thin slices of lemon and banana and walnut halves for garnish

Serves 10

Butter well a 9″ × 5″ loaf pan and sprinkle with flour; set aside.

In a large bowl cream 4 Tbs. butter until light and fluffy. Add melted butter and ½ cup of the brown sugar; cream again. Add remaining brown sugar and beat for 3 to 4 minutes.

Add eggs one at a time, beating well after each addition. Add flour, allspice, rum and lemon rind. Add bananas to the batter and blend well. Add walnuts and baking powder. Beat together for 1 minute with a wooden spoon.

Pour batter into loaf pan. Place pan on top of inverted pie pan inside preheated Dutch oven. Cover pot with foil and then with cover. Bake on a grill over a medium fire for about 50 to 55 minutes, or until a cake tester comes out clean.

When cake is done, cool in pan for about 10 minutes. Unmold onto a serving platter and spoon hot Syrup over the cake, reserving ½ cup of the syrup. Spoon syrup from around the cake over the cake again and again.

Dip several slices of lemon and banana and a few walnut halves into remaining syrup and use to decorate cake.

*Be sure to read Baking Instructions, page 8.

Syrup

    1½ cups light brown sugar
    ¾ cup water
    2 thin slices lemon
    ¼ cup dark rum or brandy

In a heavy saucepan with cover combine 1½ cups brown sugar with water. Bring to a boil over a hot fire. Reduce heat, cover and simmer for 5 minutes. Add lemon slices and cook for 3 to 4 minutes. Remove from heat. Stir in rum.

COTTAGE CHEESE PANCAKES WITH FRUIT SAUCE

8-oz. pkg. mixed dried fruits
1 cup sugar
16-oz. can peaches in heavy syrup, drained and diced
1 cup sour cream
1 cup pot cheese, sieved

4 eggs
1 cup all-purpose flour
3 Tbs. sugar
½ tsp. salt
Butter or margarine, melted
Powdered sugar

Makes 12 to 14 pancakes

Chop dried fruit. Place in medium saucepan. Add sugar and enough water to cover the fruit. Cover and simmer on a grill over a low fire for 30 to 35 minutes. Add peaches. Keep sauce warm while preparing pancakes.

In a large bowl combine sour cream and pot cheese. Beat in eggs one at a time. Add flour, sugar and salt; beat well. Let batter set 5 minutes.

Brush a griddle with melted butter. Place on fireplace grate and heat until sizzling. Drop batter by ⅓ cups onto griddle. Fry pancakes 2 to 3 minutes on each side.

Serve in stacks with hot fruit sauce sprinkled with powdered sugar.

APPLE OMELETTE FLAMBÉ

5 eggs
2 Tbs. cream
¼ tsp. salt
1 large yellow Delicious apple

6 Tbs. butter
5 Tbs. sugar
¼ tsp. cinnamon
¼ cup brandy

Serves 3

In a bowl combine eggs, cream and salt; set aside.

Peel, core and cut apple into thin slices.

In a cast-iron skillet melt ½ the butter and add apple slices. Sauté on a grill over a medium fire until golden brown. Add 3 Tbs. of the sugar and the cinnamon and cook for 2 minutes, stirring constantly.

Melt remaining 3 Tbs. butter in an omelet pan. Beat eggs with a whisk until foamy, about 30 seconds. Add apple mixture and pour into omelet pan. Cook until bottom of omelet is brown but top is still creamy.

Shake pan gently, sliding omelet forward and folding over as you slide it out of the pan onto a heated serving platter. Sprinkle with remaining 2 Tbs. sugar.

In a small pan or ladle heat brandy to lukewarm, ignite and pour over omelet. Serve as soon as the flames die down.

BAKED FRUIT CURAÇAO

1 large fresh pineapple
3 bananas
2 oranges
1 cup plus 3 Tbs. sugar

6 Tbs. butter
Grated rind of 1 orange
¼ cup orange juice
1 cup Curaçao liqueur

Serves 6

Cut off top and bottom of pineapple. Stand pineapple upright and cut off rind. Remove eyes with a small knife. Cut pineapple in ½ lengthwise. Cut out core. Slice the 2 halves into slices ½" wide.

Peel bananas and slice lengthwise, then cut each half across.

Peel oranges and separate into sections.

In a suacepan combine 1 cup sugar, the butter and grated orange rind. Cook over a medium fire, stirring constantly, until sugar is dissolved and mixture just starts to brown. Add orange juice and ½ cup of the Curaçao. Bring to a boil and remove from fire immediately.

Pour ½ the sauce into a heavy, 9" to 10" cast-iron skillet with cover. Place the pineapple slices, bananas and orange sections into the skillet in alternate rows and pour the remaining sauce over the fruit. Sprinkle with 3 Tbs. sugar.

Place skillet on a grill over a low fire and cook for about 20 minutes, basting often with the sauce. Remove from fire.

Heat the remaining ½ cup of Curaçao slightly in a small pan or ladle, ignite and pour over the fruit. Serve immediately.

COLD HAZELNUT SOUFFLÉ

1 cup hazelnuts
1½ cups sugar
¼ cup water
8 egg yolks

⅔ cup sugar
2 cups heavy cream
¼ cup brandy
2 to 3 Tbs. grated chocolate

Serves 6 to 8

Roast hazelnuts on an iron cookie sheet or in a large skillet on a grill in the fireplace or on a barbecue over slow heat for about 10 minutes. With a kitchen towel rub off the skins of the hazelnuts, then roast for an additional 5 to 7 minutes until they turn golden brown.

In an iron saucepan combine sugar and water. Place saucepan onto the grate over a medium fire. Cover and bring to a boil. Remove from fire and cool slightly.

Move some coals away to reduce heat. Replace saucepan on grill and simmer until mixture turns pale yellow. Add hazelnuts and continue cooking until sugar is golden brown. Pour mixture into a well-greased pan and cool completely until hard as rock. Crush with a rolling pin to make praline.

In a large bowl beat egg yolks for 30 seconds with a rotary or electric beater. Add sugar and beat for 5 to 7 minutes until yolks are very thick and pale yellow.

Beat cream until stiff. Reserving ½ cup, fold remaining whipped cream into egg yolks. Add brandy and 1 cup of the crushed praline.

Encircle a 1-quart glass soufflé dish with a buttered 6"-high collar of doubled wax paper. Attach it snugly to the soufflé dish with scotch tape so that the mixture will not run out.

Pour cream mixture into soufflé dish. The cream should be 2" to 3" higher than the rim of the dish. Freeze soufflé for 6 to 7 hours.

Remove frozen soufflé from refrigerator and let stand for about 5 minutes. Carefully peel off wax paper collar. Press some of the crushed praline around the edge of the soufflé which formed above the dish. Sprinkle grated chocolate on top and decorate with reserved whipped cream. Serve immediately.

FLAN DE QUESO (CHEESE CUSTARD)

1 can sweetened condensed milk
½ cup sugar
2 Tbs. water
8-oz. pkg. cream cheese
½ cup powdered vanilla sugar*

6 eggs
2 cups heavy cream
8-oz. can crushed pineapple, drained

Serves 5 or 6

Place can of condensed milk into a pot and add boiling water to cover ⅔ of the can. Simmer for 1½ hours. Cool completely.

In a saucepan cook sugar and water together until light brown. Coat bottom and sides of a 9" × 5" loaf pan with the caramel.

Soften cream cheese at room temperature. Beat until fluffy, add vanilla sugar and beat again. Add eggs one at a time, beating well after each addition. Add cooked condensed milk and the heavy cream; beat well. Fold in drained pineapple; blend well. Pour cheese mixture into caramelized pan.

Place loaf pan onto inverted pie pan or rim of a springform pan inside a Dutch oven. Pour enough water to come to top of pie pan or ring. Cover and place a few hot coals onto the lid. Place on a grill over a low fire and cook for 1 hour and 45 minutes, or until an inserted knife comes out clean.

Look into the pot a few times while flan is cooking; the water should gently simmer but never boil. If necessary push a few coals aside under the pot to cool down the heat, or add a few coals or a log to make the fire hotter.

When custard is done cool, then refrigerate for 12 hours or overnight. Unmold onto a platter. Pour excess caramel in pan over flan.

*To make vanilla sugar, place 1 or 2 whole vanilla beans with 2 to 3 cups powdered or granulated sugar into a jar with a tight lid. Within 3 days you will have vanilla sugar. Add sugar as needed. The vanilla beans last for 6 to 7 months.

STEAMED ORANGE BREAD PUDDING

6 slices stale white bread
1½ cups scalded milk
1 cup orange juice
1 Tbs. orange rind
4 eggs, beaten
⅔ cup sugar
⅛ tsp. salt

⅓ cup orange marmalade
½ tsp. vanilla extract
½ cup raisins (optional)
½ cup ground almonds (optional)
Sweetened whipped cream, custard sauce or fruit syrup

Serves 6

Cut crust off bread. Slice bread into small cubes. Scald milk, add bread cubes and soak for 10 minutes. Add orange juice and rind.

Beat eggs with sugar and salt until thick and lemon colored. Add to bread and milk.

Fold in orange marmalade, vanilla and, if desired, raisins and almonds.

Butter well a 1½-quart steamed-pudding mold or any deep baking dish. Sprinkle generously with granulated sugar. Pour bread mixture into buttered mold.

Place mold onto an inverted pie pan or trivet inside a Dutch oven with cover. Pour in hot water just to cover inverted pie pan. Cover the pot tightly. Bake pudding on a grill over a low fire or on an outdoor barbecue for 55 minutes, or until tip of knife inserted into pudding comes out clean. Cool for 10 to 15 minutes.

Loosen around edges with a knife. Invert onto a platter and unmold. Serve hot or cold with whipped cream, custard sauce or a fruit syrup.

NOTE: If you double this recipe, increase baking time to 1½ hours. Test for doneness with a knife.

WALNUT PUDDING

5 egg yolks
¾ cup sugar
¾ cup finely ground walnuts
¼ tsp. cinnamon

5 egg whites
1 cup heavy cream
2 Tbs. brandy

Serves 4 to 6

Beat egg yolks and sugar until lemon-colored and very thick. Mix walnuts with cinnamon. Add nuts to egg yolks and beat again.

Beat egg whites until thick; fold into egg yolk mixture.

Butter a 1-quart loaf pan or soufflé dish and sprinkle with sugar. Pour in egg-nut mixture and cover pan with foil.

Place loaf pan on an inverted pie pan inside a Dutch oven. Add hot water to cover ½ the loaf pan or soufflé dish. Cover and place onto a grill over a medium fire. Simmer for about 50 minutes, or until a cake tester comes out clean. Remove from oven and cool. Refrigerate for 3 to 4 hours.

Whip cream until stiff. Stir in brandy. Top chilled pudding with brandied cream and serve.

ASSORTED DESSERT COFFEES

Basic Fireplace Coffee
Use a drip pot and place it on your fireplace grill over medium fire.

Viennese Cappuccino

Serves 6 to 8

Melt 3 oz. semisweet chocolate in 2 cups strong hot coffee. Stir until completely dissolved. Use 6- or 8-oz. cups. Pour 2 to 3 Tbs. of the coffee mixture into each cup, add 2 Tbs. brandy and more strong coffee to fill (or eliminate brandy if you wish). Top with sweetened whipped cream and sprinkle with nutmeg.

Café au Cointreau

Serves 6 to 8

In a saucepan combine 2 cups very strong coffee with 3 to 4 slivers of orange peel and a stick of cinnamon. Simmer for about 2 minutes. Strain mixture into cups and add 2 Tbs. Cointreau to each cup. Fill with more coffee, top with sweetened whipped cream and grate some orange peel over the top.

Café Granita

Serves 6

In a saucepan combine 2 cups water with 1 cup sugar. Bring to a boil, reduce heat and simmer for 7 minutes. Remove from heat and cool to room temperature. Add 4 cups espresso or strong regular coffee. Pour into an icetray. Freeze for 3 hours. Every 30 minutes stir coffee, scraping frosty particles from edge of tray. The texture of the granita should resemble shaved ice. Fill 6 wine glasses ¾ full with the coffee ice and top with sweetened whipped cream or vanilla ice cream.

Café Isle Flotante
Add 2 Tbs. brandy to each cup of espresso coffee and top with sweetened whipped cream.

Café Jamaica
Pour 3 Tbs. dark Jamaican rum into each 6- to 8-oz. wine goblet. Add a pinch of ginger and nutmeg, fill with strong coffee and top with sweetened, rum-flavored whipped cream.

2
Outdoor-Indoor Grills

Grilling food over coals and cooking meats, fish or fowl on a spit or skewer is the oldest method of preparing food known to humans.

Called shashlik, shish kebab, kebabs, barbecue, saté, or just plain skewered or charcoal-grilled meat or fish, they're foods cooked over an open fire.

Ancient Greeks and Romans cherished their braziers, and the slaves of wealthy nobles cleaned all grilling services and *cena*, "skewers," before each feast to remove odors and tastes of previous meals. Roman legionnaires carried their own grills, which were placed over deep coal pits, and skewers and spits were part of each legion's equipment.

The Japanese perfected hibachi and Kamado ovens, which are oval-shaped, bowl-type barbecue units with covers, several millennia ago, and much Mediterranean cuisine is also based on grilling, as is that of most Middle Eastern countries.

American Indians were masters of pit cookery. They devised their own versions of grills and spits from the raw materials available in their regions.

However, nowhere on earth today is the barbecue as popular or as highly developed as in the United States. Many who might have invented a better mousetrap built a better grill instead. This may prove to be a real blessing, as Americans turn to the old-fashioned method of open-fire and barbecue grill cookery to save fuel costs. From now on there will be more cookouts and more people using grills and hibachis than ever before.

Small steaks, chops, sausages, disjointed chicken and fish steaks are ideal cooked right on the grill. But for new taste sensations, large pieces of meat—roasts, legs of lamb, whole chickens or ducks—may also be cooked on a barbecue grill on a spit or in a wire basket. To enhance the flavor of grilled meats or fish, try some tangy or spicy marinades and bastes. They're great flavor enhancers.

In addition to delicious main dishes, vegetables and desserts may be cooked to perfection on barbecue grills, and breads, cookies and biscuits come out great. The technique is similar to cooking in a fireplace or Franklin stove.

You don't need complicated or expensive equipment for good grill cooking. There are table-top hibachis, Mexican ceramic *braseros* and various other small grills which will be described in greater detail later in the chapter.

If your grill does not have a built-in thermometer, you can estimate the temperature by holding your hand palm down about 2 inches from the grill surface and counting to three. If you are forced to remove your palm at that count, your fire is about 350°–400°, perfect for chicken, steaks, chops or skewered meat.

But don't limit yourself to just grilling or spit roasting. If your barbecue does not have a cover, with just a bit of inventiveness you can adapt it by covering it with a dome of heavy duty foil or a foil tent placed directly over the food, making it a highly versatile cooking unit. You may cook most of your favorite dishes on your barbecue and add new and exciting recipes and gustatory sensations to your culinary repertoire.

Devices for Charcoal Cookery Outdoors

Brazier-Type Units: The most common brazier or barbecue units stand on high legs with or without wheels, are round, have bowls about 6" deep for coal and, of course, a grill. Some come with half or full hoods, others with fancy equipment—spits, motorized skewers, built-in thermometers and adjustable heat vents. In the simpler units coals are placed into the bowl, which should be lined with double foil for heat reflection and ease in cleaning. Other models come with iron grates on which coals are placed, letting the ashes fall through, leaving the bowl and grid clean.

Bowl Brazier or Covered Barbecue (also called Cooking Kettle): This is an economical device. It has adjustable dampers on the bowl and the lid, which control the heat for cooking whole chickens, roasts and large steaks using very little fuel. This unit is ideal for windy or drizzly days; just close the lid and cook as directed.

This cooker has a deep fire bowl and a lid that resembles an inverted kettle. When the lid is closed, whatever you are preparing on the grill also browns evenly on top by virtue of reflecting heat from the top bowl. The Cooking Kettle is also quite suitable for baking, but remember that it takes practice to perfect your baking technique when you're not using the familiar oven! Place a cast-iron baking sheet over the grate, put a flan ring over the sheet, open the dampers to increase heat or close to reduce heat. Close the top and then use an oven thermometer to determine inside temperature. Place whatever you are baking—bread, a simple cake, cookies, muffins, biscuits—into its pan on top of the flan ring, leave the thermometer inside, close the lid and bake as directed in the recipe. Check the thermometer for inside temperature from time to time by lifting the lid carefully, just enough to see the thermometer.

Table-Top Brazier: These are mostly round with short legs and are made of iron or steel. The bowl may be from 4"–6" deep and has a grill that fits onto a center post. Bowls should always be lined with a double thickness of foil.

Place your flat-bottomed pots and pans over the grill. You are lucky if you have an attached thermometer because you can cook as you would on a wood burning stove. Otherwise use a meat, candy or deep-fry thermometer.

Dan-Bin-Lo or Mongolian Hot Pot: This is based on the same principle as the Russian Samovar and has a center funnel containing coals, surrounded by a bowl filled with liquid. Mongolian Hot Pots are usually made of brass lined with tin. Some come equipped with a removable coal pan that fits under the funnel, while others are filled with coals from above. Be sure the bowl contains liquid before heating. Chimney extensions are often necessary; some pots come with these, or you may make a funnel about 4"–6" long from foil. Remove when the fire is going strong. Use a pan or asbestos pad under the hot pad for ashes.

Hibachi: This is used for grilling small amounts of meat, fish, vegetables and shish kebabs. It may also be used as a cooking unit for your ordinary pots, pans or wok. Most hibachis sold in this country today are made of iron, come as a single or double unit and are square in shape. There is a small vent that can be opened or closed to control intensity of heat.

The authentic Japanese hibachi is made of clay, is round in shape and may be obtained in Japanese or other Oriental stores.

Japanese Kamado Oven: This is a bake oven-smoker, and the smoke flavor may be increased by adding damp apple, plum or hickory wood chips. There are draft openings in the Kamado for regulating heat. It uses ample amounts of charcoal and generates strong heat which can be diffused by closing one of the openings.

Japanese Tempura and Sukiyaki Cooking Equipment: These round clay hibachis or braziers are marvelous as tempura or sukiyaki pans, and are also suitable for wok cookery.

Japanese Nabe Cooking Unit: This consists of several flat cast-iron grills attached to a round, cast-iron fire pot which is placed onto a wooden base or asbestos trivet. Relatively new in this country, it is imported from Japan. You may use it to grill or deep fry small pieces of meat, chicken, fish, vegetables or fruit. It is placed on a table and is a kind of Oriental fondue pot in which many delicious foods may be prepared.

Devices for Charcoal Cookery Indoors

You may use a Wok, Hibachi, Table-Top Brazier, Mongolian Hot Pot, Japanese Tempura or Sukiyaki Cooker to cook indoors. However, a word of caution is in order. The charcoal fumes should not be allowed to spread or be inhaled. Place a cookie sheet lined with an asbestos trivet on top of your regular stove, providing it has a ventilating hood above it, and set your cooking device onto the trivet. Light the coals and turn your hood fan on "low." When you are ready to cook, place your meat, fish or kebabs onto your grill and then make a shield of strong foil to channel all fumes toward the exhaust fan. Hibachis and small braziers may also be placed into a cold fireplace or Franklin stove with a flue open. Be careful of flareups and have water handy to douse any possible fire. It's always a good idea to have a portable fire extinguisher handy.

You may also place your cooking device on an asbestos trivet at an open window, being careful that the wind from the outside does not blow smoke into the room. Or use your garage for cooking on a coal grill; however don't forget to keep the door partially ajar or open the window.

Before using a grill on your apartment balcony, make sure that your city ordinance permits this. Keep all flammable objects away from the grill, including furniture with cushions and patio carpeting.

You may use your wok on a hibachi or brazier indoors as well as outdoors, just proceed as described above and make sure you have ample ventilation to disperse all fumes. Place the wok on its ring over the coals or grill when flames are high enough to touch the bottom of the wok. Heat the wok, then follow the particular recipe of your choice.

Gas and Electric Barbecues: Last but certainly not least are these popular modern cooking devices—fancy grilling-roasting gas units with ceramic briquettes, electric rotisseries, thermometers and other attachments. Portable units with gas tanks are actually easier to use than coal, cleaner and quite economical, and many have electric motor attachments for spit roasting. In addition, many new gas and electric kitchen ranges are available with built-in barbecue grills and griddles.

Rotisserie Attachments

Many brazier-type grills and barbecue units have electric rotisserie attachments. Some need an electric outlet and some do not. In fact, there are rotisserie attachments available with wind-up clockworks which turn the spit over the grill without using any electricity.

Among the most useful of these units is "Cocambroche Four," imported from France. It has a wind-up clock, two-pronged spit for large roasts, whole chickens and other large pieces of meat, two vertical notched posts attached to a drip pan to hold the spit or a wire basket called a *tambour*, which can be adjusted for whole fish, chicken halves, hamburgers and also has an attachment for shish kebab skewers. The "Cocambroche Four" is now available in specialty stores and in some fine kitchen accessory boutiques. It comes with complete directions as well as suggestions for use with your conventional electric or gas oven.

Preparing Your Grill for Cooking

First line the fire bowl with heavy-duty aluminum foil, which reflects heat, speeds up cooking and greatly facilitates cleaning. Spread a thin layer of sand, gravel or vermiculite over foil, then add charcoal or briquettes.

Lighting of charcoal cannot be rushed, and it may take from 25 minutes to an hour and 15 minutes to have the coals ready for cooking. Much depends on weather conditions. There are marvelous electric fire starters on the market, but for these you need an electric outlet.

You may want to try your hand at lighting a grill fire the same way as in your fireplace by using a "fire starter brick." Place it in the center of the fire bowl, place half a page of crushed newspaper over the brick, then place a few dry twigs or kindling over the paper. Or you may use just the paper and kindling. Put a few briquettes or coals over the kindling, light the paper and when kindling is burning and coals have caught fire, add more charcoal as needed.

Many people soak a few briquettes in a liquid fire starter, but never use gasoline. A small amount of sterno—about ⅓ cup—or a small, stubby candle may be placed under a few briquettes. As soon as they are burning, place more coal on top. The fire is ready for cooking when flames die down, the coals are covered with ash and are gray. At night they will still have a light red glow.

A shallow fire is best for broiling, and about 20–25 briquettes are ample to grill 3–4 steaks or hamburgers. Widely spaced coals provide lower heat for cooking very small amounts of food, while a large roast or an iron pot with stew requires a generous amount of coals.

When cooking shish kebab, place coals in a ring around the sides, then in parallel rows across the fire bowl between the skewers. Do this to avoid flareups. For steaks or any small pieces of meat or fowl, you should also place coals in a ring around the bowl of the grill with a small amount in the center. Shift and move the coals for even browning and minimal flareups.

Once in awhile you may have to

remove excess coals; when doing so use tongs with insulated handles. If the coals become too gray, dust them off with a wire brush with a long insulated handle.

It is an excellent idea to have a drip pan for fatty foods. These may be purchased or, for economy's sake, made out of heavy-duty aluminum foil in the shape of a baking pan with 2" sides in a size to fit your grill. The foil drip pan may also be used as a handy container for onions, potatoes and other vegetables, and even for cooking small pieces of food that would otherwise fall through the grill. It is also excellent for cooking hamburgers, because it prevents the meat from sticking to the surface of the grill.

When cooking whole fish on a grill, fish heads and tails should be wrapped in foil, which is removed just before serving, so they don't burn. The same applies to fowl—wings and tips of leg bones should be wrapped in foil to prevent scorching.

To take proper care of your grill, follow these simple suggestions for cleaning:

1. Line bowl with heavy-duty aluminum foil.

2. When grill is hot, clean it thoroughly with a wire brush just before placing food for grilling.

3. After food has been cooked, cool grill. Remove coals from the unit in foil liner and discard entire package. Wipe brazier bottom clean with a cloth.

4. When grill is cool, remove from the barbecue unit and clean again with the wire brush. Wipe with vegetable oil and then remove oil with a terry cloth or an old bath towel until grill is dry and completely free of any food particles.

5. Do not wash grill or leave it in the rain. Store indoors, if possible.

FISH AND SEAFOOD

GRILLED FISH

6 yellowtails (2 lbs. each)
6 Tbs. oil
Salt and pepper to taste

Lemon wedges
Dill Sauce (*below*)

Serves 6

Generously rub each fish with oil. Place fish on grill, leaving ½" space between each fish. Cook first one side, then the other, about 4" from the fire for about 7 to 10 minutes, or until fish flakes easily when tested with a fork.

When fish is baked, carefully remove from grill. Season with salt and pepper. Serve fish with lemon wedges and Dill Sauce.

Dill Sauce
 1 cup fresh dill
 ½ cup Dijon mustard
 ¼ cup wine vinegar

 ½ cup mayonnaise
 ¼ cup sugar
 3 Tbs. oil

Makes about 2 cups

Combine all ingredients except oil in a blender.* Blend until mixture is smooth. While blender is running, add oil slowly.

*Or beat with a whisk.

SPIT-ROASTED RED SNAPPER

4- to 5-lb. red snapper or yellowtail
3 Tbs. lemon juice
Salt and pepper to taste
2 Tbs. butter, softened
¼ cup melted butter

½ cup chicken broth
3 Tbs. minced fresh dill
2 hard-boiled eggs, sliced
Thin slices of lemon
Parsley

Serves 8

Sprinkle fish inside and out with lemon juice, salt and pepper. Rub with soft butter.

Place fish into a wire fish rack or piece of chicken wire the size of the fish. Secure well and spit fish diagonally over a medium fire. Mix melted butter and chicken broth and baste fish a few times while it is cooking. To judge doneness, use a meat thermometer inserted in thickest part of the fish. Fish is done when thermometer reads 160° to 170°.

Remove fish from spit and wire. Garnish with dill, eggs, lemon and parsley and serve.

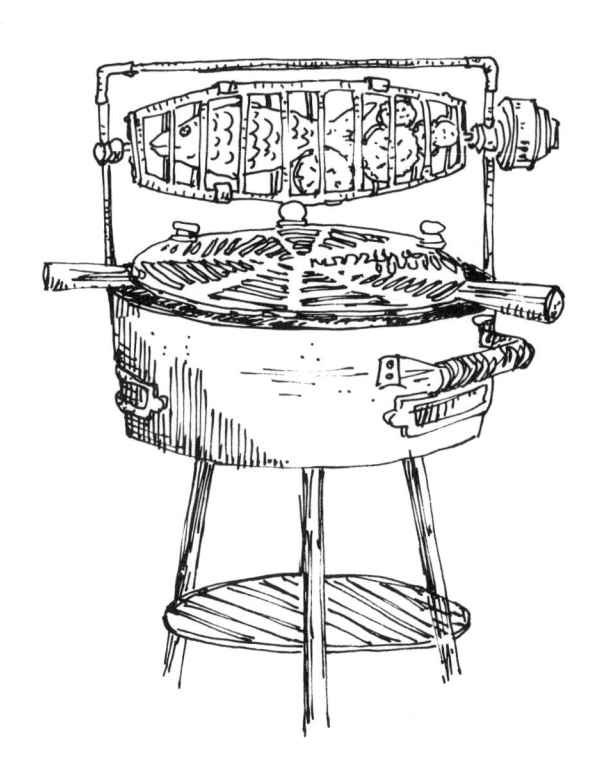

STUFFED FLOUNDER

6 medium-sized flounder
1 onion, finely chopped
1 green pepper, finely chopped
3 slices bacon, finely chopped
1 pound flaked crabmeat
3 cups flavored bread crumbs
4 eggs, well beaten

½ tsp. sage
¼ tsp. nutmeg
Salt and pepper to taste
1 cup butter
1 tsp. salt
1 tsp. paprika
3 Tbs. lemon juice

Serves 6

Wash fish in cold, salted water and pat dry.

Sauté onion and green pepper with bacon until bacon is crisp. Add crabmeat, bread crumbs, eggs, sage, nutmeg and salt and pepper to taste.

Stuff flounder with bread-crumb mixture. Secure opening with toothpicks or skewers.

Melt butter, add salt, paprika and lemon juice.

Place each fish on a square of heavy-duty aluminum foil large enough to completely wrap around the fish. Pour some of the butter on each fish, turning fish on both sides. Wrap securely in foil and place on grill over medium-hot coals. Cook for 30 to 35 minutes, or until fish flakes easily.

FISH FOIL PACKAGES

Olive Sauce (*below*)
6 halibut steaks (about 5 oz. each), ¾" thick
6 slices eggplant,* ½" thick
6 slices lemon, ⅛" thick
6 slices onion, ¼" thick
6 slices tomato, ¼" thick

Serves 6

Spoon 1 Tbs. Olive Sauce into center of 6 pieces of heavy-duty aluminum foil, 12" squares. Place halibut steaks on the sauce. Spoon 3 Tbs. of the olive sauce over each steak. Place a slice of eggplant, lemon, onion, and tomato on each steak. Wrap packages securely. Grill 3" from coals 25 to 30 minutes.

Olive Sauce
1 cup olive oil
½ cup lemon juice
2 Tbs. Worcestershire sauce
1 tsp. salt
¼ tsp. pepper
1 tsp. thyme
1 cup chopped pimiento-stuffed olives

In a bowl combine all the ingredients and mix well.

*Unpeeled.

GRILLED SHRIMP

30 to 36 large shrimp, shelled and deveined
½ cup cognac or dry white wine
½ tsp. salt
¼ tsp. freshly ground black pepper
½ tsp. basil
30 to 36 thin strips bacon
1 cup flavored bread crumbs
Lemon wedges

Serves 6

Place shrimp in a bowl, add cognac, salt, pepper and basil; marinate in refrigerator 1 hour or longer.

Wrap each shrimp in a strip of bacon and string on skewers, allowing 4 to 6 shrimp for each skewer. Place onto grill about 6" from the heat and cook about 12 minutes until bacon is partially browned, turning 2 or 3 times.

Roll shrimp in bread crumbs, return to grill and cook until golden brown, about 6 to 7 minutes. Serve with lemon wedges.

SHRIMP ITALIANO

½ cup olive oil or salad oil
½ tsp. salt
¼ tsp. freshly ground black pepper
2 Tbs. finely chopped parsley

2 lbs. large shrimp, shelled and deveined
¼ cup butter
Juice of 1 lemon

Serves 6

Mix oil, salt, pepper and parsley. Dip shrimp in oil mixture, then place on a grill over low coals. Grill 3 to 4 minutes on each side.

Place grilled shrimp on foil, sprinkle with remaining oil mixture and grill on foil for 10 minutes. Remove shrimp to a hot serving dish and keep warm.

Put the butter and lemon juice into the foil, seal tightly and heat. Remove as soon as butter is hot and pour over shrimp.

SHRIMP PIERRE

2 lbs. large shrimp, shelled and deveined
3 cloves garlic, finely chopped
1 medium onion, finely chopped
¼ cup parsley
1 tsp. basil
1 tsp. dry mustard
1 tsp. salt
½ cup olive oil or peanut oil
Juice of 1 lemon

Serves 6

Place shrimp in a bowl, add remaining ingredients and let marinate at room temperature for 1 hour.

Grill shrimp over charcoal for about 4 minutes on each side, or until the shrimp are pink and slightly charred. Baste a few times with the marinade while grilling.

CURRIED SHRIMP EN BROCHETTE

24 to 30 large shrimp, peeled and deveined, with tails removed
12 to 15 slices bacon, cut in half
6 Tbs. butter
2 tsp. curry powder
¼ tsp. salt
3 cups hot cooked rice*
½ cup thin strips pickled red sweet pepper or pimiento
½ cup julienne strips cooked ham

Serves 6

Wrap each shrimp in ½ slice bacon and thread on skewers.

Melt ½ the butter in a small saucepan, add the curry powder and salt and cook, stirring, for ½ minute. Brush the curry butter over both sides of the shrimp and arrange them on a grill over low heat 6" from the fire. Cook 4 to 5 minutes on each side. Brush both sides again with the curry butter. Turn and grill 3 minutes longer.

Toss rice with pepper, ham and the remaining butter. Spoon rice into a serving dish. Arrange the skewers of shrimp on the rice.

*See page 255.

MONGOLIAN HOT POT

2 cups condensed chicken broth
2 cans condensed beef bouillon
¾ cup pale dry sherry
2 cloves garlic
½ cup soy sauce
1 Tbs. peanut butter
1 tsp. horseradish
½ lb. raw shrimp, shelled and deveined

½ lb. boned chicken breasts, pounded thin and thinly sliced
½ lb. sirloin steak, sliced into strips ⅛" thick
4 stalks celery, thinly sliced into 1" pieces
6 scallions, sliced into 1" pieces
2 green peppers, thinly sliced into 1" strips

Serves 8

Pour into bowl of hot pot chicken broth, beef bouillon, ½ cup of the sherry, garlic and enough water to fill bowl. Heat to boiling point, using charcoal fire inside pot.

Mix soy sauce, remaining ¼ cup sherry, the peanut butter, and horseradish.

Using fondue forks, dip shrimp into the sauce, then into boiling broth. Swish around for a few seconds; then, if you wish, dip into sauce again and eat. Follow shrimp with chicken, then beef, then vegetables. Finish by pouring broth into soup cups and drinking with remaining vegetables and meat.

NOTE: Other vegetables, fish and seafood may be used with the above.

POULTRY

CURRIED BARBECUED CHICKEN

2 Tbs. salt
2 cups warm water
2 broiler-fryer chickens (3 lbs. each), quartered
2 tsp. curry powder

3 Tbs. lemon juice
¼ cup apple juice
½ cup melted butter
¼ tsp. pepper

Serves 6 to 8

Combine salt and warm water. Grill chicken 25 minutes over low heat, basting with salt water every 5 minutes.

Combine curry powder, lemon juice, apple juice, melted butter and pepper; blend well. Grill chicken an additional 20 minutes, turning frequently and basting with butter sauce.

SAFFRON CHICKEN ESPAÑOL

2 broiler-fryer chickens (3 lbs. each), quartered
½ tsp. salt
½ tsp. pepper
½ tsp. thyme
½ tsp. tarragon

½ cup butter, melted
⅓ cup soy sauce
½ cup dry white wine
2 Tbs. honey
1 tsp. dry mustard
⅛ tsp. saffron

Serves 8

Sprinkle chicken with salt, pepper, thyme and tarragon.

Mix together melted butter, soy sauce, wine, honey, mustard and saffron. Marinate chicken in butter sauce for 3 hours or overnight.

Broil chicken over medium charcoal fire about 10 to 12 minutes on each side, starting with the skin side up. Baste with marinade frequently. Serve with yellow rice.

CHICKEN NORMANDY STYLE

2 cups dry white wine
½ tsp. garlic powder
½ tsp. basil
1 broiling chicken (2½ to 3 lbs.), cut into serving pieces
½ tsp. salt
Topping (*below*)
2 cans (16 oz. each) peeled tomatoes, drained and cut up

Serves 3 or 4

Make a large pan out of double foil, folding up the sides so the wine cannot pour out. Pour wine into foil, add garlic and basil. Place chicken, skin side down, into the wine and sprinkle with salt. Seal foil carefully. Place onto a hot barbecue grill for 40 minutes, or until chicken is tender.

While chicken is baking, prepare Topping.

When chicken is tender open foil and fold it back without tearing. Place ½ the tomatoes on top of the chicken. Spread Topping over the tomatoes. Top with remaining tomatoes. Seal foil.

Wrap entire package in another layer of foil if necessary. Place back onto the grill and cook for another 35 minutes.

Topping

8 scallions, finely chopped
1 onion, thinly sliced
1 green pepper, diced
2 cloves garlic, crushed
½ cup oil
½ lb. mushrooms, sliced
¼ tsp. basil
Salt and pepper to taste

In an iron skillet over a hot grill sauté scallions, onion, green pepper and garlic in oil until just limp. Add mushrooms and seasonings. Cook until mushrooms are just tender, about 8 to 10 minutes.

CHICKEN FROM TICINO

2 frying chickens (2½ to 3 lbs. each), cut into serving pieces
½ lb. bacon, chopped
6 scallions, chopped
1 tomato, peeled and chopped
1½ cups dry white wine
½ tsp. rosemary
Salt and pepper to taste
Cooked spaghetti or boiled rice

Serves 6

Place chicken and bacon into heavy double foil and wrap securely. Cook over low coals on a grill until the chicken pieces are tender, about 35 to 40 minutes.

Open foil and add scallions, tomato, wine, rosemary and salt and pepper. Rewrap chicken and cook for about 30 to 35 minutes.

Place chicken on a heated serving platter. Pour a little sauce from the foil over the chicken. Pour remaining sauce over spaghetti or rice.

GRILLED TURKEY

12- to 14-lb. turkey
Salt and white pepper
½ cup apple juice
1½ cups honey
2 Tbs. prepared mustard

¼ cup soy sauce
2 Tbs. dark brown sugar
1 Tbs. tomato paste
½ tsp. nutmeg

Serves 8 to 10

Defrost turkey as directed on package or for 36 hours in the refrigerator. Take giblets out of turkey. Rinse with cold water and pat dry with paper towels. Sprinkle with salt and pepper on the inside and the outside.

If possible use a bowl-type grill (cooking kettle) or cook turkey under a dome of double foil sealed around the edges. Light a large number of coals and let them get all gray. Push coals in a circle around the bowl. Put an aluminum pan in the center surrounded by coals.

In a bowl combine apple juice, honey, mustard, soy sauce, brown sugar, tomato paste and nutmeg. Beat with a whisk until smooth and well blended. Brush turkey generously with honey mixture inside the neck and body cavity. Baste turkey generously on all sides.

Place turkey onto grill over drip pan. Insert a meat thermometer into the thickest part of breast without touching the bone. Close the bowl or cover with a foil hood. Baste turkey every 20 to 25 minutes. Grill turkey for about 2½ to 3 hours, until thermometer shows 185° to 190°.

BARBECUED TURKEY THIGHS

6 turkey thighs, about 4 lbs.
Salt and pepper to taste
12 bacon strips
4 acorn squash, cut into ½" slices

2 cups barbecue sauce
1 cup chopped onions
½ cup brown sugar
2 cloves garlic, crushed
3 Tbs. lemon juice

Serves 6

Season turkey thighs on all sides with salt and pepper. Place thighs, side by side, into double foil large enough to cover turkey. Place 2 bacon strips over each thigh. Place onto a grill over low heat and cook for 1½ hours covered, or until meat is easily pierced, adding acorn squash slices at end of 1 hour.

In a bowl combine barbecue sauce, onions, brown sugar, garlic and lemon juice. Let stand at room temperature while turkey is cooking. After 1½ hours open foil and pour sauce over turkey. Grill 50 minutes longer, basting every 15 minutes with juices which have formed in foil.

Arrange turkey thighs on platter. Spoon juices over turkey and garnish with acorn squash slices.

MEATS

ROAST IN FOIL

2 onions, sliced into thin strips
5 Tbs. minced celery
2 carrots, thinly sliced
2 cloves garlic, crushed
3 Tbs. butter
3 Tbs. soy sauce

1 cup tomato sauce
1 Tbs. prepared mustard
1 tsp. salt
1 tsp. pepper
4- to 5-lb. rib eye roast

Serves 6 to 8

In a heavy skillet over a hot grill sauté onion, celery, carrots and garlic in butter until tender.

Mix together soy sauce, tomato sauce, mustard, salt and pepper. Add to vegetables.

Brown beef on all sides over hot coals. Put ½ the vegetable sauce on a large piece of heavy duty foil. Put roast in center of foil and pour rest of sauce over it. Fold foil over meat and seal edges so no sauce can pour out.

Cook roast over low coals for 2 to 2½ hours, turning several times. Use a meat thermometer inserted through top of sealed foil for correct temperature—140° for rare, 160° for medium.

GRILLED FILET MIGNONS

6 filet mignons, about 6 to 7 oz. each
½ cup dry red wine
1 Tbs. crushed bay leaves
1 tsp. fennel seeds
½ tsp. salt
½ tsp. pepper
4 Tbs. butter, melted
½ tsp. coarsely crushed peppercorns
2 cloves garlic, crushed
½ tsp. oregano

Serves 6

In a bowl mix together wine, bay leaves, fennel, salt and pepper. Pour over filet mignons and marinate overnight in refrigerator.

One hour before grilling, remove meat from refrigerator and let stand at room temperature. Grill over hot coals 3 to 4 minutes on each side, basting with marinade a few times. Filet mignon should be rare to medium rare.

Mix together melted butter, pepper, garlic and oregano. Just before serving brush steaks with seasoned butter.

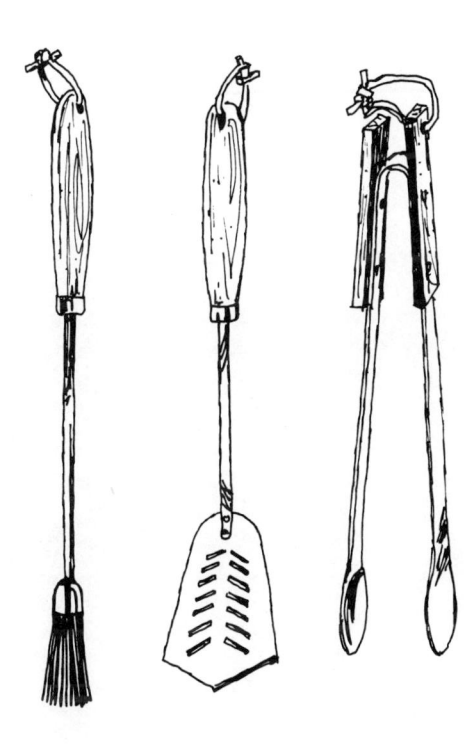

BLUE CHEESE STEAK

3 lbs. sirloin steak, 1½" to 2" thick
¼ cup olive oil
3 Tbs. wine vinegar
½ tsp. salt
½ tsp. pepper
½ tsp. thyme
½ tsp. basil
¼ cup butter
½ cup blue-veined cheese
2 garlic cloves, crushed
2 Tbs. chopped scallions
2 Tbs. brandy

Serves 6

Marinate steak in oil, vinegar, salt, pepper, thyme and basil for 6 hours in the refrigerator.

Cream butter and cheese together. Add garlic, scallions and brandy.

Grill steak over very hot coals, 6 minutes on each side. Place on a heated platter. Spread blue cheese butter onto steak and let it melt a bit. Slice steak into ¼" strips and serve.

OYSTER-STUFFED STEAKS

2 cloves garlic, crushed
¼ cup butter
¼ cup minced celery
3 Tbs. minced onion
¼ cup dry white wine
1 can (8 oz.) small oysters, drained and with liquid reserved

½ pkg. (8 oz.) herb-seasoned stuffing mix
Salt and pepper to taste
6 boneless rib steaks (about ½ lb. each), cut 1" thick

Serves 6

In a skillet placed on a grill over hot coals, sauté garlic in butter, but do not let it brown. Add celery and onion and cook until just soft. Add white wine to reserved oyster liquid to make ½ cup of liquid. Pour into skillet. Add oysters, stuffing mix and salt and pepper to taste. Toss lightly.

Cut a horizontal pocket in each steak. Leave enough rim around outer edge of meat so filling will not break through. Stuff pockets in steaks lightly with oyster filling. Secure edges of steaks with toothpicks or little metal skewers. Grill over hot coals about 5 minutes on each side for rare steaks or 6 to 7 minutes for medium rare.

HAWAIIAN MEATBALLS ON SKEWERS

1 lb. ground beef
1 lb. ground lean pork
⅔ cup bread crumbs
⅔ cup evaporated milk or light cream
½ tsp. salt
¼ tsp. pepper
1 egg
Sauce (*below*)

Makes 30 to 40 meatballs

Place all ingredients except Sauce into a bowl and blend into a very smooth paste. With wet hands, roll mixture into 1" meatballs. Thread 3 to 4 meatballs on each wooden skewer and refrigerate until ready to cook (or place on ice for 1 to 2 hours in an ice chest).

Place meatballs onto a hot hibachi or grill. Baste generously with Sauce and broil for 7 to 8 minutes. Turn, baste and broil for an additional 8 minutes. Serve immediately.

Sauce

1 cup barbecue sauce
½ cup honey
2 Tbs. soy sauce
1 Tbs. dry mustard
½ cup pineapple juice
½ tsp. ginger

In a saucepan combine all the ingredients. Mix well and simmer for 7 to 8 minutes on the hibachi, stirring frequently. Cool before using.

SHISH KOFTESI (ARMENIAN KEBABS)

2 lbs. lean ground beef
1 cup finely minced onion
3 eggs
¼ tsp. cumin
1 tsp. thyme
2 tsp. salt
1 clove garlic, crushed
Olive oil

Serves 6 to 8

Combine ground beef, onion, eggs, cumin, thyme, salt and garlic and mix well; chill.

Form meat into sausage-shaped pieces about 3" long and 1" in diameter. Thread lengthwise on skewers, 2 or 3 to a skewer.

Brush with olive oil and grill over hot coals for 8 to 10 minutes, turning to brown all sides.

GRILLED LAMB ROAST

1 leg of lamb (about 6 to 7 lbs.), boned and butterflied
3 or 4 slivered garlic cloves
1 cup olive oil
1 Tbs. rosemary
1 Tbs. coarsely ground black pepper
Juice of 3 lemons
2 tsp. grated lemon rind
1 large onion, sliced into thin circles
Salt to taste
Lemon and Rosemary Butter (*below*)

Serves 8 to 10

Make several incisions in the meat on both sides. Stick slivered garlic into incisions. Brush meat generously with olive oil on both sides. Sprinkle with rosemary and pepper on one side and with a mallet or heel of your hand, pound the seasonings lightly into the meat. Turn the meat over and repeat pounding the rosemary and pepper into the meat. Generously sprinkle with juice of 2 lemons and grated lemon rind on both sides.

Spread ½ the onion on a large piece of double foil and place meat on top of the onion. Spread remaining onion on top of the meat. Cover with foil and refrigerate for 18 to 24 hours.

Build a good coal fire in a brazier-type barbecue unit large enough to accommodate the flattened out leg of lamb. Place a drip pan in the center of the fire bowl and surround the pan with hot coals covered with ashes.

Remove lamb from foil and discard onions. Dab meat with paper towel to blot up excess oil. Sprinkle with salt on both sides and place flat on grill. Insert a meat thermometer into the thickest part of the meat and grill for about 15 minutes per pound, turning twice, or until thermometer reaches 170° for medium and 180° for well done. Baste occasionally with the remaining olive oil and lemon juice.

Place lamb onto a cutting board and cut across the grain on a slight diagonal into thin slices. Serve on heated platter with Lemon and Rosemary Butter (below) and Deep-Fried Zucchini (page 129).

Lemon and Rosemary Butter
In a saucepan placed on a grill combine ½ lb. butter with juice of 2 lemons and 3 Tbs. fresh minced rosemary or 1 Tbs. dried rosemary. Cook together stirring occasionally until well blended, foamy and hot.

LAMB SHISH KEBAB

2 lbs. leg of lamb, cut into 1½" cubes
1 cup dry red wine
3 onions, quartered
3 Tbs. olive oil
2 Tbs. fresh mint leaves or 1 Tbs. dried mint
½ tsp. basil
2 Tbs. lemon juice
Salt and pepper to taste
2 green peppers
4 tomatoes

Serves 6

Place lamb into a large bowl. Pour wine over meat and toss. Add onions, olive oil, mint, basil, lemon juice and salt and pepper. Toss and refrigerate overnight.

Drain meat and onions well and blot with paper towels. Cut up green peppers and tomatoes into 1" pieces. Thread meat, onions, peppers and tomatoes onto 6 skewers. Sprinkle with more salt and pepper.

Place kebabs on a grill over hot charcoals and cook turning often, for 10 to 15 minutes. Serve immediately over rice.

MACEDONIAN SHISH KEBABS

3 lbs. lean leg or shoulder of lamb, cut into 1½" cubes
Salt and pepper to taste
3 garlic cloves, crushed
½ tsp. sage
½ tsp. rosemary
¼ cup olive oil
3 Tbs. wine vinegar
3 Tbs. prepared mustard
3 Tbs. minced scallions
2 large green peppers, cut into 1½" squares
2 large red peppers, cut into 1½" squares
¼ cup melted butter
½ cup minced parsley

Serves 6

Place lamb into a bowl and sprinkle with salt and pepper. Combine garlic, sage, rosemary, olive oil, vinegar, mustard and scallions and mix until smooth. Pour over the lamb. Cover bowl and refrigerate for 3 to 4 hours.

Thread lamb cubes onto skewers alternating with green and red peppers. Sprinkle with salt. Place onto a hot barbecue grill. Brush a few times with butter. Brown on all sides. Cut a small slit with a sharp knife to test for doneness.

Serve over a bed of rice, sprinkled with parsley.

EAST INDIAN SATÉ

1 Tbs. ground coriander
1 Tbs. salt
½ tsp. ground cayenne pepper or to taste
1 onion, chopped
4 cloves garlic, crushed
½ cup soy sauce
¼ cup lime juice
½ cup peanut butter
¼ cup brown sugar
½ cup peanut oil
Tabasco sauce to taste
2 lbs. boneless pork, lamb or chicken, cut into 1" cubes

Serves 6

In a bowl combine all ingredients except meat. Beat with a whisk until smooth or purée in a blender.

Marinate meat in this mixture for 1 to 2 hours. String meat onto wooden skewers.

Grill satés over hot coals until brown but not dry, about 3 to 4 minutes on each side. Baste often with marinade. Place onto a serving platter. Heat remaining marinade in a saucepan and pour over meat.

CHINESE PORK KEBABS

½ cup soy sauce
2 Tbs. peanut oil
3 garlic cloves, mashed
½ small dried chili pepper, crushed
2 tsp. sugar
¼ tsp. ginger
¼ tsp. allspice

Salt and pepper to taste
2 lbs. lean pork, cut into 1½" cubes
24 to 30 pineapple chunks, well drained
2 medium green peppers, cut into chunks

Serves 6

In a bowl mix together soy sauce, oil, garlic, chili pepper, sugar, ginger, allspice and salt and pepper. Put meat into marinade. Marinate pork for 5 hours in the refrigerator stirring a few times.

Remove pork from marinade and thread onto skewers, alternating with pineapple chunks and green pepper. Barbecue 5" above hot coals turning often, for about 15 minutes, or until pork is thoroughly cooked.

BUTTERFLIED PORK ROAST

1 boned pork butt, butterflied
Salt and pepper to taste
¼ cup olive oil
½ cup vinegar
2 Tbs. dark brown sugar

⅓ cup chopped parsley
2 cloves garlic, minced
1½ tsp. salt
¼ tsp. pepper

Serves 10 to 12

Sprinkle pork with salt and pepper. Place meat fatty side up on a cutting board and score with a knife in a diamond pattern.

In a bowl mix remaining ingredients. Place pork into a baking dish and pour on the marinade. Refrigerate for 8 hours.

Place meat, scored side down, on the grill over low heat and cook for 1 hour, basting frequently with marinade. Turn meat and cook for another hour, continuing to baste frequently. Slice into 1" slices and serve.

MAPLE-FLAVORED BARBECUE SPARERIBS

2 lemons
3-lb. rack of spareribs or loin ribs
1¼ cups maple syrup
½ cup wine vinegar
2 Tbs. soy sauce

2 Tbs. Worcestershire sauce
1 tsp. salt
2 tsp. dry mustard
½ tsp. cayenne pepper
½ cup water

Serves 6

Place lemon slices on ribs. Combine remaining ingredients and simmer over low heat until ingredients are thoroughly dissolved and mixture is slightly thickened.

Place ribs onto a grill about 6" above coals that have just turned gray. Baste with sauce every 15 minutes. If sauce thickens too much, add a little hot water to prevent ribs from burning. Turn ribs over 2 or 3 times, cooking them 20 to 25 minutes on each side.

HAM STEAK BARBECUE

1 ham steak, 2" thick
2 Tbs. oil
1 cup grapefruit juice
2 Tbs. sugar
½ tsp. salt
1 tsp. oregano

¼ tsp. pepper
¼ cup soy sauce
1 tsp. grated grapefruit rind
2 Tbs. chopped parsley
¼ cup chopped scallions

Serves 6

Place ham steak in shallow dish. Mix remaining ingredients and pour over ham. Cover and refrigerate for 2 hours.

Remove ham from marinade and place on grill when coals have reached light-gray ash stage. Grill 25 minutes on one side, basting with marinade. Turn and grill 20 minutes longer. Remove from grill and serve with Grapefruit Sauce.

Grapefruit Sauce
½ cup light brown sugar
2 Tbs. cornstarch
¼ tsp. salt

¾ cup water
1¼ cups grapefruit juice
1 grapefruit, sectioned

In a saucepan mix brown sugar, cornstarch and salt. Gradually stir in water and grapefruit juice. Cook on the grill over low fire, stirring constantly, until mixture thickens and comes to a boil. Simmer for 1 minute. Remove from grill and stir in grapefruit sections.

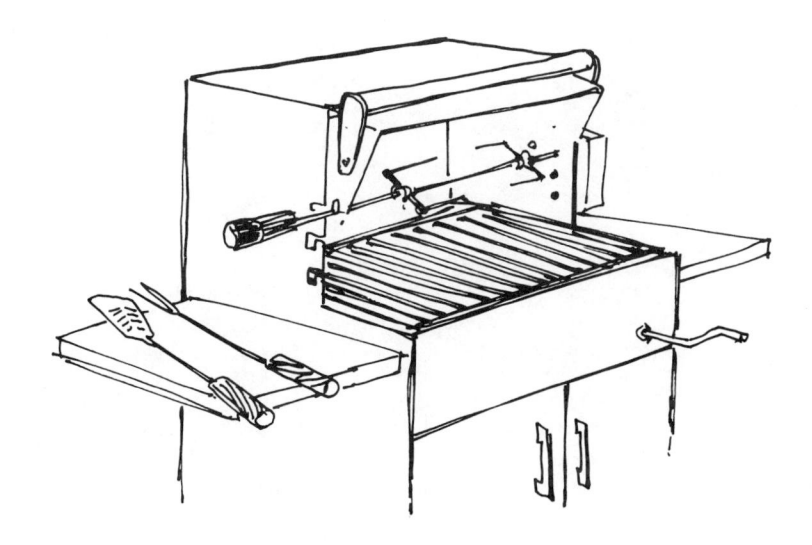

VEGETABLES

LEMONY CAULIFLOWER

1 large head cauliflower, separated into flowerets
½ tsp. salt
⅓ cup salad oil
Grated peel and juice of ½ fresh lemon

3 Tbs. chopped green pepper
2 Tbs. chopped pimiento
1 small clove garlic, crushed
¼ tsp. oregano
⅛ tsp. pepper

Serves 6

Place cauliflower on a large square of double foil and turn up edges. Sprinkle with salt and pour on ½" boiling water. Wrap up tightly and place directly on grill. Cook until tender about 7 to 12 minutes; drain.

In a bowl combine remaining ingredients. Add cooked cauliflowerets and refrigerate. Toss slightly before serving.

HERBED VEGETABLES

4 medium zucchini, cut into ½" rounds
2 large tomatoes, diced
2 medium onions, thinly sliced
½ tsp. salt
½ tsp. basil
¼ tsp. thyme
¼ tsp. marjoram
¼ tsp. pepper
½ cup creamy Italian dressing
Garlic salt to taste

Serves 8

Place zucchini, tomatoes, onions and remaining ingredients except garlic salt in the center of a large square of heavy-duty aluminum foil. Seal foil tightly. Cook on grill about 30 minutes. Sprinkle with garlic salt before serving.

VEGETABLES WITH FENNEL

2 tomatoes, cut into wedges
1 eggplant, cut into cubes
2 medium onions, sliced
2 zucchini, sliced
1 Tbs. brown sugar

2 chicken bouillon cubes, crushed
½ tsp. crushed fennel seed
½ tsp. salt
⅛ tsp. pepper
4 Tbs. butter, cut into pieces

Serves 6

In a bowl toss all ingredients together. Pour onto the center of a large square of heavy-duty aluminum foil. Seal package securely. Place on grill 5″ from coals and cook about 40 minutes, turning package from side to side twice.

DEEP-FRIED ZUCCHINI

7 large zucchini
Salt
2 cups flour
Oil for deep frying

1 tsp. paprika
½ tsp. salt
¼ tsp. pepper

Serves 8 to 10

Pare and slice zucchini into long strips ½" wide. Spread on a board and sprinkle generously with salt. Let stand for 10 minutes. Dry well with a kitchen towel.

Place a deep fryer with a basket onto a grill, or use an electric deep fryer. Heat oil to 365°–370°. Be careful if heating oil on the grill. It shouldn't flow over, and the pots should be deep enough so that if it sputters, it does not cause a flareup or fire. Use a candy or oil thermometer to check temperature.

Mix flour, paprika, salt and pepper. Coat zucchini with seasoned flour.

Fry small amounts at a time until pale golden brown. Remove the basket without dripping oil onto the coals. Drain zucchini on paper towels and serve immediately.

BAKED POTATOES WITH BACON AND CHEESE

8 large baking potatoes, well scrubbed
8 slices bacon
2 large onions, minced

½ lb. American cheese, shredded
1 cup sour cream
Salt and pepper

Serves 8

Wrap each potato in foil and bake on a grill, turning often, until soft to the touch.* (These may also be baked in a covered Dutch oven suspended over a fire.) Unwrap the potatoes and let cool slightly.

While potatoes are baking, cook bacon until crisp in a heavy iron skillet placed on the grill. Remove bacon with a slotted spoon and crumble. Fry onions in the bacon drippings until soft but not brown. Add cheese and sour cream, stir well and let the cheese melt slowly, shaking the pan several times. Add salt and pepper to taste and the crumbled bacon.

Slit open each potato. Scoop out the insides and add to the pan with the cheese and sour cream, tossing slightly with 2 forks. Fill potato skins with potato mixture, wrap in foil and heat over the grill for about 10 minutes. Serve immediately.

*Cooking time may range anywhere from 45 minutes to 1½ hours depending on the size of your potatoes and the intensity of your fire.

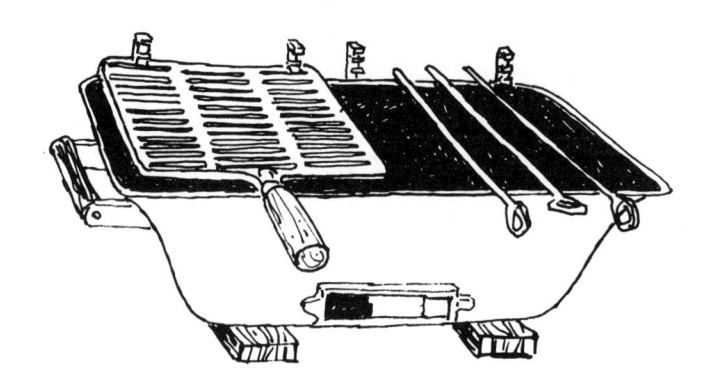

DILLED POTATOES

6 medium potatoes, peeled
Salt and pepper to taste
½ cup butter, softened

2 Tbs. parsley, minced
2 Tbs. fresh dill, minced, or 1 tsp. dried dill weed

Serves 6

Cut each potato into 1" slices and place on 6 squares of heavy-duty aluminum foil. Sprinkle slices generously with salt and pepper and spread with butter. Sprinkle with parsley and dill.

Reassemble slices to shape of whole potato; wrap in foil, sealing tightly. Place on grill 3" from coals and cook about 35 minutes, turning foil packages several times.

BAKED SWEET POTATOES OR YAMS

6 medium-sized sweet potatoes
or yams

Serves 6

Scrub sweet potatoes well and blot dry. Wrap in foil and bake on a grill over medium coals for 1 to 1½ hours, or until potatoes feel soft to the touch.

DESSERTS

BANANAS MAFOLIE

⅔ cup finely crushed vanilla wafers
½ cup finely crushed cashew nuts
¼ cup granulated sugar
6 firm, ripe bananas
2 Tbs. lemon juice

1 cup light brown sugar
½ tsp. nutmeg
½ tsp. cinnamon
½ tsp. ginger
½ cup guava jelly
½ cup rum

Serves 6

Mix together crushed wafers, nuts and sugar and set aside.

Peel a thin strip of skin from each banana. Scoop out the flesh, reserving the skins.

In a bowl break bananas into coarse pieces with a spoon. Combine with remaining ingredients and stir well. Fill banana skins with banana mixture almost to the top. Sprinkle with wafer-nut mixture and place each banana onto well-buttered foil; seal well.

Bake bananas for 15 to 20 minutes on a hot barbecue grill, turning packets on their sides. Unwrap and serve immediately in the skins. Or, chill bananas and serve topped with Coconut Cream and coconut flakes.

To make Coconut Cream:
Add 2 cups hot water to 3 cups grated coconut. Steep 1 hour, strain through cheesecloth, then squeeze the flakes dry. Let milk stand until cream rises to the top, about 1½ hours. Skim off cream with a spoon. Use as directed.

3
Wood- or Coal-Burning Range

The invention of the wood-burning stove in the early eighteenth century changed the mode of cooking completely.

By the end of the nineteenth century, the coal-burning stove became a standard item, especially in city kitchens. Most of these stove-oven combinations, which burned wood or coal, were fancy affairs, inlaid with tiles and adorned with scrollwork and other designs. Some had built-in water heaters, two baking ovens and four to six flat-top burners with rings, which regulated the heat for cooking. There was also a shelf above the stove where foods could be kept warm for hours.

The new old-fashioned ranges available today are combination stove and oven, have several burners on top covered with movable rings, a baking oven, water heater and warming oven box. They are compact and functional, and some are even equipped with oven thermometers. Fueled by wood or coal (or adapted to the use of oil), these stoves have the added dividend of heating the kitchen.

If you are the new owner of a wood burning stove it's a good idea to check with your local fire department for further information and regulations.

If you have a coal- or wood-burning range, especially a modern one with an attached thermometer, you can cook and bake all your favorites. Here are a few tips on temperature-testing without a thermometer.

To test the top of the stove for frying, sprinkle a few drops of water on the stove. If they bead, you are ready to cook. For simmering or boiling, place ½ cup water in a pan on top of the stove. When the water simmers or boils, depending on the heat you need, you are ready to cook.

To test the oven, sprinkle a little flour onto a cookie sheet and put it into the oven. If it blackens and burns in about two minutes, your oven is about 450°–500°. If it turns dark brown, it's about 400°. If the flour comes out beautifully golden brown, your oven is about 300°, ready to be used for most of the recipes in this chapter. There are usually hot spots in wood-burning stoves, particularly on the top of the range. Temperature can be adjusted by moving pots around to hotter or cooler areas, as desired.

Of course, a more accurate method

for determining temperature is an oven thermometer, a wise investment for the iron-stove cook, particularly if you are interested in more delicate baking and soufflés. To use an oven thermometer in a wood-burning stove, place the thermometer in the center of the oven. When it reaches the desired temperature, place the food to be baked in the oven and keep the stove stoked with the same amount of fuel as when you measured the temperature. Try to keep the fire constant by adding a few logs or coals at a time. For hints on how to buy wood for your stove and light a good fire, see pages 2–3 and 5. Also, check the literature that comes with your new wood- or coal-burning stove or, if you have an old one, request literature from the companies and foundries listed in the appendix.

Most of your favorite recipes are suitable for wood-burning ranges, and with just a bit of trial and error, you will learn to adjust the temperature and length of cooking time. To create more heat on top of the stove, remove a ring or cook right over the rings. To lower heat, move pan away from rings. From steaks to soufflés, you can prepare even delicate and complicated dishes on these old-fashioned new-fangled ranges. However, the process of cooking on the range is a slow one, so keep canned goods and convenience foods on hand for when you are in a big hurry!

For utensils, most modern pots and pans are fine, even heavy-cast aluminum, stainless steel with copper bottoms and enameled cast iron or tin-lined copper; but do not use lightweight aluminum. Ovenproof glass cookware is a bit tricky, but do not discard your favorite bake-and-serve utensils. You will soon determine how best to adapt them to your range through trial and error.

APPETIZERS

CHEESE WITH MUSHROOMS

6 slices white bread
12 Tbs. butter
1 lb. fresh mushrooms, quartered
2 Tbs. lemon juice
1 large onion, minced
¼ cup flour

1½ cups milk
1 cup light cream
1 tsp. salt
¼ tsp. pepper
6 slices Swiss cheese, same size as the bread
6 poached eggs

Serves 6

Sauté bread slices on both sides in 5 Tbs. of the butter until golden brown. Grease a 10″ × 12″ shallow baking dish. Line bottom of dish with bread slices in one layer.

Sprinkle mushrooms with lemon juice. Cook mushrooms and onion in 3 Tbs. of the butter over low heat until just tender, about 5 minutes.

In another saucepan melt the remaining 4 Tbs. butter. Stir in flour and cook, stirring, for 2 to 3 minutes until smooth and bubbly. Slowly stir in milk and cream. Cook over low heat, stirring constantly, until thick and smooth. Season with salt and pepper. Add mushrooms and onion.

Pour sauce over bread in baking dish. Top with cheese slices. Bake in a preheated 350° oven for 10 to 15 minutes, or until cheese is melted.

Top each serving with a poached egg and serve immediately.

DUTCH CHEESE STEAKS

6 Edam or Gouda cheese slices (each about 1½″ thick)
Flour
3 eggs, well beaten
2 cups seasoned bread crumbs
¼ cup butter or margarine
¼ cup oil
⅓ cup brandy
Juice of 1 lemon
2 tsp. grated lemon rind
Watercress and lemon wedges for garnish

Serves 6

Dredge cheese slices in flour to coat all sides. Dip slices into beaten eggs, then into bread crumbs. Press crumbs firmly into cheese to make them adhere. Place slices on foil-lined cookie sheet; chill for 30 minutes.

In a large iron skillet heat together butter and oil. Brown cheese slices 1 to 2 minutes on each side. Remove to a large, heated platter.

Heat brandy, ignite and ladle over cheese slices. Sprinkle with lemon juice and grated lemon rind and garnish with watercress and lemon wedges.

FRIED CHEESE

4 eggs
¼ cup milk
¼ tsp. salt
¼ tsp. pepper
1 loaf Italian bread

1½ to 2 lbs. mozzarella cheese
1 cup flour
1 cup Italian seasoned bread
 crumbs
1 cup vegetable oil

Serves 8

In a bowl beat eggs with milk, salt and pepper.

Cut the crust off the bread, and slice loaf into equal squares ½" thick. Cut cheese into ¼" slices about ⅛" smaller around than the bread. Place 1 slice cheese between 2 slices bread, sandwich fashion. Dust with flour, dip into egg mixture and press the edges together to seal. Roll in bread crumbs.

In a large skillet heat oil. Place a cube of bread in skillet. When it turns golden brown, the oil is ready for frying. Fry the sandwiches, 3 or 4 at a time, turning once, until golden brown on both sides. Remove with a slotted spoon and drain on paper towels. Serve immediately.

CHICKEN WINGS WITH PLUM SAUCE

1 cup beer
2 cups flour
1 Tbs. paprika
½ tsp. garlic powder
1 tsp. salt
½ tsp. white pepper
3 eggs

2 to 3 cups vegetable oil or vegetable shortening
20 to 30 chicken wings (use only first joint, closest to breast; cut off tips)
20 to 30 decorative paper frills
Plum Sauce (*below*)

Serves 10

In a bowl beat together beer, flour, paprika, garlic powder, salt, pepper and eggs until smooth. Add more flour if necessary to produce a thick batter.

Heat oil in a large skillet or deep fryer with a basket. Place a bread cube in oil; when it turns brown oil is ready for use (about 375° on a thermometer). Dip each wing into the batter* and fry on both sides until golden brown, or deep fry. Drain on paper towels. Keep warm in an approximately 200° oven. Cool oven by opening door slightly.

Just before serving, place paper frills onto the exposed bones. Serve Plum Sauce on the side.

* *NOTE:* When dipping wings into the batter, leave a bit of bone exposed so that you may place paper frills on the bone after frying the chicken.

Plum Sauce

1 cup plum preserves
3 Tbs. wine vinegar
1 tsp. prepared mustard
½ tsp. garlic powder

¼ tsp. white pepper
¼ tsp. ginger
Salt to taste

In a small saucepan heat preserves; add vinegar, mustard, garlic powder, pepper, ginger and salt. Simmer for 5 minutes. Cool before serving.

SOUPS

AVGOLEMONO (GREEK EGG AND LEMON SOUP)

2 quarts chicken broth
2 to 3 cups cooked rice*
4 eggs

Juice of 2 lemons
Salt and white pepper

Serves 6 or 7

Bring chicken broth to boil in a soup pot. Add 2 or 3 cups of cooked rice, depending on how thick you would like the soup to be. Return to boil and remove from heat.

In a bowl beat eggs until very smooth. Beat in lemon juice and add 2 cups of the broth from the pot, beating steadily.

Add egg mixture to soup in pot, beating continuously. Heat but do not boil, or soup will curdle. Season with salt and pepper to taste. Serve immediately.

*See page 255 for a quick recipe.

HEARTY BEAN SOUP

¼ cup chopped onion
1 cup coarsely chopped ham
2 Tbs. butter

1 can (28-oz.) brick-oven baked beans
1 cup beef broth
¼ tsp. pepper

Serves 6

In a large iron kettle sauté onion and ham in butter for 5 minutes, or until onion is soft and transparent. Combine 2 cups of the beans and the beef broth in a blender;* purée until smooth. Add to kettle with the remaining beans and the pepper. Simmer for 15 minutes. If a thinner soup is desired, add more beef broth.

*If blender is not available, purée in a hand-operated food mill.

CREAM OF CARROT SOUP

1 cup sliced carrots (about 6 carrots)
1 large onion, sliced
2 stalks celery with leaves, sliced
3 cups chicken broth
1 tsp. salt

Generous pinch cayenne pepper
⅔ cup cooked rice
1 cup heavy cream
2 Tbs. gin
1 cup unsweetened whipped cream

Serves 6 to 8

Place carrots, onion, celery and ½ cup of the chicken broth in a saucepan. Bring to a boil, cover, reduce heat and simmer for 20 minutes.

Pour into container of an electric blender, add salt, cayenne and rice.* Cover and purée mixture at high speed. Remove cover of blender and, with the motor running, pour in remaining broth and the heavy cream.

Pour soup back into saucepan and heat but do not allow to boil. Add gin and top each serving with a dab of whipped cream.

*If blender is not available, purée in a hand-operated food mill.

MINESTRONE (HEARTY ITALIAN SOUP)

6 strips bacon, diced
1 large onion, diced
2 large potatoes, diced
3 carrots, sliced
3 stalks celery, diced
2 quarts beef bouillon
2 cans (15 oz. each) Great Northern beans
2 cups finely sliced cabbage
1 tsp. basil
1 tsp. oregano
½ tsp. rosemary
3 cloves garlic, crushed
Salt and pepper
1 cup grated Parmesan cheese

Serves 8 to 10

In a large soup pot cook bacon until it begins to brown but is still limp. Add onion and cook until golden brown. Add potatoes, carrots, celery and bouillon. Cook covered over low heat for 45 minutes to 1 hour.

Add beans, cabbage, basil, oregano, rosemary, garlic and salt and pepper to taste. Cover and simmer for 15 minutes, or until cabbage is tender. Serve sprinkled with Parmesan cheese.

SOUR AND HOT SOUP

2 Chinese mushrooms*
1 leek, white part only
3 slices baked ham
5 cups chicken stock or broth
¼ cup shredded bamboo shoots
12 shrimp, shelled and deveined
1½ Tbs. soy sauce
1 Tbs. vinegar or more to taste

1 Tbs. cornstarch mixed with 2 Tbs. water
3 eggs, beaten
6 snow peas, cleaned and cut into thin strips
1½ tsp. Tabasco sauce
½ tsp. pepper
Salt to taste
2 Tbs. finely chopped scallions

Serves 4 or 5

Soak mushrooms as directed on package. Cut mushrooms, leek and ham into thin strips.

Bring chicken stock to a boil in a heavy pot. Add mushrooms, leek, ham and bamboo shoots; cook for 3 minutes. Add shrimp, soy sauce, vinegar and cornstarch mixture; cook for 2 minutes.

Stir in beaten eggs. Add snow peas, Tabasco, pepper and salt. Simmer for 1 minute and serve sprinkled with scallions.

*Available in specialty and Chinese grocery stores.

SALADS

INSALATA DI BROCCOLI (BROCCOLI SALAD)

1½ to 2 lbs. (1 large bunch) broccoli
¼ cup olive oil
3 Tbs. lemon juice
2 cloves garlic, minced
½ tsp. salt
½ tsp. pepper
½ tsp. oregano
3 Tbs. scallions, minced
3 Tbs. parsley, minced
1 cup thinly sliced pimiento
½ cup grated Parmesan cheese

Serves 4 or 5

Separate broccoli into flowerets; cut off thick stems. Cook in boiling salted water 5 to 8 minutes, or until just tender. Drain well and refrigerate.

Place broccoli in a salad bowl; toss with oil, lemon juice and garlic. Sprinkle with salt, pepper and oregano. Add scallions, parsley, pimiento and cheese. Toss and serve.

BRUSSELS SPROUTS SALAD

2 lbs. fresh Brussels sprouts or 2 pkgs. (10 oz. each) frozen sprouts
2 cups chicken broth
⅓ cup wine vinegar
⅓ cup olive oil
½ tsp. tarragon
½ tsp. thyme
½ tsp. oregano
1 tsp. salt
¼ tsp. pepper
1 dozen cherry tomatoes, halved
1 Tbs. minced chives
1 Tbs. minced fresh dill or 1 tsp. dried dill weed

Serves 6

Use an aluminum or stainless steel saucepan.

If using frozen Brussels sprouts, cook as directed on package, using chicken broth instead of water. If using fresh sprouts, wash well; trim off outer leaves. Bring chicken broth to a boil, add sprouts and cook uncovered for 5 minutes.

Cover and cook 10 to 15 minutes, or until tender. Drain well and place in a bowl.

Pour vinegar and oil over the hot sprouts. Sprinkle with tarragon, thyme, oregano, salt and pepper. Chill for 2 to 3 hours or overnight.

Halve the tomatoes; add to sprouts. Taste for seasoning. Sprinkle with chives and dill.

Brussels Sprouts with Brown Butter and Bread Crumbs
Cook sprouts as for salad. Melt ½ cup butter; add ½ cup bread crumbs. Brown butter and crumbs. Pour over drained Brussels sprouts and toss well.

RUSSIAN SALAD

3 cups diced cooked red beets*
2 cups diced cooked carrots*
3 cups diced cooked potatoes*
2 cups cooked navy beans*
3 large dill pickles, diced

3 Tbs. minced scallions
Dressing (*below*)
Quartered hard-boiled eggs, sliced tomatoes and thinly sliced pickles for garnish

Serves 8

Place all ingredients except Dressing and garnish in a large bowl.

Pour Dressing over vegetables and toss lightly. Refrigerate. Serve as part of a buffet or as a salad in individual portions decorated with quartered eggs and sliced tomatoes and pickles.

Dressing

4 hard-cooked egg yolks, mashed
1 Tbs. prepared mustard
2 Tbs. sugar
½ cup mayonnaise
½ cup sour cream

½ cup olive oil
¼ cup wine vinegar
¼ cup minced parsley
½ tsp. salt
½ tsp. black pepper

In a mixing bowl, mash egg yolks; add mustard, sugar and mayonnaise. Mix into a smooth paste, then beat in sour cream, olive oil, vinegar, and add parsley, salt and pepper.

*Cook in usual manner or use canned.

FISH

CHINESE FISH WITH PEPPER SAUCE

5 black Chinese mushrooms*
1 cup hot water
2 tsp. salted black beans*
½ cup cold water
Two 1-lb. pomfrets, butterfish or flounder
2 Tbs. peanut oil
1 Tbs. sesame seed oil

2 Tbs. soy sauce
1 small red hot chili pepper, minced
1 Tbs. minced scallions
¼ lb. cooked ham, cut into thin slivers
2 Tbs. minced fresh ginger root
2 oz. rice wine or pale dry sherry

Serves 4

Place mushrooms in a bowl with the hot water and let stand for 15 minutes. Drain and slice into thin slices.

Soak black beans in the cold water for 5 minutes. Squeeze dry and mince.

Place fish on an oiled rack in a baking pan. Pour 2 cups water into pan. Sprinkle fish with mushrooms and beans. Brush with peanut oil, sesame oil and 1 Tbs. of the soy sauce. Spread ¼ of the chili pepper over the fish, then put remainder into water in pan. Spread scallions, ham and 1 Tbs. of the ginger root over fish.

Cover pan with foil and bake in a 375° oven for about 30 minutes or until fish flakes easily. Place fish onto a serving platter.

Pour water remaining in baking pan into a saucepan. Add remaining soy sauce and ginger root and the sherry. Salt to taste and, if desired, add more hot pepper. Bring to boil and boil for 2 to 3 minutes. Pour over fish.

*Available in specialty and Chinese grocery stores.

RED SNAPPER TROPICAL

8 red snapper fillets (about ½ lb. each)
4 Tbs. melted butter, or more as needed
Salt and white pepper to taste
½ tsp. each nutmeg, allspice and ginger
1 cup pale dry sherry
1 Tbs. cornstarch
½ cup orange juice
Grated rind of 1 orange
2 grapefruits, peeled and sectioned
2 oranges, peeled and sectioned
1 cup lightly toasted coconut flakes

Serves 8

Place fish fillets in a large, well-buttered baking dish. Brush generously with melted butter and sprinkle with salt, pepper and ¼ teaspoon each nutmeg, allspice and ginger. Cover with foil and bake in a preheated 350° oven for 25 minutes; uncover.

In a bowl mix sherry, cornstarch, orange juice and orange rind. Pour ½ of the liquid over the fish. Arrange grapefruit and orange sections on top, sprinkle with salt, pepper and the remaining nutmeg, allspice and ginger.

Bake uncovered, basting often with the remaining liquid for about 10 minutes, or until fish flakes easily.

Serve sprinkled with toasted coconut flakes.

BAKED FISH IN COCONUT SAUCE

4 lbs. thick red snapper steaks, cut into chunks
Salt and pepper to taste
½ cup lemon juice
3 Tbs. soy sauce
½ tsp. ginger
3 cups thick coconut milk*
Juice of 1 lemon
¼ tsp. allspice

Serves 10

Place fish in a buttered baking dish. Sprinkle with salt and pepper. Mix ½ cup lemon juice, the soy sauce and ¼ tsp. of the ginger and pour over fish. Place into a preheated 350° oven and bake for 10 minutes.

Mix coconut milk, juice of 1 lemon, remaining ginger and the allspice and pour over fish. Continue baking for 10 to 15 minutes, or until fish flakes easily. Adjust seasoning, adding more salt and pepper to taste.

To make coconut milk: Place 6 cups shredded coconut (fresh, if possible) into a large bowl. Pour 3 cups boiling water over the coconut and let steep for about 10 minutes. Strain the liquid through a double thickness of cheesecloth into a bowl, squeezing well to get all the coconut milk out of the flakes. Refrigerate until ready to use.

FILLETS OF SOLE BURGUNDY STYLE

2 sole fillets (½ lb. each)
Salt and pepper
¾ cup dry red wine
2 tsp. flour
2 Tbs. butter, softened
½ tsp. Kitchen Bouquet
16 small white onions, boiled
¼ lb. whole button mushrooms, sautéed in 2 Tbs. butter

Serves 4

Sprinkle both sides of fillets with salt and pepper. Place in a buttered skillet with cover. Add wine, cover and simmer 8 to 10 minutes, or until fish flakes easily.

Drain off cooking liquid, strain it into a saucepan and boil down until reduced by half. Blend flour and butter to make a smooth paste; add to the reduced cooking liquid and mix well. Cook, stirring, for 2 minutes, or until thickened. Color with Kitchen Bouquet. Season to taste with salt and pepper.

Transfer fish to a warmed platter and surround it with onions and mushrooms. Coat fish and vegetables with the sauce. Serve immediately.

FILLETS OF SOLE IN WHITE WINE

8 sole fillets
1½ cups white wine
1½ cups water
Salt and pepper
¼ lb. unsalted butter
6 shallots, finely chopped
2 dozen mussels, precooked* and shelled or use canned
2 dozen small shrimp, shelled and deveined
2 dozen small mushroom caps with stems cut off
1 cup Velouté Sauce (*below*)
Juice of 1 lemon
1 cup unsweetened whipped cream

Serves 8

In a large skillet with cover poach the fillets 10 minutes in white wine and water. Add salt, pepper, butter and shallots, simmer for 5 minutes. Remove fillets with a slotted spoon to a buttered ovenproof serving dish.

Cook shelled mussels, shrimp and mushroom caps in the same skillet with the poaching liquid for 5 minutes. Remove with a slotted spoon and place around the fish.

Boil down the poaching liquid until it is reduced by two-thirds; stir in Velouté Sauce and lemon juice. Strain sauce through a fine sieve.

Fold whipped cream into sauce, pour over fillets. Reheat briefly until just golden brown.

Velouté Sauce
3 Tbs. butter
3 Tbs. flour
1 cup light cream
1 cup chicken broth
Salt and white pepper to taste

In a saucepan melt butter and add flour, stirring constantly with a wooden spoon. When butter and flour bubble up, add cream and broth, stirring constantly. Bring to a boil, stirring constantly. Cook for about 3 minutes on low heat until sauce thickens. Add salt and pepper. If sauce thickens too much add a little more broth.

*Cook in 1 quart simmering water until they open, about 10 to 15 minutes. Discard unopened mussels.

FILLETS OF SOLE À LA CRÈME

6 sole fillets (about ½ lb. each)
24 large raw shrimp, shelled and deveined
Salt and white pepper
1½ cups dry white wine
1 cup heavy cream
3 Tbs. butter or margarine
⅛ tsp. thyme
⅛ tsp. crushed fennel seed
Salt and white pepper to taste
2 egg yolks, slightly beaten
Lemon slices, capers and parsley for garnish

Serves 6

Place fish and shrimp in a large, heavy-cast aluminum or stainless-steel skillet. Sprinkle with salt and pepper. Pour in wine, bring to a boil and simmer for 4 to 5 minutes, or until fish flakes easily.

Remove fillets with a slotted spoon and place on a heatproof, well-buttered serving platter or shallow casserole; reserve cooking liquid. Place 4 shrimp onto each fillet.

Bring reserved liquid to a boil and cook until reduced to 1 cup; add cream, butter and seasonings. Bring just to boiling point and stir in the egg yolks. Do not let sauce boil.

Remove sauce from heat and pour over fish and shrimp. Garnish with lemon slices, capers and parsley.

Serve immediately with a tossed green salad, white rice and French bread.

TROUT AMANDINE

2 trout (about 10 oz. each)
Salt and pepper to taste
½ cup flour
1 tsp. paprika
6 Tbs. butter

½ cup thinly sliced almonds
2 tsp. lemon juice
2 Tbs. minced parsley
6 thin lemon slices

Serves 2

Sprinkle trout with salt and pepper inside and out. Mix flour and paprika; dredge fish in flour. In a large skillet melt 4 Tbs. of the butter and sauté fish on each side for 5 to 7 minutes, or until fish flakes easily.

While fish is cooking, in small skillet melt 2 Tbs. butter, add almonds and sauté until golden brown. Just before serving, sprinkle lemon juice, almonds and parsley over the trout and garnish with lemon slices.

PERUVIAN FISH MEDLEY

1 lb. red snapper fillets
1 lb. flounder fillets
1 lb. halibut fillets or steaks
1 lb. medium shrimp, shelled and deveined
1 lb. shucked raw oysters*
Juice of 1 lemon
1 large onion, finely chopped
3 cloves garlic, crushed
¼ tsp. coriander
¼ tsp. thyme
¼ tsp. nutmeg

1 tsp. crushed bay leaves
⅛ tsp. red pepper flakes
1½ cups tomato sauce
1 cup dry sherry
½ cup finely chopped fresh parsley
1 cup chopped walnuts
1 cup bread crumbs
½ cup olive oil
1 jar (5 oz.) pimientos, cut into strips

Serves 7 or 8

Cut fillets into 4" pieces. Place in a shallow dish, add shrimp and oysters and sprinkle with lemon juice. Butter well a 2½ to 3 quart ovenproof baking dish with a cover.

In a bowl combine onion, garlic, seasonings, tomato sauce and sherry. In another bowl mix together parsley, walnuts and bread crumbs.

Divide fish and seafood into 3 parts. Place a layer of fish and seafood in bottom of baking dish, pour ⅓ of the liquid over the fish, then sprinkle with ⅓ of the dry ingredients. Repeat layering twice, finishing with dry ingredients.

Dribble olive oil over top and decorate with pimientos. Cover and bake for 35 minutes in a 350° oven. Uncover and bake for 15 minutes. Serve immediately.

*You may substitute 6 to 8 oz. crabmeat, clams, mussels or cut-up lobster meat for the oysters.

SCAMPI FRA VINTONE

2 Maine lobsters (about 2 lbs. each) or 2 large lobster tails
10 scallions, finely chopped
½ large Spanish onion, diced
2 cloves garlic, finely chopped
¼ cup olive oil

8 to 10 large shrimp, peeled, deveined and butterflied
Salt and pepper to taste
2 tsp. oregano
4 cups canned tomatoes, chopped
½ cup dry white wine

Serves 4

Pull all the meat out of the lobster tails. Crack the claws and remove the meat.

In a large stainless steel skillet sauté scallions, onion and garlic together in oil until golden brown. Add lobster meat and shrimp, stirring gently and cook until just pink, about 5 to 6 minutes.

Add salt, pepper, oregano, tomatoes and wine. Cook until done, about 10 minutes.

Serve over bed of rice.

SHRIMP TOLLIVER

1 lb. small raw shrimp, shelled and deveined
¼ cup olive oil
3 Tbs. lemon juice
2 Tbs. butter
1 clove garlic
½ cup chopped almonds
Few dashes of Tabasco sauce
2 Tbs. dry white vermouth
2 cups hot cooked rice
Pinch of saffron
2 Tbs. chopped chives

Serves 3

Marinate shrimp in olive oil and lemon juice for 2 hours in the refrigerator, turning shrimp once. Drain, reserving the marinade.

In a skillet heat butter, add shrimp and garlic and cook until shrimp turns pink. Discard garlic and transfer shrimp to a hot platter.

To the skillet add almonds, reserved marinade, Tabasco and vermouth. Heat and pour over shrimp.

Serve with rice mixed with saffron and chives.

POULTRY

BAKED SPANISH CHICKEN

3-lb. frying chicken, cut into serving pieces
2 Tbs. butter
¼ cup olive oil
3 medium onions, cut into strips
2 medium green peppers, cut into strips
2 cloves garlic, crushed
16-oz. can tomato purée

½ cup cooked lean pork or ham, cubed
½ cup black olives, halved and pitted
½ cup green olives, halved and pitted
Salt and pepper
2 pimientos, cut into strips

Serves 4 or 5

In a large skillet sauté chicken in butter and olive oil until golden brown. When chicken is golden, place into an ovenproof casserole with cover and set aside.

Sauté onions, peppers and garlic in remaining oil in skillet until tender but not brown. Pour off excess oil.

Add tomato purée, pork, olives and salt and pepper to taste. Mix well and pour over chicken in casserole. Lift chicken pieces to coat with the mixture. Garnish with pimiento strips. Cover and bake in 350° oven for about 30 minutes, or until chicken is tender.

PINEAPPLE CHICKEN

3 frying chickens (2½ to 3 lbs. each), cut into serving pieces
2 cups flour
Salt and pepper to taste
½ Tbs. crushed fennel seed
¼ lb. butter
2 cups crushed pineapple, well drained
1 cup pineapple juice
½ cup sugar
¼ tsp. ginger
¼ tsp. cinnamon
1½ lbs. raisins
1½ cups pale dry sherry
2 cups chopped walnuts

Serves 8

Pat chicken dry with a paper towel. Mix flour, salt, pepper and fennel seed. Dredge chickens in the seasoned flour.

Melt butter in a skillet and brown chickens on both sides. Place chickens into a well-buttered baking pan.

Combine pineapple, pineapple juice, sugar, ginger, cinnamon, raisins and sherry. Pour into skillet used to brown chickens. Bring to a boil, season to taste and pour over chickens.

Bake in a preheated 350° oven for 35 to 40 minutes. Sprinkle with walnuts and serve.

DUCK WITH OLIVE SAUCE

5- to 6-lb. duck, cut into serving pieces
2 tsp. salt
½ tsp. pepper
½ tsp. oregano
½ tsp. rosemary
1 cup chopped onions
1 cup finely chopped celery
1 cup dry red wine
2 bay leaves
1 cup pitted black olives, halved

Serves 4

Wash duck, remove as much fat as possible and dry. Rub duck pieces with a mixture of salt, pepper, oregano and rosemary.

In a heavy pot, brown duck pieces on all sides. Pour off fat. Add onions and celery and cook for 15 minutes. Pour off fat again.

Add wine and bay leaves. Bring to a boil, cover and simmer for 1 hour or until tender, basting frequently. Place duck on a heated serving dish and keep warm.

Skim fat off sauce in pot. Remove bay leaves. Add olives and cook for 5 minutes. Pour some sauce over the duck and serve the rest on the side.

DUCK WITH ORANGES

1 cup dry red wine
1 clove garlic, mashed
1 Tbs. lemon juice
2 Tbs. minced parsley
2 Tbs. minced scallions

1 duckling (4 to 5 lbs.)
Salt and white pepper to taste
4 Tbs. butter, softened
1 cup fresh orange juice
5 oranges, peeled and sectioned

Serves 4

In a large bowl, mix wine, garlic, lemon juice, parsley and scallions. Marinate duck in the mixture overnight in the refrigerator, turning occasionally.

Drain duck, reserving marinade, pat dry, sprinkle with salt and pepper and rub well with butter. Place on a rack in a baking pan and bake in a 350° oven for 1 to 2 hours, or until the joints move easily. While duck is roasting, strain reserved marinade and mix with orange juice. Baste duck often with marinade mixture.

Place duck on a heated platter and keep warm. Pour remaining marinade into baking pan and swish it around to deglaze pan. Add orange slices and turn to coat with liquid in pan. Bake for 5 minutes. Serve duck decorated with orange slices.

MEATS

PAN-COOKED STEAK

⅔ cup all-purpose flour
½ tsp. salt
¼ tsp. pepper
¼ tsp. oregano
2 lbs. boneless round steak, sliced into 12 slices, ½" thick
3 Tbs. vegetable oil
1 large onion, finely chopped
½ cup tomato sauce
1 Tbs. brown sugar

2 tsp. wine vinegar
1 tsp. dry mustard
1 cup beef bouillon
½ tsp. salt
¼ tsp. oregano
⅛ tsp. pepper
24 small potatoes, peeled and cooked
1 lb. sliced green beans
1 cup thinly sliced pimiento

Serves 6

Mix together flour, salt, pepper and oregano. Coat steaks with the seasoned flour, then pound flat with a mallet.

Heat oil in a 10" skillet with cover and brown steaks on both sides. Push steaks aside, add onions and cook until just tender, about 5 minutes.

While onions are cooking, in a bowl mix tomato sauce, brown sugar, vinegar, mustard and beef bouillon. Add salt, oregano and pepper.

Cover steaks with onions and pour tomato mixture over steaks. Stir gently, cover and cook over medium heat for about 1½ hours, or until steaks are tender. You may have to push a log or coals aside to reduce heat. Stir once in a while.

Add potatoes, green beans and pimiento to skillet. Stir and cook until beans are tender, about 15 minutes. Add more salt and pepper to taste. Serve with crusty French bread.

STUFFED PEPPERS

12 green peppers
½ lb. lean ground beef
½ lb. lean ground pork
½ cup cooked rice
1 egg
½ tsp. salt
¼ tsp. pepper
3 cloves garlic, mashed
2 Tbs. ice cold water

1 small onion, minced
3 Tbs. olive oil
1 Tbs. paprika
16-oz. can or jar Italian tomato sauce with meat
½ tsp. oregano
½ tsp. tarragon
1 Tbs. sugar
2 cloves garlic, mashed

Serves 6

Core peppers and boil in salted water for 10 minutes; drain and let cool.

In a bowl combine beef, pork, rice, egg, salt, pepper, 3 cloves garlic and water; mix well. Sauté onion in oil until tender, add paprika and stir into meat mixture.

Stuff each pepper with meat mixture. Pour tomato sauce into a deep casserole with a cover, stir in oregano, tarragon, sugar and 2 cloves garlic and place the peppers in the casserole.

Bake in a 350° oven for 1 to 1½ hours, or until meat is cooked through and peppers are tender. Serve hot as an appetizer or main dish.

SCALLOPINI OF VEAL WITH MARSALA

2 lbs. thinly sliced veal cutlets
Salt and pepper to taste
1½ cups flour
1 Tbs. paprika
5 Tbs. butter
1 cup Marsala wine
¼ cup chicken stock

½ lb. chanterelle mushrooms, sliced or ½ lb. fresh mushrooms, sliced
½ cup heavy cream
Salt and pepper
1 Tbs. butter, softened
1 Tbs. flour
Chopped parsley

Serves 6

Pound veal cutlets as thin as possible between waxed paper. Sprinkle with salt and pepper. Combine flour and paprika.

Melt 5 Tbs. butter in a large skillet. Coat meat with flour and brown on both sides. Pour ½ cup of the Marsala wine and the chicken stock into skillet. Cover and simmer for 10 minutes. Remove meat to a warm platter.

Put sliced chanterelles in the skillet and cook for 2 minutes. Add remaining ½ cup wine, the cream and salt and pepper to taste.

Mix softened butter and flour to a smooth paste; add to skillet. Stir until butter is melted and sauce slightly thickened.

Pour sauce over veal and sprinkle with chopped parsley. Serve immediately.

STUFFED SCALLOPINI OF PORK MARENGO

6 boneless loin pork chops
Stuffing (*below*)
Salt and pepper to taste
2 tsp. paprika
1 cup flour
¼ cup vegetable oil
2 tsp. butter or margarine

3 Tbs. minced onion
12 mushrooms, sliced
½ cup wine
1½ cups heavy cream
1 tsp. Worcestershire sauce
3 Tbs. minced parsley

Serves 6

Butterfly each pork chop by cutting horizontally almost all the way through; leave about ¼" attached and spread open the two pieces. Flatten the pork pieces with a mallet and set aside while preparing Stuffing.

Place Stuffing on ½ of each chop, cover with the other ½ and secure with 2 toothpicks. Sprinkle with salt and pepper to taste and paprika. Dredge in flour.

In a skillet heat oil and butter and brown chops until golden brown on both sides. Cover and cook on low heat* about 35 minutes, or until chops are very tender. With a slotted spoon remove chops to a heated platter; cover with foil to keep warm.

Cook onions in remaining fat in same skillet as chops until they are just limp. Add mushrooms and wine. Simmer for 2 to 3 minutes.

Add cream and cook until sauce has been reduced by about ⅓. Add the Worcestershire and salt and pepper to taste. Bring to a boil. Pour over pork chops and sprinkle with parsley.

Stuffing

8 large fresh mushrooms, minced
3 Tbs. minced onion
½ cup bread crumbs
3 Tbs. minced celery
3 Tbs. minced parsley

2 cloves garlic, crushed
3 eggs
¼ tsp. basil
2 tsp. Worcestershire sauce
Salt and pepper to taste

In a bowl combine all the ingredients and blend with a wooden spoon into a smooth paste.

*Lower heat by pushing pan away from rings to a cooler part of stove.

PORK CHOPS MARGARITA

8 lean pork chops, 1" thick
Salt and pepper to taste
2 cups crushed pineapple, drained and with juice reserved
1 cup bread crumbs
1 cup finely chopped pecans
6 Tbs. melted butter
1 cup raisins
½ tsp. allspice
¼ lb. butter, softened
1 cup pineapple juice
1 Tbs. cornstarch
Salt and pepper to taste

Serves 8

Cut a pocket in each pork chop. Sprinkle chops with salt and pepper and set aside.

Place pineapple in a bowl. Add bread crumbs, pecans, melted butter, raisins and ¼ tsp. allspice; blend well. Stuff chops with bread-crumb mixture. Close the opening with a toothpick.

Grease a baking pan with 4 Tbs. of the soft butter. Butter chops on both sides with the remaining soft butter. Place chops in baking pan. Cover with foil and bake in a 400° oven for 25 minutes.

Uncover and bake for 10 to 15 minutes, until well browned and very tender. Transfer chops to a heated platter and keep warm while preparing the sauce.

Pour ½ of the pineapple juice into the baking pan. Swish around to deglaze and pour into a saucepan. Dissolve cornstarch in the remaining ½ cup juice and add to saucepan. Add salt, pepper and remaining allspice. Cook until slightly thickened. Taste for seasoning.

Pour sauce over chops or serve on the side in a sauceboat. Serve with buttered noodles or white rice.

SWEET AND SOUR SPARERIBS

3 lbs. baby pork spareribs
¼ cup soy sauce
1 cup flour
Salt and pepper to taste
4 cloves garlic, crushed
¼ cup shortening
½ cup light brown sugar
3 Tbs. finely chopped ginger root

½ cup vinegar
½ cup water
1 cup pineapple juice (reserve ½ cup for mixing with cornstarch)
1 cup drained crushed pineapple
2 Tbs. cornstarch

Serves 6

Separate spareribs into individual pieces. Sprinkle ribs with soy sauce. Combine flour, salt, pepper and garlic; dredge spareribs in seasoned flour.

In a large aluminum or stainless steel pot heat shortening and brown spareribs on both sides. Add brown sugar, ginger root, vinegar, water and pineapple juice and cook for about 1 to 1½ hours, or until spareribs are very tender.

Add crushed pineapple and stir well. Add cornstarch mixed with the pineapple juice. Simmer for about 5 minutes, or until sauce is slightly thickened. Taste for seasoning.

STEWS

KESHY YENA (STUFFED CHEESE)

1 large onion, finely chopped
4 Tbs. butter
¼ lb. ground beef
¼ lb. ground pork
1 green pepper, diced
1 small chili pepper, minced
¼ cup stuffed green olives, chopped

2 Tbs. chopped capers
3 Tbs. piccalilli
2 Tbs. catsup
⅓ cup raisins, chopped
2 beaten eggs
Salt to taste
1 whole Edam cheese (2 to 3 lbs.)

Serves 6 or 7

In a skillet sauté onion in butter until golden brown. Add beef and pork and cook, stirring, for 5 minutes.

Add green pepper and chili pepper. Cook, stirring frequently, until peppers are limp and meat is brown. Add olives, capers, piccalilli, catsup and raisins. Stir well and simmer for 2–3 minutes.

Add beaten eggs and salt. Cook for 5 minutes longer, stirring occasionally. Set aside and let cool.

Remove wax from edam cheese. Cut off about ¼″ to ½″ from the top and reserve. Carefully scoop out the inside of the cheese, leaving a shell about ¼″ to ½″ thick all around.* Soak cheese shell in cold water for 1 hour.

Butter an ovenproof baking dish just large enough to hold the cheese. Stuff hollowed cheese with meat mixture; replace top. Cover dish with foil and place in a pan of hot water. Bake in a 350° oven for 1 hour.

Serve hot from the baking dish.

*NOTE: Scooped-out cheese may be cut up and served as an appetizer or used for cooking.

PASTEL DE CHOCLO (VENEZUELAN MEAT PIE)

¼ cup peanut oil
2 medium onions, thinly sliced
2 lbs. ground chuck
3 Tbs. flour
3 green peppers, sliced into thin strips
1 tsp. salt

¼ tsp. red pepper flakes (optional)
½ cup beef broth
1 cup green olives, sliced
2 Tbs. butter for greasing
Topping (*below*)

Serves 6 to 8

In a large skillet heat oil, add onions and sauté until golden brown. Add ground chuck and cook until all red disappears, stirring constantly to prevent lumping. Sprinkle with flour and stir well. Add peppers, salt, pepper flakes and beef broth and cook until peppers are tender, about 10 to 15 minutes. Add olives and blend well.

Butter well a 10" ovenproof baking dish with 3" sides or a deep pie pan. Place meat mixture in baking dish.

Spread Topping over meat and bake in a preheated 350° oven for 25 to 30 minutes, until the topping is firm and slightly browned.

Serve hot, cut into wedges like pie.

Topping

1 medium onion, minced
2 Tbs. peanut oil
½ cup minced pimientos
3 cups canned yellow corn kernels, well drained

3 eggs
½ cup heavy cream
½ tsp. salt
Pinch red pepper flakes

In a large skillet sauté onion in oil until golden brown. Add pimientos and corn. Blend well and simmer for 2 to 3 minutes; remove from heat. In a bowl beat well eggs and cream, add salt and pepper flakes; then stir into vegetables in skillet.

SOUTH AMERICAN BOILED DINNER

- 3 lbs. beef short ribs
- ½ lb. salt pork cut into 2" pieces
- 2 Tbs. salt
- 4 qts. water
- 1 stewing chicken cut into serving pieces*
- 2 lbs. spicy Italian sausage or if available Spanish chorizos, cut into 3" pieces
- 10 sweet chili peppers, sliced
- 5 carrots, peeled and quartered
- 5 onions, quartered
- 2 cups canned garbanzos (chick peas), drained
- 5 cloves garlic, minced
- 1 large cabbage, cut into large chunks
- 6 large boiling potatoes, peeled and quartered
- 6 tomatoes, quartered
- 4 medium zucchini, cut into pieces, 2" long and 1" wide
- ½ tsp. coriander
- ½ tsp. oregano
- ¼ tsp. red pepper flakes (optional)
- Salt and pepper to taste
- ½ cup minced parsley
- ½ cup minced scallions

Serves 5 or 6

Place beef and pork into a stainless steel soup pot; add salt and water. Bring to a boil, reduce heat and simmer for 1½ hours. Skim off some of the fat and foam that form on top.

Add chicken and sausage and cook for ½ hour. Then add peppers, carrots, onions, garbanzos, garlic, cabbage and potatoes. Add more water if necessary. Cook for ½ hour.

Add tomatoes, zucchini, coriander, oregano and red pepper. Be careful with the red pepper; add a few flakes at a time. Cook for 15 to 20 minutes longer, or until zucchini is just tender. Season with salt and pepper.

Serve in soup plates sprinkled with parsley and scallions. Or take out of the liquid and place meats on a heated platter surrounded with the vegetables, sprinkled with parsley and scallions. Pour the liquid into soup plates and let family or guests help themselves to meat and vegetables. Serve rice and bread on the side.

*In Argentina, this dish is made without chicken and sausage.

BLACK BEANS WITH CHICKEN CASSOULET

6 strips bacon, cut up
1 large onion, sliced
1 green pepper, sliced
⅔ cup diced ham
4 chicken breasts
6 chicken thighs
Salt and pepper to taste
1 to 2 Tbs. vegetable oil, if needed
½ cup white wine
16-oz. can whole tomatoes, drained and cut up
¼ tsp. coriander, crushed
¼ tsp. oregano
4 cans (15 oz. each) black beans, drained (or 12-oz. pkg. dried beans, cooked)
3 Tbs. butter

Serves 6

In a heavy pot sauté bacon until crisp. With a slotted spoon, remove bacon and discard.

Sauté onion and green pepper in bacon drippings until limp; add ham and cook for 2 to 3 minutes. With a slotted spoon, remove onion, peppers and ham and reserve.

Sprinkle chicken with salt and pepper and brown in the remaining bacon drippings for 25 to 30 minutes, or until chicken is tender. If necessary, add 1 to 2 Tbs. oil to the pot.

When chicken is tender remove from pot; cool and bone chicken and slice. Return chicken to pot, add onion, pepper, ham, wine, tomatoes, coriander, oregano and salt and pepper to taste. Simmer for 10 minutes.

Add beans and stir. Adjust seasoning. Dot with butter and bake in a medium oven (325° to 350°) for 1½ to 2 hours.

Cool and refrigerate for 2 to 3 days, or let stand in a cool place for 24 hours. Heat for about 45 minutes in a medium oven before serving.*

Serve with white rice, crisp French or Cuban bread and a green salad.

*This dish may also be cooked over a low fire in your fireplace. Check to make sure that the bottom does not scorch.

CHOUCROUTE GARNIE (SAUERKRAUT ALSATIAN STYLE)

6 to 7 strips bacon
2 bags (16 oz. each) fresh sauerkraut
1 large onion, diced
3 Tbs. bacon drippings
2 Tbs. caraway seed
1½ cups pale dry sherry
1 lb. knockwurst, halved lengthwise
1½ lbs. small smoked links
Salt and pepper
2 lbs. small potatoes, boiled
4 Tbs. melted butter

Serves 6 or 7

Cut bacon into small pieces. In a large pot fry bacon until crisp. Reserve 3 Tbs. bacon drippings.

Drain sauerkraut, reserving the juice, and rinse under cold water. Squeeze out excess water. Add sauerkraut to the pot, stir well and simmer for 20 minutes.

In a small skillet sauté onion in the bacon drippings; add to large pot.

Add caraway seed, 1 cup of the sherry, knockwurst and small smoked links to pot. Simmer for 30 minutes. Season to taste with salt and pepper and add some sauerkraut juice if too bland. Add potatoes. Sprinkle with remaining ½ cup sherry and the melted butter. Cover and cook another 15 to 20 minutes.

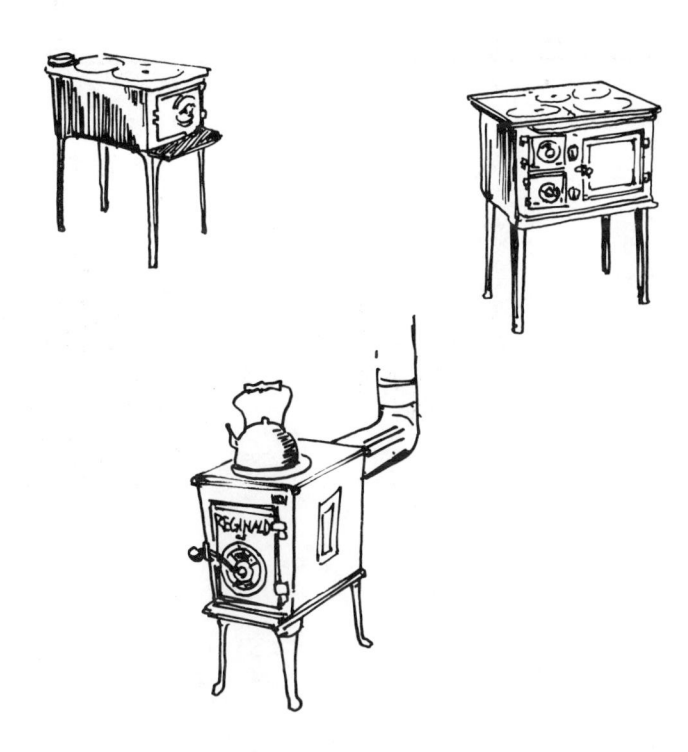

BURRIDA (GENOESE FISH STEW)

4 lbs. assorted fish fillets of your choice—red snapper, haddock, mackerel, salmon, white fish
¾ cup olive oil
2 cloves garlic, minced
1 large Spanish onion, finely chopped
2 anchovy fillets, minced
½ cup chopped parsley
16-oz can sliced, peeled tomatoes with their liquid
14 walnut halves, mashed
2 cups dry white wine
2 bay leaves
¼ tsp. crushed fennel seed
¼ tsp. crushed saffron
Salt and pepper to taste
Slices of toasted Italian bread

Serves 6

Cut fillets into 3″ pieces.

Heat oil in a heavy pot. Cook garlic until soft but not brown. Add onions and cook until just tender, about 5 to 6 minutes. Add anchovies, parsley and the tomatoes with their liquid.

Mix walnuts with wine and add to the pot. Simmer for 10 minutes. Add fish, bay leaves, fennel seed, saffron, salt and pepper. Simmer for an additional 20 minutes.

Serve in soup bowls with bread slices.

VEGETABLES

BRAISED BELGIAN ENDIVES

12 Belgian endives
¼ lb. butter
Salt and pepper to taste
½ cup plus ¼ cup heavy cream

¼ tsp. lemon juice
1 Tbs. butter, softened
2 Tbs. minced parsley

Serves 6

Wash, dry and trim endives. In a large skillet melt butter. Add endives to butter, sprinkle with salt and pepper and cook over low heat, turning often until just limp. Carefully remove endives and place into a saucepan.

Pour ½ cup cream over the endives. Simmer for 10 minutes uncovered, basting occasionally until the liquid is reduced by half. The sauce will look curdled. Remove endives with a slotted spoon to a heated platter.

Add ¼ cup cream to the sauce by tablespoons and stir until the sauce smoothes out. Season to taste with salt and pepper. Add a few drops of lemon juice and the butter.

Pour sauce over endives and serve sprinkled with parsley.

SPICED CARROTS

6–8 carrots, cut into ¼" rounds
1 cup water
½ tsp. salt
3 Tbs. butter
2 Tbs. light brown sugar

1 tsp. grated lemon peel
2 Tbs. lemon juice
4 whole cloves
Thin lemon slices

Serves 6

In a covered saucepan cook carrots in boiling salted water until just tender, 10 to 15 minutes; drain. Add remaining ingredients; heat, stirring occasionally. Garnish with lemon slices if desired.

CHUCHUS RECHEADAS (STUFFED CHAYOTES)

6 chayotes*
1 tsp. salt
¼ cup vegetable oil
1½ lbs. lean ground beef
1 large green pepper, diced
1 medium onion, diced
½ cup raisins

Red pepper flakes to taste
Salt and pepper
1 cup flour, or more as needed
3 eggs, beaten
1 cup seasoned bread crumbs
Oil for frying

Serves 6

Wash chayotes well. Place in a large pot with water to cover and add salt. Cook covered over medium heat for about 20 minutes. Drain, cool and peel.

Cut off tops about ½" thick from the narrow end to make a lid. With a grapefruit knife cut out seed and pulp carefully, leaving about ¼" of the shell intact. Set the chayotes aside.

Heat oil in a large skillet. Add beef, stirring to break up lumps. Add pepper and onion, continuously stirring until beef is brown. Add raisins, pepper flakes and salt and pepper to taste. Cook, stirring occasionally, for 2 to 3 minutes; cool.

Stuff chayotes with meat mixture. Cover with the lids and secure lids with two toothpicks. Dredge each chayote in flour. Beat eggs in a bowl. Dip chayotes into beaten eggs, then roll on all sides in bread crumbs.

Heat oil about 2" deep in a large iron pot. To test temperature, drop a piece of bread into the oil. If it browns quickly, oil is ready for frying, 325° on a frying thermometer. Place chayotes in the hot oil and fry on all sides until golden brown. Remove with a slotted spoon onto absorbent paper. Serve immediately.

*Chayote is a squash-type vegetable. Very large zucchini or any other squash may be substituted.

STUFFED EGGPLANTS

3 medium-sized eggplants
1 cup olive or salad oil
3 tomatoes, peeled and chopped
1 cup chopped onion
2 cloves garlic, mashed
¼ cup chopped parsley
¼ cup chopped scallions

1 cup cooked brown or white rice
8 oz. small-curd cottage cheese
½ tsp. oregano
½ tsp. thyme
Salt and pepper to taste
1 cup seasoned bread crumbs
1 cup water

Serves 6

Slice eggplants in half lengthwise. With a sharp knife remove center, leaving a shell ½" thick. Dice removed eggplant.

In large skillt heat oil; sauté diced eggplant until soft. Add tomatoes, onion, garlic, parsley and scallions. Cook, stirring for 5 minutes, or until vegetables are soft and tender. Add rice, cottage cheese, oregano, thyme, salt and pepper. Stuff eggplant shells. Sprinkle tops with bread crumbs.

Pour water into a shallow pan. Place eggplant halves in pan. Cover with aluminum foil and cook over low heat for 45 minutes.

SPINACH SOUFFLÉ

2 pkgs. chopped frozen spinach
3 Tbs. butter or margarine
3 Tbs. flour
2 cups milk
5 egg yolks

Salt and pepper to taste
⅛ tsp. nutmeg
1 oz. vodka
6 egg whites
Pinch of cream of tartar

Serves 6

Butter well a 1½-quart soufflé dish.

Defrost spinach and squeeze as dry as possible.

In a saucepan melt butter, add flour and cook stirring until well blended and bubbly. Add milk and cook over low heat, stirring continuously, until slightly thickened; remove from heat.

Add egg yolks one at a time, beating well with a whisk after each addition. Add salt, pepper, nutmeg, vodka and spinach; blend well.

In a mixing bowl beat egg whites with cream of tartar until stiff but not dry. Fold into spinach mixture. Pour into buttered dish and run a knife around the soufflé.

Bake in a preheated 350° oven for 50 to 60 minutes, or until an inserted knife comes out clean. Do not open oven door for the first 25 minutes of baking. Check after 35 minutes if soufflé is rising. You may have to make the fire a bit hotter.

SWEET POTATOES ORANGÉ

6 sweet potatoes
½ cup coconut milk*
½ cup orange juice
¼ cup dark rum
2 Tbs. butter
3 Tbs. dark brown sugar

2 Tbs. grated orange rind
½ tsp. salt
¼ tsp. nutmeg
¼ tsp. cinnamon
6 large oranges

Serves 6

In a cast aluminum or stainless steel pot cook unpeeled sweet potatoes for 35 to 40 minutes, or until tender. Drain, peel and mash. Add coconut milk, orange juice, rum, butter, brown sugar, orange rind and seasonings to the potatoes and beat until smooth.

Cut tops off oranges and scoop out pulp without breaking the skin. Fill orange skin shells with sweet potato mixture and place in a shallow baking dish.

Bake in a 350° oven for 25 minutes, or until browned on top. Decorate with sections of orange and serve hot.

To make coconut milk: Place 2 cups grated coconut into a bowl. Pour 2 cups boiling water over coconut. Let steep for 1 hour. Drain well and squeeze out all liquid from coconut flakes through a double thickness of cheesecloth.

PASTA, GRAINS AND RICE

HAM AND NOODLE CASSEROLE

1 lb. medium noodles
¼ lb. butter, melted
1 lb. boiled ham, diced
5 eggs
½ tsp. salt
¼ tsp. pepper
Pinch each of ground cloves and nutmeg

½ cup heavy cream
1 cup sour cream
⅔ cup grated Parmesan cheese
4 Tbs. butter
¼ cup flour
2 cups milk
2 egg yolks (optional)
Salt and pepper

Serves 6 to 8

Cook noodles as directed on package; drain.

Add ¼ lb. butter and the ham and toss with noodles.

Beat eggs; add salt, pepper, cloves, nutmeg, cream and sour cream and beat until smooth. Add to noodles. Sprinkle 2 Tbs. of the Parmesan cheese into a heavily buttered ovenproof casserole. Pour noodle mixture into casserole.

Melt 4 Tbs. butter, add the flour and stir; add milk and stir until smooth and slightly thickened; cool slightly. Add yolks, if desired, and the remaining cheese. Season with salt and pepper to taste; mix well.

Pour sauce over noodles. Bake in a preheated 350° oven for 40 to 45 minutes.

KASHA CASSEROLE (BUCKWHEAT GROATS CASSEROLE)

4 cups water
1 cup whole or coarse kasha (buckwheat groats)
½ tsp. salt
4 Tbs. butter or margarine
2 onions, finely chopped
1½ cups sliced mushrooms
1 clove garlic, crushed
¼ tsp. pepper
¼ tsp. thyme
¼ tsp. oregano
4 eggs
½ cup minced parsley

Serves 6 to 8

Bring water to a boil, add kasha, salt and 1 Tbs. butter. Return to a boil, cover and cook until kasha is completely thickened, about 12 to 15 minutes. If necessary, add a bit more water.

Sauté onions in 3 Tbs. butter until lightly browned, add mushrooms and cook until mushrooms are tender, about 4 to 6 minutes. Add garlic, pepper, thyme and oregano; stir into kasha and blend well.

Butter a 1½- to 2-quart casserole or ovenproof dish. Beat eggs well. Blend into kasha and add parsley. Pour kasha into casserole and bake for 35 to 40 minutes in a 350° oven.

RICE VENETIAN STYLE

5 Tbs. olive oil
5 Tbs. butter
1 cup chopped onions
2 cups raw long-grain rice
¼ cup pale dry sherry
4 cups hot chicken broth

4 cups shelled fresh peas (or 2 pkgs. frozen thawed peas)
1½ tsp. salt
¼ tsp. white pepper
½ cup grated Parmesan cheese

Serves 6 to 8

Heat oil and 3 Tbs. of the butter in a heavy skillet; sauté onions until tender. Add rice and stir until translucent.

Add sherry, 2 cups of the broth, the peas, salt and pepper. Cover, bring to boil and cook over low heat for 15 minutes.

Add the remaining broth, cover and cook for 10 minutes, or until rice is tender and dry. Stir in cheese and the remaining butter; taste for seasoning.

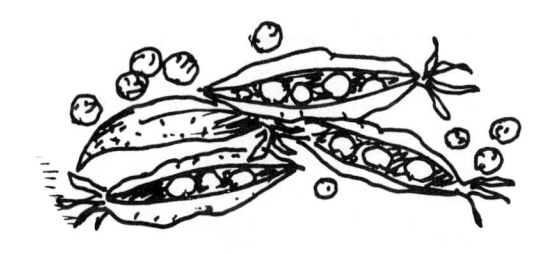

FAST RICE PILAF

1 medium onion, minced
4 Tbs. butter or margarine
4 cups instant rice

4 cups boiling water
4 chicken bouillon cubes
White pepper to taste

Serves 8

In a medium-sized iron pot with cover sauté onion in butter until golden brown. Add rice and stir to coat with onions. Sauté for 2 to 3 minutes, stirring constantly.

Add water, crumbled chicken bouillon cubes and pepper; stir once or twice. Cover, remove from heat and let stand for 5 minutes. Fluff with fork.

SHRIMP RISOTTO WITH CURRY

1 large onion, chopped
7 Tbs. butter
1 cup rice
5 cups chicken broth
1 tsp. salt
¼ tsp. thyme
¼ tsp. basil
1 lb. small shrimp, cooked and shelled

3 Tbs. flour
½ cup heavy cream
1 Tbs. curry, or more to taste
½ cup white raisins
½ cup blanched, slivered almonds

Serves 6

Sauté onion in 4 Tbs. of the butter until soft. Add rice and stir until rice is translucent. Add 3 cups of the chicken broth, the salt, thyme and basil. Cook, stirring occasionally, for about 30 minutes. Add a little more liquid if necessary. Add shrimp, stir and set aside.

In a saucepan melt remaining 3 Tbs. butter; add flour and cook stirring constantly, for about 1 minute. Add cream and remaining 2 cups chicken broth. Cook, stirring constantly, until thickened. Mix curry powder with about ¼ cup of the sauce and add to the sauce in the skillet. Add salt to taste. Add raisins and almonds.

Butter well a heated 1½ quart charlotte mold or 9" × 5" loaf pan. Place rice in mold. Unmold onto a heated platter. Pour ½ cup of sauce over rice and serve rest of the sauce on the side.

BREADS

FEATHER-LIGHT BREAD

1½ cups scalded milk
¼ lb. butter or margarine
2 tsp. salt
½ cup sugar

2 pkgs. granulated yeast
½ cup lukewarm water
3 eggs, well beaten
About 9 cups all-purpose flour

Makes 3 loaves

Pour scalded milk into a bowl over butter, salt and sugar. Mix until butter is melted; cool.

Dissolve yeast in lukewarm water and let stand until it bubbles, about 5 minutes.

Add yeast and beaten eggs to cooled milk. Add flour, 1 cup at a time beating thoroughly after each addition. Add just enough flour to make an easy-to-handle dough.

Turn out onto a floured board and knead until smooth, blistery and elastic. Place into a greased bowl, cover and let rise until doubled in bulk, about 1½ hours.

Punch down and turn out onto lightly floured board. Shape into 3 loaves and place in buttered, 8" loaf pans. Cover and let rise until dough comes to the tops of the pans.

Bake in a 375° oven for 50 to 60 minutes, or until bread is well browned and a cake tester comes out clean.

FRENCH CHEESE GANNAT BREAD

2 pkgs. granulated yeast
½ cup warm water
6 cups all-purpose flour
2 Tbs. sugar
1 tsp. salt

12 Tbs. butter or margarine
2 cups grated Gruyère cheese
1 cup warm mashed potatoes
5 eggs
½ cup scalded milk

Makes 2 loaves

Dissolve yeast in water.
　Combine flour, sugar and salt.
　In a large bowl combine butter, cheese, potatoes, eggs and milk. Beat until blended. Add yeast and dry ingredients. Mix thoroughly.
　Turn onto a floured board and knead for 6 minutes. Place in a buttered bowl, cover and let rise until doubled in bulk. Punch down and knead again for about 2 minutes.
　Shape dough into 2 loaves. Place on a buttered and floured baking sheet. Cover and let rise until doubled. Bake in a 375° oven for 25 to 45 minutes, or until loaves are golden and a cake tester comes out clean.

SALLY LUNN

¼ lb. butter or margarine
½ cup sugar
1½ tsp. salt
1 cup scalded and cooled light cream

1½ pkgs. granulated yeast
½ cup lukewarm water
3 eggs plus 1 egg yolk, beaten
4½ cups unbleached all-purpose flour

Makes 1 ring

Cream butter with sugar and salt. Add cream.

Dissolve yeast in water. Add yeast and eggs to creamed butter.

Add flour, a little at a time, beating thoroughly after each addition. Cover and let rise until doubled.

Punch dough down and place in a well-greased and floured 9″ or 10″ tube pan. Cover and let rise again.

Bake in a 350° oven for about 40 minutes, or until loaf is golden brown and a cake tester comes out clean.

SOUR CREAM MUFFINS

¼ lb. butter or margarine
1½ cups sugar
½ tsp. salt
1 tsp. baking soda

3 cups all-purpose flour, sifted
4 eggs, well beaten
1 cup sour cream

Makes 12 to 14 muffins

In a bowl cream butter and 1 cup of the sugar until light. Combine salt, baking soda and flour. Add dry ingredients to butter and sugar alternately with the eggs and sour cream, starting and ending with flour mixture. Mix lightly.

Pour into buttered muffin tins and sprinkle with remaining sugar. Bake in a preheated 425° oven for 15 minutes, or until browned.

DESSERTS

BUÑUELOS

3 cups unsifted, all-purpose unbleached flour
¼ cup sugar
½ tsp. salt
3 eggs

½ cup light cream
3 Tbs. unsalted butter, melted
¼ tsp. cinnamon
Vegetable oil for frying
Cinnamon Syrup (*below*)

Makes 30 to 36 pieces

In a bowl combine flour, sugar and salt. In another bowl beat eggs with cream for about 30 seconds, using a whisk or rotary hand beater.

Add melted butter and cinnamon. Beat well for another 30 seconds. Add to flour mixture and blend swiftly but gently with a fork until the mixture holds together.

Turn dough out onto a lightly floured board and knead gently for about 3 minutes. Shape into a ball. Cover with an inverted bowl and let rest for 10 to 15 minutes. Divide dough into 30 to 36 pieces and roll each piece into a ball.

Pour 1½" to 2" vegetable oil into a large iron skillet. Heat until a haze appears, or candy (frying) thermometer reaches 370° to 375°.

Quickly roll each ball on a floured board into a thin 5" round disk. Carefully place 2 to 3 rounds at a time into hot oil and fry, turning once with 2 slotted spatulas, until golden brown on both sides. Remove with slotted spatula onto absorbent paper towel. Place Buñuelos onto a heated platter and sprinkle with Cinnamon Syrup while still hot. Serve immediately.

Cinnamon Syrup
2 cups sugar
1½ cups water

¼ cup light corn syrup
1 tsp. cinnamon

In a saucepan combine all the ingredients. Stir over low heat until sugar has melted and cinnamon has been completely absorbed. Simmer covered for about 15 minutes, or until syrup has thickened.

CALAS (RICE BALLS)

1 cup flour
1 tsp. baking powder
½ tsp. baking soda
½ tsp. cinnamon
½ tsp. allspice
¼ tsp. salt
2 eggs plus 1 egg yolk

¼ cup sugar
1½ cups cooked long-grain rice, cooled to room temperature
Vegetable oil for frying
Cane syrup, preserves, or sugar mixed with cinnamon

Makes 8 balls

Into a bowl sift together flour, baking powder, baking soda, cinnamon, allspice and salt. Beat eggs and sugar for 2 to 3 minutes, add rice and blend well. Add flour mixture a little at a time, mixing well after each addition. With moist hands make 2½" balls.

In a large skillet fry rice balls in oil until golden brown on all sides. Serve with cane syrup or preserves or sprinkle with sugar and cinnamon.

VERSATILE COOKIES

½ cup unsalted butter or margarine
½ cup brown sugar
¼ cup granulated sugar
1 egg, well beaten
1 tsp. vanilla
2 cups sifted all-purpose flour
½ tsp. baking powder
¼ tsp. baking soda
1 Tbs. milk
½ cup sesame seeds or ¼ cup ground walnuts or ¼ cup ground hazelnuts (optional)
4 oz. semisweet chocolate bits, melted
Candied cherries and walnut halves for decoration

Makes about 24 cookies

Cream butter, brown sugar and granulated sugar until very fluffy. Add egg and vanilla and beat well. Add flour, baking powder, baking soda and milk; mix well. If desired, stir in sesame seeds or nuts.

Either use a cookie press or roll out cookie dough on a lightly floured board to ½″ thickness and cut with a 2″ cookie cutter. Place cookies onto an ungreased cookie sheet. Bake in a preheated 400° oven for 10 minutes. Glaze with melted chocolate and decorate with candied cherries or walnuts.

LAYERED APPLE PANCAKES

8 eggs
1¼ cups all-purpose flour
1 tsp. salt
½ tsp. nutmeg
1 cup light cream
¼ cup butter or margarine, melted

6 apples peeled, cored and sliced
¼ cup butter or margarine
½ cup sugar
2 tsp. grated lemon peel
Powdered sugar
Warm raspberry or boysenberry syrup

Serves 6

Beat eggs thoroughly in a large bowl. Add flour, salt, nutmeg, cream and ¼ cup melted butter; beat well.

Heavily butter two 9" omelet pans with metal handles. Pour even amounts of batter into each pan. Bake in a preheated 350° to 375° oven until pancakes are light brown and puffy, 15 to 20 minutes. Repeat with remaining batter.

Cook apples in ¼ cup butter for 5 minutes; add sugar. Cook until apples are tender, about 10 minutes.

Place 1 pancake on serving plate and top with ⅓ of the apple mixture. Sprinkle with lemon peel, place another pancake on top, then ½ the remaining apple mixture, another pancake, the remaining apples and top with last pancake. Sprinkle with confectioners' sugar. Serve cut in wedges with syrup.

SOUFFLÉ DE BRAZIL* (BRAZILIAN PRUNE AND BANANA SOUFFLÉ)

1 pkg. (12 oz.) pitted prunes
1 cup ruby port
2 Tbs. rum
2 large bananas

1 cup sugar
⅓ cup water
4 egg whites

Serves 6

Butter well a 2-quart soufflé dish and sprinkle generously with sugar.

Chop the prunes. Place into a saucepan, add port and simmer until port has cooked down and mixture has thickened.

Remove from heat and mash prunes with a wooden spoon. Add rum and set aside.

Mash the bananas.

In a saucepan combine sugar and water and cook over low heat to soft-ball stage, 235° on a candy thermometer.

Beat egg whites until soft peaks appear. Pour in the hot syrup slowly and beat until very stiff.

Fold prunes and bananas into egg whites. Pour mixture into prepared soufflé dish.

Bake in a preheated 350° oven for 35 minutes, or until a cake tester comes out clean. Serve immediately or cool and serve at room temperature.

*This is not a conventional soufflé, so don't expect it to rise as high.

BANANAS FLAMBÉ

6 bananas
¾ cup sugar
⅓ cup butter
4 oranges

Grated peel of 1 lemon
Juice of ½ lemon
½ cup brandy
Vanilla ice cream (optional)

Serves 6

Peel bananas and cut lengthwise in half.

In a skillet combine sugar and butter. Cook over low heat, stirring continuously until pale golden brown. Grate peel of 1 whole orange and add to sugar-butter mixture. Cut oranges in half and squeeze juice of the peeled orange into skillet, stirring constantly to prevent lumping. Add grated lemon peel and lemon juice; stir well.

Add banana halves to butter sauce and simmer until bananas are tender, about 2 to 3 minutes. Place bananas with sauce in a serving dish and decorate with remaining orange halves.

In a ladle or small pot, heat the brandy to lukewarm, ignite and pour flaming over the bananas. Serve immediately. If you wish, serve bananas over scoops of vanilla ice cream. Pour flaming brandy over bananas and ice cream.

STRAWBERRY TART

1½ cups flour
1 tsp. salt
6 Tbs. chilled shortening
¼ cup ice water, or more as needed
2 cups heavy cream, chilled
1 tsp. vanilla
⅔ cup plus ½ cup powdered sugar
40 large, ripe strawberries
2 to 3 Tbs. kirsch
Red Currant Glaze (*below*)

Serves 6

Sift flour into a bowl. Add salt and shortening. Blend quickly and lightly until it resembles a coarse meal. Add ice-cold water and toss lightly, just to moisten mixture. Do not handle pastry too much. Form into a ball, wrap in wax paper and refrigerate for 2 to 3 hours.

Roll out pastry as thin as possible. Fill a 9" pie pan with the pastry and crimp the edges. Chill for ½ hour. Prick with a fork and bake in a preheated 350° oven for 15 to 20 minutes or until delicately browned. Cool completely.

Whip cream until slightly thickened. Add vanilla and ⅔ cup powdered sugar. Beat until stiff but do not overbeat; refrigerate.

Wash and hull strawberries. Place on a platter, sprinkle with ½ cup powdered sugar and the kirsch. Refrigerate for ½ to 1 hour.

Fill baked pastry shell with whipped cream. Drain strawberries well and place side by side on top of cream. Coat generously with Red Currant Glaze. Serve immediately.

Red Currant Glaze

½ cup red currant jelly
2 Tbs. water
2 Tbs. granulated sugar

In a small saucepan combine jelly with water and sugar; stir until very smooth. Boil over medium heat for 3 to 4 minutes. Cool completely. Brush onto strawberries with a pastry brush.

CRÊPES MELBA

Crêpe Batter

- 4 eggs
- 1 cup light cream
- 1 cup club soda
- 2 Tbs. melted butter
- ¼ tsp. salt
- 1 Tbs. sugar
- 1 cup sifted all-purpose flour
- 2 Tbs. brandy
- ½ cup clarified butter* for baking the crêpes

Makes about 25 to 30 crêpes

In a blender combine eggs and cream and mix for a few seconds.** Add soda, butter, salt, sugar, flour and brandy. Blend until very smooth. Scrape down sides of blender and mix again. Let stand covered for 1 hour.

Use 5" or 6" crêpe pans. Brush a little clarified butter on the pans. Pour 2 to 3 Tbs. batter into pan and tip pan to the left and right, so that batter covers the bottom evenly. Pour off excess batter. Brown slightly on one side, then turn and brown other side. Stack crêpes on a platter. Serve with Melba Sauce, page 198.

If you plan to refrigerate or freeze the crêpes, place wax paper between them and seal with foil. Refrigerate for 3 to 4 days or freeze. To defrost crêpes, place still wrapped into 250° oven for 25 to 30 minutes until heated through. Separate carefully.

*To clarify butter, melt butter and let stand ½ hour. Remove white sediment from top and strain off golden liquid. Discard sediment from bottom.
**If blender is not available, beat eggs and cream in a bowl with a whisk or a rotary beater.

Melba Sauce

    2 pkgs. frozen raspberries in heavy syrup
    ¼ lb. butter
    1 cup sugar
    ¼ cup frozen orange juice
    ¼ cup light corn syrup
    ¼ cup plus ⅓ cup brandy

Defrost raspberries and press through a sieve; set aside.

In a large skillet melt butter and sugar together until golden in color. Add sieved raspberries, undiluted orange juice and corn syrup. Add ¼ cup brandy.

Place crêpes into sauce and fold in thirds. Simmer for 2 or 3 minutes.

Heat remaining ⅓ cup brandy in a small pot until lukewarm. Ignite and pour over crepes. Serve immediately.

MOCHA BAVARIAN CREAM

2 pkgs. ladyfingers
1½ envelopes unflavored gelatin
½ cup cold water
6 egg yolks
1¼ cups sugar
1 Tbs. cornstarch
1½ cups light cream
4 Tbs. instant coffee dissolved in ¼ cup hot water
4 oz. semisweet chocolate bits
½ cup coffee liqueur
1 tsp. vanilla
6 egg whites
⅛ tsp. cream of tartar
3 cups whipped cream
Additional whipped cream, grated chocolate or chocolate curls for garnish

Serves 6

Line sides and bottom of a 1½-quart soufflé dish with ladyfingers.

Sprinkle gelatin over cold water; set aside.

In a bowl beat egg yolks for 1 to 2 minutes. Add sugar and cornstarch. Beat for 1 minute, then pour into the top of a double boiler. Beat with a whisk for 1 more minute.

Scald light cream and add gradually to the egg yolks, beating steadily with a wooden spoon. Simmer, stirring constantly, until mixture coats the spoon.

Add instant coffee; blend well. Add chocolate, stirring until chocolate is melted. Add softened gelatin and blend well. Cool, then refrigerate.

When cream is cold, add coffee liqueur and vanilla. Refrigerate again. As soon as mixture starts to set, about 35 to 45 minutes, beat egg whites with cream of tartar until stiff but not dry. Fold whipped cream alternately with egg whites into coffee-chocolate mixture until well blended.

Pour into prepared soufflé dish and refrigerate for at least 6 hours or overnight. Decorate with additional whipped cream, grated chocolate or chocolate curls.

4
Saving Energy in the Modern Kitchen: Conventional Stoves and Small Appliances

It may well happen that a scientific wizard will soon discover the secret of harnessing the energy of the sun, wind or atom efficiently enough for us to stop worrying about our energy-eating lifestyle. Until then, however, "making do" or returning to the sensible ways of a past era is simply not everyone's bag. The multitude of kitchen gadgets available in this country provides an alternative route to saving previous energy. After all, why preheat a conventional oven when a small toaster-oven will do the job just as well and more economically (in fact, a toaster-oven can cook an entire meal in 35 to 40 minutes using the same amount of energy it would take to preheat a large, conventional oven for 10 or 15 minutes), or when a slow cooker will prepare your evening meal while you're away all day and save energy as well. If you already own lots of major and minor appliances or gadgets, you should learn how to use them efficiently, without any undue waste of energy.

To conserve energy with a conventional refrigerator-freezer, insulation is the key word. If yours is a few years old, you may want to replace the gaskets, and the compressor coils and motor casing should be vacuumed once a year. Be sure not to open the doors unnecessarily, and cool foods before placing them in the refrigerator or freezer. Keep your freezer about ⅔ to ¾ full at all times, because frozen foods help keep the temperature stable, thereby saving energy.

Gas or electric ovens should be checked for good insulation and accurate temperature. When you use your oven, try to cook several meals at once, or prepare large amounts and freeze the extra meals or surplus. When cooking on an electric or gas stove, fit your pans to burner size in order to prevent heat loss. Use lids on sauté pans and skillets; this speeds up cooking and saves energy.

Choosing the proper pots and pans with maximum heat efficiency is a smart way to conserve. Flat-bottomed aluminum pans (especially cast aluminum), stainless steel pans with copper bottoms or copper pots lined with tin are better heat conductors than cookware made of plain stainless steel or light-weight aluminum. Pots with ridged bottoms and cast-iron utensils, plain or with enameled coating, as well as pots with non-stick surfaces, actually use more energy in spite of the fact that cast iron distributes heat evenly, because they take longer to heat up.

Lift the lids of pots and skillets as infrequently as possible during cooking. By all means use small, individual electrical appliances whenever feasible—but use them individually, not all at once, or you'll defeat your efforts at energy saving!

Whenever possible, steam your vegetables and fish. A small amount of water boils up quickly, and vegetables will taste better and crisper when steamed. Steamed or poached fish is superb. You may want to make a good investment in a steamer basket and a fish poacher.

Would you believe that the pilot light on an average gas range accounts for 25% to 30% of the gas normally used by a stove or oven for cooking or baking? That's why pilotless ranges and ovens are real energy savers. In addition, there are gas ranges with built-in broilers that convert gas heat to infra-red rays and greatly reduce broiling time.

Professional kitchens have been using so-called convection ovens for years. Hot air is recirculated through these ovens almost continuously, and they bake and cook at about 50° lower temperature than conventional ovens, thereby reducing fuel consumption considerably. They are available in both gas and electrical models, and the latter may be readily changed from a convection to regular oven with the flick of a switch.

Not everyone is attuned to using a microwave or radar oven, but these are certainly real energy savers. For many families the ideal solution is a combination of conventional and microwave ranges, one on top and the other on the bottom, or a true microwave-electric oven combo in one appliance. Just push a buttom and cook fast or slow the old-fashioned way!

Small appliances can often do double, triple and quadruple duty, such as Toaster Ovens, which come in all sizes and some of which even have continuous cleaning cycles. Most smaller models are used primarily for toasting or broiling, while larger types are ideal for broiling, baking and roasting. They are a boon for singles, students and apartment dwellers, but even a super hostess with a large, well-equipped kitchen considers the broiler-oven combo a tremendous convenience, especially on the eve of a big party!

Griddles are useful both as energy savers on the stove and as handy small appliances. A non-electric griddle placed over one burner can do the work of two burners at the same time. Most electric griddles have thermostatic controls. Griddles will also keep food warm when set on "low" for a long time; just cover with foil to prevent drying out.

An *Electric Frying Pan* is a marvelous energy saver and can be used for broiling, frying, baking and stewing. You use much less energy to make a hamburger in an electric frying pan than on an electric range. Pancakes, eggs, bacon, vegetables and even steaks are easily prepared on a coated, non-stick *Crock Plate*, which may also be used as a server.

The *Slow Cooker*, or *Crock Pot*, has been around for awhile. For people who haven't time to stand over a stove for hours, it's a veritable mealtime marvel. The slow cookers don't brown meat, but stews, soups and bean dishes come out perfectly, and there are many interesting meals which you may prepare in a slow cooker.

One of the most versatile gadgets, a real energy saver, is a stack-up *Steamer Unit*. Meat or fish and two side dishes are magically finished at the same time, in about 30 minutes, and according to the manufacturer, this appliance uses only 1/6 the wattage of an oven and two burners.

The *Chinese Wok* is perhaps the supreme energy saver, and happily many people are now head over heels in love with this versatile Oriental utensil. Stove-top models suitable for cooking on electric or gas burners and plug-in *Electric Woks* both cook tasty dishes quickly while preserving most of the vitamins and nutrients.

There are also several fuel-saving cooking devices that are familiar to campers, hikers and boaters and are available in sporting-good or hardware stores:

Sterno Cookers do not generate much heat and are mostly used in emergency situations or for heating water or small amounts of food, as well as for making fondue or tabletop dishes.

Alcohol Stoves must be primed before using, and this takes time and patience. There are one, two and three-burner alcohol stoves, some with good-sized ovens, available in marine supply stores.

There are also portable ovens which fit over the burners of your regular stove. The best of these is the French "*Le Diffuseur*," available in some utensil and marine supply stores. A *Stove-Top Ovenette* can be used in emergencies for baking potatoes, heating foods and even browning rolls.

The old-fashioned *Primus* or *Kerosene Stoves* with one or two burners, widely used in Europe, generate enough heat for any kind of cooking, but are not considered very safe in this country and are, therefore, not readily available.

You may find other types of stove-oven combos in your camping supply stores which are suitable for gas and electric energy saving. Look them over. You may prefer their performance to that of alcohol burners.

APPETIZERS

STUFFED ARTICHOKES
(Conventional Stove and Toaster Oven)

2 cans (14 oz. each) artichoke hearts
½ cup olive oil
2 cloves garlic, crushed
1 large onion, minced
2 medium green peppers, minced

1 cup minced parsley
½ tsp. Italian seasoning
Salt and pepper
2 cups minced mushrooms* sautéed in 4 Tbs. butter
½ cup grated Parmesan cheese

Serves 6

Drain artichokes; gently squeeze out excess liquid. Remove centers and level off the cone-shaped side with a knife.

In a saucepan combine olive oil, garlic, onion and peppers. Simmer until vegetables are just limp. Add parsley, Italian seasoning and salt and pepper to taste. Simmer for 2 to 3 minutes.

Remove ½ the sauce and reserve. Add mushrooms to remaining sauce and boil until liquid is reduced by ⅓; remove from heat.

Stuff artichokes with mushroom mixture. Sprinkle with Parmesan cheese.

Pour reserved sauce into a small baking pan. Place artichokes into pan and bake in a 350° toaster oven for 15 minutes. Cool, then chill in the refrigerator. Serve as an appetizer on lettuce leaves.

*Approximately ½ lb.

BANANA FRITTERS
(Electric Skillet)

6 bananas	3 eggs
Salt and pepper to taste	3 Tbs. milk
¼ tsp. nutmeg	¼ tsp. salt
¼ tsp. ginger	⅛ tsp. pepper
¼ tsp. allspice	2½ cups flavored bread crumbs
2 cups flour	Vegetable oil for deep frying

Serves 10

Peel bananas and slice lengthwise; then cut crosswise into 2" pieces. Sprinkle with salt, pepper, nutmeg, ginger and allspice. Dip into flour.

Beat eggs with milk, salt and pepper. Dip banana pieces thoroughly into egg mixture and dredge in bread crumbs. Be sure pieces are completely covered with bread crumbs. (May be prepared in advance to this point.)

Place bananas onto paper towel–lined cookie sheet and refrigerate before using or use immediately as soon as the bananas are breaded.

Heat 1" of oil to 375° in an electric skillet or small deep fryer. If deep frying, heat oil to 375° and drop banana pieces 5 to 6 at a time, (depending on size of the deep fryer) into hot oil. Cook until crust is golden brown.

Remove with slotted spoon and place on absorbent paper towels. To keep warm, line a jelly roll pan with absorbent paper towels. Place bananas onto it and keep in a 200° oven or toaster oven until ready to serve.

OPEN HAM 'N CHEESE SANDWICH
(Toaster Oven)

¼ lb. cooked ham, minced
½ cup finely chopped celery
¼ cup chopped pimiento-stuffed olives
3 Tbs. butter
4 slices rye or pumpernickel bread
4 slices American-style cheese
16-oz. pkg. frozen fried onion rings

Serves 4

In a bowl blend together ham, celery, olives and butter. Place bread in toaster oven and toast on both sides. Spread enough ham mixture on each slice to cover evenly to the very edge.

Cut each cheese slice into 3 strips. Place 3 strips diagonally across each sandwich. Top each sandwich with frozen onion rings. Return to oven until cheese melts and onions are crispy, about 3 to 4 minutes.

PEPPER APPETIZERS
(Crock Plate)

3 dozen small, mild green Italian or Cuban peppers
2 cups water
1 tsp. salt
1 cup oil
2 cups Cheddar cheese
¼ cup crumbled blue-veined cheese

4 eggs, well beaten
⅛ tsp. white pepper
¼ tsp. basil
¼ tsp. salt
¼ tsp. pepper
1 cup flour

Serves 6

Cut off tops of peppers. Remove seeds and ribs. Pour water into crock plate and add salt. Place peppers onto the rack* in a single layer. Put rack into water on plate. Cover and turn to high. Steam peppers for 15 minutes. Remove peppers from rack, pour out water and dry crock plate.

Pour oil into crock plate and heat on high for 10 minutes. In a bowl combine cheddar and blue cheeses with 1 egg, white pepper and basil. Stuff peppers with cheese mixture.

Beat remaining eggs with salt and pepper. Dredge peppers in flour, then dip thoroughly into eggs. Drop into hot oil and fry on both sides until golden brown. Serve immediately.

*Rack comes with crock plate.

SWISS FONDUE
(Conventional Stove or Sterno)

2 cloves garlic, halved
1 cup dry white wine
1½ lbs. Swiss cheese, grated
2 tsp. cornstarch
Dash of cayenne pepper
1 tsp. Worcestershire sauce

Dash of nutmeg
1 tsp. dry mustard
Salt
⅓ cup kirsch
French or Italian bread, cut into 1" cubes, or apple wedges

Serves 6

Rub fondue pot with garlic. Add wine and heat on stove (or over sterno unit) until bubbles begin to rise; do not let boil.

Combine cheese with cornstarch and add to hot wine, ¼ cup at a time, stirring over low heat until cheese is melted and smooth. Add cayenne pepper, Worcestershire sauce, nutmeg, mustard, salt to taste and kirsch and stir well.

If you have been using stove, light burner on fondue unit and set pot over flame. Spear bread or apple wedges with fondue fork and dip into cheese fondue.

FISH

STEAMED FISH, SEAFOOD AND VEGETABLES
(Steamer Unit*)

1 cup water
½ cup pale dry sherry
2 bay leaves
1 tsp. fennel seed
2 Tbs. chopped scallions
3 cloves garlic, minced
2 dozen medium shrimp, shelled and deveined

3 flounder fillets, cut into 2" chunks
Salt and pepper to taste
3 medium zucchini, thinly sliced
1 green pepper, diced
1 onion, diced
½ tsp. oregano

Serves 5 or 6

Pour water and sherry into base unit. Add bay leaves, fennel seed, scallions and garlic.
 Place shrimp and fish into perforated container. Sprinkle with salt and pepper.
 Place ½ the vegetables into each section of divided container. Season with oregano and more salt and pepper to taste.
 Steam for about 10 minutes, or until vegetables are just tender. Place shrimp and fish onto a platter and surround with vegetables.

*Always follow exact cooking directions that come with the unit. Be careful not to burn yourself. Use protection for your hands.

STUFFED YELLOWTAIL
(Toaster Oven)

3-lb. yellowtail or red snapper
Salt, pepper and oregano to taste
1 medium onion, minced
⅓ cup butter or margarine
2 Tbs. minced parsley
2 cups bread crumbs

½ tsp. salt
¼ tsp. sage
¼ tsp. oregano
¼ tsp. pepper
¼ cup melted butter

Serves 3 or 4

Sprinkle fish with salt, pepper and oregano.

Sauté onion in butter until tender. Add parsley, bread crumbs and seasonings and blend well. Stuff fish with bread-crumb mixture.

Butter well a baking dish. Place fish into dish, pour on melted butter and bake in a 375° oven for 25 to 30 minutes, or until fish flakes easily.

SEAFOOD FONDUE
(Conventional Stove or Sterno)

Vegetable oil for frying
¼ lb. butter
1 lb. medium shrimp, peeled and deveined
1 lb. scallops or halibut or scrod, cut into 1" cubes
Tartar Sauce or Remoulade Sauce (*below*)

Serves 4 to 6

Heat 2" of oil in fondue pot on stove or over fondue burner until nearly smoking. Add butter and cover until sizzling quiets down; remove from heat. Just before serving, light fondue burner and reheat oil at the table.

Spear shrimp and scallops with fondue fork and cook in hot oil until done (until fish becomes opaque and firm). Sprinkle with salt and dip in Tartar Sauce or Remoulade Sauce.

Tartar Sauce

2 Tbs. chopped capers
2 Tbs. chopped parsley
2 Tbs. chopped pickle
1½ cups mayonnaise
2 Tbs. minced scallions
Salt and pepper to taste

In a bowl mix all the ingredients together and chill.

Remoulade Sauce

1 cup mayonnaise
2 tsp. prepared mustard
2 cloves garlic, minced
Tabasco sauce to taste
2 tsp. tarragon
2 tsp. capers
½ cup catsup

In a bowl mix all the ingredients together and chill.

POULTRY

POTTED LEMON CHICKEN
(Slow Cooker)

3-lb. broiler-fryer chicken
Salt and pepper to taste
½ tsp. basil
3 cloves garlic

2 Tbs. butter
¼ cup water
¼ cup lemon juice

Serves 6

Wash chicken and pat dry. Sprinkle with salt, pepper and basil. Place garlic inside cavity of chicken.

Melt butter in a large skillet and brown chicken on all sides for 10 minutes, or until golden. Place into the slow cooker. Deglaze skillet with water and pour into pot; cover.

Cook at 200° for 6 to 8 hours, adding lemon juice during last hour of cooking. Serve with cooking juices poured over chicken.

CHICKEN AND LEEKS
(Conventional Stove and Slow Cooker)

2½- to 3-lb. broiler-fryer chicken, cut up
2 Tbs. peanut oil
1 large onion, chopped
2 cloves garlic, minced
4 leeks, washed well and cut into 3" pieces

5 carrots, pared and cut into 2" pieces
1 tsp. marjoram
1 bay leaf
¼ tsp. pepper
¾ cup dry white wine
2 Tbs. cornstarch
½ cup minced parsley

Serves 4

In a large skillet, brown chicken in oil; remove with slotted spoon and reserve. Sauté onion and garlic in remaining oil until soft.

Place chicken, onion and garlic into slow cooker. Add leeks, carrots, marjoram, bay leaf, pepper and ½ cup of the wine; stir. Cover and cook on low heat (190°–200°) for 8 hours, or on high heat (290°–300°) for 4 hours, or until chicken is tender. Remove chicken and vegetables to a heated platter with a slotted spoon and keep warm.

Turn heat control to high (290°–300°). Combine cornstarch and remaining ¼ cup wine in a cup; stir into liquid in slow cooker until well blended. Cover and simmer for 15 minutes. Pour sauce over chicken and serve sprinkled with chopped parsley.

CHICKEN AND RICE ESPAÑOL
(Steamer Unit*)

¾ cup water
1 cup dry white wine
3 Tbs. minced parsley
1 tsp. thyme
1 tsp. basil
2 bay leaves
½ tsp. salt
¼ tsp. pepper
2½- to 3-lb. broiling chicken, cut up

12 medium shrimp, shelled and deveined
Salt and pepper to taste
2 cups yellow rice
2 cubes chicken broth
1 Tbs. butter
1 plastic pouch of frozen peas in butter

Serves 4

Pour water and wine into base unit. Add parsley, thyme, basil, bay leaves, salt and pepper.

Place chicken and shrimp into perforated container; sprinkle with salt and pepper.

In one part of the divided container, combine rice with water as directed on package. Add 2 crushed cubes chicken broth and butter; stir well.

Place pouch with frozen peas into other section of divided container. Cover steamer and steam for about 35 to 45 minutes, or until chicken is tender.

To serve, combine chicken, shrimp and rice on a heated platter. Drain peas and add to chicken; toss lightly.

*Always follow exact cooking directions that come with steamer unit. Be careful not to burn yourself. Use protection for your hands.

CHICKEN IN SPICY SAUCE
(Electric Skillet)

3½ lb. frying chicken, cut up
¼ cup olive oil
4 cloves garlic, minced
1 tsp. salt
⅛ tsp. pepper
½ tsp. basil

½ cup dry white wine
3 Tbs. wine vinegar
½ cup sliced black olives
¼ cup boiling water
3 anchovy fillets, chopped

Serves 4

Wash chicken and pat dry.

Heat oil in electric skillet. Add chicken and garlic, sprinkle with salt and pepper and brown over low heat on all sides. Add basil, wine and vinegar; cook for 5 minutes. Add olives, water and anchovies. Cook over low heat for 45 minutes, or until chicken is tender. Taste for seasoning and serve with rice.

TOASTER CHICKEN
(Toaster Oven)

¼ cup soy sauce
¼ cup catsup
3 Tbs. honey
3 Tbs. oil
2 Tbs. lemon juice

Salt and pepper to taste
½ tsp. basil
2 cloves garlic, crushed
2½- to 3-lb. chicken, cut up

Serves 4

Remove oven pan from toaster oven. Preheat toaster oven to 350°. Cover oven pan with foil and turn up the edges. Butter the foil.

Combine soy sauce, catsup, honey, oil, lemon juice, salt, pepper, basil and garlic and mix well.

Put chicken pieces on oven pan and brush generously with sauce. Bake, basting frequently, for about 1 hour, or until chicken is very tender.

CHICKEN ORLOFF
(Crock Plate)

1 large onion, chopped
3 Tbs. butter
½ cup light cream
2 Tbs. flour
½ lb. fresh mushrooms, sliced
Salt and pepper to taste

5 cooked chicken breasts, skinned and sliced into strips, 2″ wide
1 cup sour cream
⅓ cup pale dry sherry

Serves 6

Preheat crock plate on low for 8 minutes.

In preheated crock plate sauté onion in butter until soft. Blend cream and flour until smooth; add to onions. Add mushrooms, salt and pepper. Simmer for 6 to 7 minutes. Add chicken and simmer for 3 minutes. Turn crock plate off.

Mix sour cream and sherry. Season with salt and pepper to taste and pour over chicken. Heat to serving temperature and serve with noodles.

MEATS

STEAK DIANE
(Electric Skillet)

2 boneless club steaks or a 12-oz. sirloin steak, ¾" thick
5 Tbs. butter
2 Tbs. minced chives
2 tsp. prepared mustard
2 Tbs. minced parsley
2 Tbs. lemon juice
2 Tbs. Worcestershire sauce
½ tsp. salt
⅛ tsp. coarsely ground black pepper
¼ cup heavy cream
¼ cup brandy

Serves 2

Cut the steak horizontally through its thickness, leaving the two parts connected at one side. Open the steak and pound with a mallet until thin and flat.

Melt 2 Tbs. of the butter in electric skillet. Sear steak on both sides quickly.

Mix remaining butter with chives and mustard; spread on top of steaks. Add parsley, lemon juice, Worcestershire sauce, salt and pepper and cream to skillet. Cook for 2 minutes.

Warm brandy slightly, ignite and pour over steaks. Serve immediately.

MINUTE STEAKS
(Toaster Oven)

2 thin Delmonico steaks
Salt, pepper and garlic powder to taste
1 large tomato, cut crosswise in ½
2 cling peach halves

4 Tbs. butter
1 Tbs. minced scallions
2 tsp. drained horseradish
2 Tbs. strawberry jam or preserves
1 Tbs. slivered almonds

Serves 2

Season steaks with salt, pepper and garlic powder. Place on foil-lined baking pan with tomato and peach halves.

Blend butter, scallions and horseradish. Dot top of each tomato with 1 Tbs. butter mixture. Spoon 1 Tbs. jam into each peach half. Broil steak in toaster oven for 5 minutes. Turn steaks, add almonds to peach halves and broil for 5 minutes longer. If tomatoes and peaches brown too quickly, cover with foil.

BEEF FONDUE
(Conventional Stove or Sterno)

3 lbs. sirloin steak or filet, cut into 1" cubes
Garlic salt and pepper to taste
Vegetable oil for frying

¼ lb. butter
Sauce Espagnole (*below*) and any other sauces of your choice

Serves 6

Sprinkle steak with garlic salt and pepper. Heat oil in fondue pot on the stove or fondue burner until nearly smoking. Add butter and cover until the sputtering slows down. If heating on stove, light fondue burner and bring pot with oil to the table.

Place steak cubes and sauces on the table. Spear beef cubes with fondue fork and dip into hot oil. Cook for 10–20 seconds for rare and 40–50 seconds for well done. Dip cooked steak cubes into Sauce Espagnole or your favorite sauce. Serve with a salad or French bread.

Sauce Espagnole

3 scallions, minced
1 clove garlic, crushed

½ cup dry red wine
½ cup beef gravy

In a saucepan boil scallions and garlic in wine until wine is reduced by ½. Stir in beef gravy and simmer for 7 minutes.

GREEK MEAT PATTIES
(Electric Skillet)

½ lb. lean ground beef
½ lb. lean ground lamb
4 slices white bread, with crust cut off and moistened with ¼ cup water
1 medium onion, finely chopped
Salt and pepper to taste
3 cloves garlic, minced
½ cup olive oil
1 cup flour
1 lemon

Serves 4 or 5

In a bowl combine beef, lamb, bread, onion, salt, pepper and garlic. Mix until smooth and well blended. Form into 3" patties.

Heat olive oil in electric skillet. Coat meat patties with flour and sauté in oil until well browned on both sides. Squeeze lemon on top just before serving.

PICCATA DI VITELLO (VEAL IN LEMON SAUCE)
(Electric Skillet)

1 cup flour
1½ tsp. salt
¼ tsp. pepper
½ tsp. oregano
1 lb. veal scallops, pounded thin

3 Tbs. olive oil
2 Tbs. butter
¼ cup lemon juice
3 Tbs. minced parsley

Serves 6

Combine flour, salt, pepper and oregano. Dip veal into seasoned flour.

Heat oil and butter in electric skillet until it sizzles. Brown veal in a single layer on both sides, about 5 minutes each side. When browned and tender, remove veal.

Pour off ½ the fat and add lemon juice and parsley. Return veal to skillet and heat, stirring to coat well with sauce.

VEAL STEAK
(Electric Skillet)

6 veal steaks, 1½" thick
Salt and pepper to taste
2 tsp. paprika
2 tsp. rosemary

Flour
5 Tbs. butter
2 cups dry red wine
1 cup heavy cream

Serves 6

Rub veal with salt, pepper, paprika and rosemary. Dredge in flour.

Heat butter in electric skillet and brown meat quickly on both sides. Add wine and simmer, covered, about 15 minutes, or until meat is tender.

Place meat on a heated platter. Stir cream into pan juices in skillet and bring to a boil. Pour sauce over veal steaks and serve.

LAMB SHANKS
(Conventional Stove and Slow Cooker)

6 lamb shanks (about 1½ lbs.)
3 Tbs. oil
20 small white onions, peeled (or 2 large onions, cut into chunks)
3 cloves garlic, minced
1 lb. green beans
1 tsp. basil
1 cup chicken broth
2 Tbs. Dijon mustard
Salt and pepper to taste

Serves 6

Trim excess fat from lamb shanks. In a large skillet brown lamb shanks in oil; remove with a slotted spoon. Sauté onions and garlic in remaining oil in skillet for 5 minutes.

Place lamb shanks, onions, garlic and green beans in slow cooker. Add basil, chicken broth, mustard, salt and pepper; stir. Cover cooker and cook on low heat (190°–200°) for 8 hours, or on high heat (290°–300°) for 4 hours, or until lamb shanks are very tender.

PORK CHOPS MELMO
(Electric Skillet)

4 Tbs. butter
6 loin pork chops, ¾" thick
Salt and pepper to taste
½ cup honey
½ cup tawny port

⅛ tsp. nutmeg
⅛ tsp. thyme
5 large apples, peeled and sliced
Salt and pepper to taste
Juice of ½ lemon

Serves 6

In a large electric skillet heat the butter. Sprinkle chops with salt and pepper and sauté on both sides until golden brown. Add honey, port, nutmeg and thyme. Cover and simmer for 5 minutes.

Add apples to skillet. Stir and mix until apples are coated with wine and honey. Sprinkle apples with salt and pepper. Simmer, stirring occasionally, until apples are tender and sauce is slightly thickened, about 7 to 8 minutes.

Sprinkle with lemon juice and simmer for 2 to 3 minutes longer.

NEAPOLITAN BEAN BAKE
(Conventional Stove and Slow Cooker)

1 lb. Great Northern beans
1 lb. hot or sweet Italian sausage, sliced
2 large onions, chopped
3 cloves garlic, minced

16-oz. can Italian tomatoes
2 bay leaves
2 tsp. Italian seasoning
2 tsp. salt
½ tsp. pepper

Serves 6

Rinse beans, place in a large kettle and add water to cover; bring to a boil. Cover and cook for 2 minutes. Remove from heat and let stand for 1 hour. Pour beans into an electric slow cooker.

Brown sausage in a large skillet. Push sausage to one side, add onion and garlic and sauté until soft. Add tomatoes, bay leaves, Italian seasoning, salt and pepper. Bring to a boil and stir contents of skillet into beans. Cover and cook on low heat (190°–200°) for 10 hours, or on high heat (290°–300°) for 5 hours, until beans are tender.

VEGETABLES

SKIN-FRIED POTATOES
(Electric Skillet or Deep Fryer)

2 lbs. medium potatoes
Salt and pepper to taste

Vegetable oil for frying

Serves 6

Quarter unpeeled potatoes and sprinkle with salt and pepper.

In a large electric skillet or deep fryer heat the oil. Drop potatoes into hot oil and cook 8 to 12 minutes, or until golden brown and tender. Drain on paper towels and serve wrapped in a napkin.

FRITTO MISTO (FRIED MIXED VEGETABLES)
(Electric Skillet or Deep Fryer)

3 medium zucchini, cut into ½" × 2½" fingers
1 medium cauliflower, separated into flowerets
½ lb. green beans
2 dozen mushroom caps
1 eggplant, cut into ½" × 2½" fingers
10-oz. pkg. frozen artichokes, defrosted and cut in ½
Salt and pepper to taste
2 cups or more flour
3 eggs, well beaten
2 cups bread crumbs
2 to 3 cups oil for frying

Serves 6

Sprinkle vegetables with salt and pepper. Dredge in flour, dip into beaten eggs, and roll in bread crumbs.

Preheat oil in an electric deep fryer or large electric skillet to 375°–380°. Drop breaded vegetables into hot oil and fry until golden brown on all sides. Keep cooked vegetables covered on a heated platter until all are cooked.

CARROT FRITTERS
(Electric Skillet)

2 cans (16 oz. each) sliced carrots, drained
½ cup sugar
2 eggs
Salt to taste
2½ cups all-purpose flour

1 tsp. grated lemon rind
1 tsp. baking powder
¼ tsp. cinnamon
¼ tsp. nutmeg
Vegetable oil for frying

Makes 24 to 30 pieces

Put carrots, sugar, eggs and salt into a blender and purée at high speed until smooth; pour into a bowl. Add flour, lemon rind, baking powder, cinnamon, and nutmeg; mix well.

Heat oil in electric skillet to 375°. Drop carrot mixture by tablespoons into hot oil. Fry 5 to 6 minutes until deep brown, turning frequently. Drain well on paper towels.

BREADS

POPPY SEED BISCUITS
(Toaster Oven)

2 cups packaged biscuit mix	3 Tbs. poppy seeds
1 cup grated sharp cheese	¾ cup milk

Makes 10 to 12 biscuits

In a bowl combine biscuit mix, cheese and 2 Tbs. of the poppy seeds. Add milk all at once and stir lightly with a fork to form a soft dough.

Working quickly to prevent dough from hardening, turn onto a floured board. Knead lightly a few times and form dough into a smooth ball. Pat or roll out to ½" thickness. Cut with a 2" cookie cutter and place on a small ungreased pan.

Bake in preheated 400° toaster oven for 15 to 20 minutes, or until biscuits are puffed and browned. If desired, brush with a little milk and sprinkle with additional poppy seeds 5 minutes before end of baking time.

CROCK PLATE BISCUITS
(Crock Plate)

2½ cups all-purpose flour
1 Tbs. double-acting baking powder
1 tsp. salt
¼ lb. butter or margarine
⅓ to ½ cup buttermilk

Makes 12 to 14

In a bowl combine flour, baking powder and salt. Add butter and cut in quickly with 2 forks until mixture resembles coarse meal. Add just enough buttermilk to moisten dry ingredients.

Turn out onto a floured board and pat to ½" thickness. Cut with a 2" or 2½" cookie cutter.

Preheat crock plate on low, covered, for 10 minutes. Place biscuits onto hot plate, cover and bake for 4 to 5 minutes, or until browned. Turn and bake for an additional 3 minutes.

WAFFLES GERMAN STYLE
(Toaster Oven)

4 frozen waffles
⅔ cup cream cheese
4 Tbs. apple butter
4 Tbs. light brown sugar

Serves 4

Toast waffles in toaster oven, following directions on the package; remove from oven. Spread each waffle with cream cheese, then top with apple butter and sprinkle with brown sugar.

Return waffles to toaster oven and cook at 350° for about 3 minutes, or until topping is hot.

DESSERTS

CHESTNUT REFRIGERATOR TORTE
(Conventional Stove)

16-oz. can chestnut purée
3 eggs
⅔ cup sugar
2 cups light cream

1 oz. semisweet chocolate bits
3 Tbs. brandy
1 tsp. vanilla extract
1 cup heavy cream, whipped

Serves 6 to 8

Press chestnut purée through a sieve.

Beat eggs and sugar in top of a double boiler. Stir in cream and chocolate. Place over hot water and cook, stirring constantly, until thickened. Beat chestnuts, 1 Tbs. of the brandy and the vanilla into chocolate mixture. Cool slightly; then pour into well-greased 7" tube pan. Chill for 5 hours or until firm.

Carefully unmold torte onto a serving dish. Fill center with whipped cream flavored with remaining brandy.

CHOCOLATE FONDUE
(Conventional Stove or Sterno)

12-oz. pkg. semisweet chocolate bits
½ cup heavy cream
¼ cup brandy
1 Tbs. instant coffee
⅛ tsp. cinnamon
Mixed fresh fruit*—washed, dried and cut into large bite-size pieces; and pound cake, cut into bite-size cubes

Serves 6 to 8

Melt chocolate with cream in a fondue pot or small chafing dish over low heat on a stove or over an alcohol or sterno flame. Add remaining ingredients (except fruit) and stir well.

Place the pot on low alcohol or sterno flame. Dip fruit and cake into the chocolate mixture with fondue forks. Eat immediately. Keep chocolate warm and fruit cold.

*You may use any selection of fruits you wish: strawberries, oranges, bananas, pears and apples go especially well.

STUFFED BAKED APPLES
(Toaster Oven)

8-oz. pkg. mixed dried fruit
½ cup chopped nuts
½ cup apricot preserves
4 baking apples

¼ cup sugar
½ cup ruby port
1 cup sweetened whipped cream

Serves 4

Cook packaged fruits according to directions on package; drain and chop. Mix fruit with nuts and apricot preserves.

Peel and core apples. Cut each apple into 3 crosswise slices. Spoon fruit mixture between apple slices. Restack each apple into original shape.

Line baking pan with foil. Place apples in pan. Sprinkle with sugar and bake in preheated 350° toaster oven for 30 to 35 minutes. Pour a little port over each apple. Bake for 10 minutes, or until apples are tender. Serve apples warm or cold with pan juices and whipped cream.

BEIGNETS MAMMA JEANNETTE
(Conventional Stove and Electric Skillet)

1½ cups milk
½ cup water
12 Tbs. butter or margarine
2 cups all-purpose flour, sifted
½ tsp. vanilla extract

½ tsp. salt
7 eggs
Vegetable oil for frying
Powdered sugar and cinnamon

Makes about 24 to 30 pieces

In a saucepan combine milk, water and butter. Bring to a boil, reduce heat and stir until butter is melted; remove from heat.

Add flour, vanilla extract and salt. Stir and beat until batter leaves sides of pan and forms a ball. Beat in eggs one at a time, beating well after each addition.

Pour 1" to 1½" oil into a large electric skillet. Heat the oil to 375°. To test the temperature, drop in a piece of bread. If it turns golden brown, oil is hot enough.

Using a tablespoon, drop batter from spoon into hot oil, flattening it into small pancakes. Fry until golden brown on both sides. Remove with slotted spoon onto paper towels. Sprinkle generously with powdered sugar and cinnamon.

CANDY-COATED FRITTERS
(Electric Skillet and Conventional Stove)

1½ cups all-purpose flour
⅔ cup ice water
2 eggs, beaten
Oil for deep-fat frying
2 medium apples
2 firm bananas
1 cup sugar

1 cup light corn syrup
½ cup water
2 Tbs. cooking oil
2 Tbs. sesame seeds
Large bowl filled with ice water
 and ice cubes

Serves 6

In a bowl combine flour, ice water and eggs; beat until smooth.

Peel and core apples; cut into ¼" thick slices. Cut bananas into 1" slices.

In a large electric skillet heat 2" to 3" of oil to 365°. Dip fruit into prepared batter, coating well. Fry fruit, a few pieces at a time, in hot oil for 1 to 2 minutes, or until lightly golden. Drain on paper towels.

Just before serving prepare syrup: In a saucepan combine sugar, corn syrup, water and oil. Bring to a boil, stirring until sugar dissolves. Boil, stirring occasionally, until mixture turns a light caramel color (280° on candy thermometer). Add sesame seed.

Keep hot over low heat. Quickly dip fruit, one or two at a time into hot syrup. Plunge immediately into large bowl of ice water. Remove and serve at once.

RICE FRITTERS
(Conventional Stove and Electric Skillet)

1¼ cups rice
2½ cups water
2 Tbs. brown sugar
1 tsp. vanilla extract
2 egg yolks
¼ tsp. nutmeg
¼ cup rum

1 cup flour
2 eggs, well beaten
1 cup bread crumbs
Vegetable oil for frying
Sugar
Coconut flakes

Serves 5 or 6

Combine rice and water in a saucepan. Add brown sugar and vanilla. Cook for 25 minutes on low heat until rice is tender and water is absorbed; cool completely.

Beat egg yolks with nutmeg and rum. Add to rice and mix well; chill thoroughly. Roll rice mixture into 2" fingers. Dredge fingers in flour, dip in beaten eggs and roll in bread crumbs.

Heat oil in electric skillet to 375°. Fry rice fingers until crisp and golden brown. Sprinkle with sugar and coconut flakes.

5
Little-or-No-Cook Recipes

The most efficient way of saving energy is, of course, to use none at all. Salads are natural no-cookers, as are many desserts. When planning menus, try to minimize your use of appliances and stoves by coordinating cooked foods with recipes that require little or no cooking. Once you've prepared a dish over a fire or on a grill or stove, the residual heat can be used to dissolve gelatin or melt chocolate.

For main dishes, many meats and poultry are available precooked, and there is a whole variety of smoked and canned fish and seafood. Experiment with composed salads, mixing cooked meat, fish or cheese with garden vegetables, tossing them together with a freshly prepared vinaigrette or mayonnaise. If you have your own garden, you'll welcome the chance to show off your green thumb as well as your culinary artistry. Canned vegetables, often dreary by themselves, perk up surprisingly when drained well, rinsed in fresh water and marinated overnight.

The following is just a sampling of appetizers, salads and desserts that require minimal cooking or no cooking at all. They may be combined with any of the other recipes in the book to compose a complete menu. Use them, too, as inspiration to think about the no-cook possibilities that really do exist. After all, saving energy is largely dependent on your own desire and ingenuity.

APPETIZERS

BLUE CHEESE AND BEEF CANAPÉS

8 oz. cream cheese
5 Tbs. crumbled blue-veined cheese
1 Tbs. minced chives
3 Tbs. sour cream
Pinch of cayenne pepper

24 to 30 thin slices party rye or pumpernickel bread, toasted
1 lb. very thinly sliced filet of beef cooked to desired doneness
Olives, capers and small pickled onions for garnish

Makes 24 to 30 canapés

Mix cream cheese, blue cheese, chives, sour cream and cayenne pepper into a smooth paste. Spread bread slices with the mixture. Place 1 or 2 slices of beef on top of each canapé. Decorate with olives, capers or small pickled onions.

COCONUT CREAM-CHEESE BALLS

8 oz. cream cheese
½ tsp. garlic salt
¼ cup pale dry sherry
1 Tbs. soy sauce
Pinch of cayenne pepper

½ cup ground Macadamia nuts or walnuts
1½ cups coconut flakes, lightly toasted

Makes about 30 to 35 cheese balls

Soften cream cheese at room temperature for about 1 hour and add all the other ingredients except coconut flakes. Place into refrigerator for another hour or 2 or overnight.

Roll cream cheese mixture into small balls. Roll each ball in toasted coconut flakes. Place onto serving platter, cover and refrigerate. Before serving you may want to sprinkle more coconut over the cheese balls.

LITCHI NUTS STUFFED WITH CREAM CHEESE

2 cans (18 oz. each) litchi nuts
2 pkgs. (8 oz. each) cream cheese
2 Tbs. blue cheese, crumbled
½ cup chopped walnuts
¼ cup pale dry sherry
¼ tsp. salt
2 Tbs. brandy
Watercress leaves or walnut halves

Serves 10

Drain litchi nuts well on paper towels. Mix all remaining ingredients into a smooth paste. Stuff each litchi nut with 1 tsp. of the cheese mixture. Decorate with watercress leaves or walnut halves. Refrigerate for at least 1 hour.

ORANGE PICKLED HERRING

2 jars (12 oz. each) herring in wine sauce
2 cups sugar
½ cup white vinegar
6-oz. can frozen orange juice
2 bay leaves
4 peppercorns
2 oranges
2 onions, thinly sliced

Serves 6

Drain herring and set aside. Mix sugar and vinegar in a bowl; add undiluted orange juice, bay leaves and peppercorns. Pare oranges, cut peel into thin strips. Add peel to marinade. (Save oranges for another recipe.) Add herring and onions and mix. Refrigerate overnight.

Serve with rye crackers or thinly sliced pumpernickel.

SALADS AND VEGETABLES

AVOCADO AND PAPAYA SALAD

1 papaya or cantaloupe, cut into 1" cubes
1 large or 2 small avocados, cut into 1" cubes
14-oz. can of hearts of palm, drained and sliced (if available, use fresh hearts of palm)
2 tomatoes, cut into chunks
Juice of 2 lemons, or more to taste
1 cup watercress leaves
¼ tsp. salt or more
¼ tsp. coriander
¼ tsp. allspice
¼ tsp. white pepper
½ cup mayonnaise
3 Tbs. honey

Serves 3 or 4

Place papaya, avocado, hearts of palm and tomatoes into a bowl and sprinkle with juice of 1 lemon. Add watercress leaves and seasonings; toss gently. Refrigerate for 1 to 2 hours, or until chilled.

Combine mayonnaise, remaining lemon juice and the honey; beat with a whisk. Pour over salad and toss gently.

AVOCADO AND TOMATO SALAD

4 large ripe tomatoes, cut into large chunks
2 large avocados, peeled and cut into chunks
3 Tbs. lime juice
3 Tbs. lemon juice
¼ cup olive oil
2 Tbs. minced scallions
1 tsp. salt
¼ tsp. pepper
3 heads Bibb lettuce, separated into leaves and washed
3 hard-boiled eggs, minced
3 Tbs. minced parsley

Serves 6

In a bowl combine tomatoes and avocados; sprinkle with lime and lemon juice. Add olive oil, scallions, salt and pepper; toss gently.

Line a salad bowl with lettuce leaves. Place tomatoes and avocados into salad bowl. Sprinkle with minced eggs and parsley.

FENNEL AND CUCUMBER SALAD

1 bulb fennel
1 cucumber
¼ cup olive or corn oil
2 Tbs. lemon juice or vinegar

½ tsp. salt
½ tsp. pepper
1 clove garlic, finely chopped (optional)

Serves 4

Wash fennel and slice very thinly. Peel cucumber and slice very thinly. Place fennel and cucumber in salad bowl, add remaining ingredients and toss well.

BOSTON LETTUCE SALAD

2 heads Boston lettuce
½ lb. fresh mushrooms, thinly sliced
¼ cup wine vinegar
½ cup olive oil
½ tsp. salt
¼ tsp. pepper

½ tsp. Italian seasoning
3 Tbs. chopped scallions
¼ cup chopped parsley
2 Tbs. minced fresh dill
½ cup black olives, cut in half
¼ cup capers

Serves 6

Separate lettuce, wash well, tear into 3" pieces, wrap in paper toweling and chill for 2 to 3 hours or overnight.

Place mushrooms in a bowl and sprinkle with 3 Tbs. of the vinegar, ¼ cup of the olive oil and ½ the salt, pepper and Italian seasoning. Refrigerate for 1 hour.

Just before serving, assemble the salad. Place lettuce into a salad bowl; add scallions, parsley, dill and mushrooms. Pour the remaining vinegar and oil over the salad and sprinkle with remaining salt, pepper and Italian seasoning. Add olives and capers. Toss lightly and serve immediately.

SALAD ESPAÑOL

14-oz. can artichoke hearts, drained and quartered
2 cups cooked green peas
2 cups diced carrots, cooked
20-oz. can garbanzos (chick peas), drained
1 cup chopped green olives
1 cup chopped black olives
½ cup chopped pimientos
2 Tbs. capers
½ cup olive oil
3 Tbs. wine vinegar
Salt and pepper to taste
½ tsp. oregano
½ tsp. basil
Romaine lettuce

Serves 6

Place artichoke hearts, peas, carrots, garbanzos, olives, pimientos and capers in a bowl. In another bowl, mix olive oil, vinegar, salt, pepper, oregano and basil. Pour over the vegetables, toss and refrigerate for 2 hours. Serve over crisp lettuce.

CHICKEN ASPIC SALAD

2 envelopes unflavored gelatin
3½ cups chicken broth, unheated
½ tsp. basil
2 cloves garlic, chopped
5 scallions, minced
2 bay leaves
5 whole peppercorns
5 Tbs. lemon juice
3 cups diced cooked chicken
16-oz. can sliced carrots
2 pkgs. (10 oz. each) frozen peas, cooked
1 cup chopped parsley
1 cup diced cooked ham
2 Tbs. capers
Parsley, cherry tomatoes

Serves 6

Sprinkle gelatin on ½ cup chicken broth; set aside.

Heat 1½ cups of the chicken broth in a small saucepan. Add basil, garlic, scallions, bay leaves and peppercorns. Bring to a boil and simmer for 2 to 3 minutes; remove from heat.

Add gelatin to chicken-broth mixture and stir until dissolved. Strain into a bowl through a sieve lined with cheesecloth. Add lemon juice and remaining chicken broth. Cool but do not let set.

Place diced chicken into a bowl and add 1 cup of chicken broth with gelatin; mix well.

Oil a 9" × 5" loaf pan. Pour about 1" of gelatin mixture into loaf pan and refrigerate until almost set (do not let set completely). Place about 12 carrot pieces on top of gelatin in 2 corners of the pan; spread the cooked peas evenly over exposed gelatin. Pour a bit of liquid gelatin over the vegetables. Sprinkle ½ the diced chicken mixture over the vegetables. Sprinkle ½ the parsley over the chicken. Then spread another layer of vegetables and let set completely. Place ham over gelatin, then remaining parsley, remaining chicken, capers and remaining vegetables. Pour remaining gelatin over vegetables and chill overnight.

To unmold, loosen gelatin around edges with a knife. Dip pan into hot water quickly, invert onto a platter and shake loose. Decorate with parsley and cherry tomatoes.

TURKEY SALAD WITH PINEAPPLE-HORSERADISH SAUCE

2 lbs. cooked turkey breast
1 can (20 oz.) pineapple chunks, drained
2 pints blueberries or strawberries

Pineapple-Horseradish Sauce (*below*)
Bibb lettuce or Romaine lettuce

Serves 12 to 14

Slice turkey breast into julienne strips. In a bowl combine turkey and pineapple chunks.

Wash and hull berries; toss with turkey and pineapple. Add Horseradish-Pineapple Sauce and toss well.

Line a large salad bowl with lettuce leaves and fill with turkey salad. Decorate with more berries and pineapple chunks.

Pineapple-Horseradish Sauce

15-oz. bottle prepared hot horseradish
1 cup mayonnaise
1 cup sour cream
½ tsp. garlic salt
Pinch of white pepper
1 Tbs. sugar or to taste
¼ tsp. nutmeg
¼ tsp. ginger
¼ tsp. allspice
2 cups crushed pineapple, drained
2 cups whipped cream

In a large mixing bowl beat horseradish and mayonnaise together with a wire whisk. Add sour cream and beat again. Add garlic salt, pepper, sugar, nutmeg, ginger and allspice and beat lightly.

Add pineapple and purée in a blender or food processor until very smooth. Fold in whipped cream.

GARDEN SALAD MOLD

1 large pkg. (7 oz.) lime gelatin
16-oz. can peas and carrots
1 large cucumber, diced
1 green pepper, diced
2 dill pickles, diced
½ cup pitted green olives, chopped
3 scallions, minced
2 Tbs. minced fresh dill (optional)
1 cup apple cider vinegar
½ tsp. dry mustard
1 tsp. Worcestershire sauce
½ tsp. salt
½ tsp. pepper
½ tsp. oregano
1 cup salad oil

Serves 6 to 8

Prepare gelatin as directed on package but reduce liquid by using only ½ cup cold water. Cool and place into refrigerator until gelatin is the consistency of thick cream.

In a large bowl combine cucumber, green pepper, pickles, olives, scallions and dill; toss lightly.

In a glass jar with a tight lid mix vinegar with mustard, Worcestershire, salt, pepper and oregano. Add oil and shake well.

Pour ½ the dressing over the vegetables; toss lightly. Reserve the remaining dressing to use on salads.

Fold vegetables into partially set gelatin. Pour into your favorite mold. Refrigerate for at least 3 to 4 hours. To unmold, invert the mold over a platter, hold a hot towel over the mold for about 2 to 3 seconds, repeat if necessary and shake the mold from side to side. Decorate with cucumbers, radishes, etc.

SPECIAL MINUTE RICE

4 cups water
4 cubes chicken broth, crushed
3 Tbs. butter

4 cups Minute Rice
10-oz. pkg. frozen peas
(optional)

Serves 6 to 8

In a saucepan combine water, crushed chicken broth cubes and butter. Bring to a boil, add rice and, if you wish, the frozen peas. Cover and simmer for 2 to 3 minutes. Remove from heat and let stand covered for about 5 minutes.

NOTE: This dish cooks so fast that I've put it in this chapter! So easy to do, not only on your conventional or wood-burning stove but on your fireplace grate or outdoor grill.

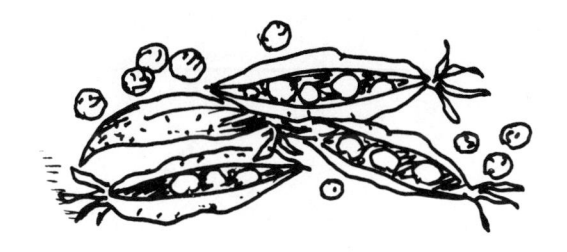

DESSERTS

BISCUIT MAXIM

3 eggs, separated
1½ cups sugar
¼ lb. butter

1 pkg. Social Tea biscuits
1 cup very strong coffee, cooled

Serves 6 to 8

To prepare cream, beat egg yolks with ½ cup of the sugar until thick. Beat egg whites with another ¼ cup sugar until stiff. In a large bowl beat butter until fluffy. Add egg yolks and whites alternately to the butter, blending well.

Dip 20 biscuits quickly into ½ cup of the coffee. Place side by side on a platter in 4 rows, 5 to a row. Spread ⅓ of the cream over the biscuits, dip and place another layer of 20 biscuits and spread with ½ the remaining cream. Repeat with another layer of biscuits and remaining cream.

Combine remaining coffee and sugar and cook for 5 to 7 minutes, or until slightly thickened. Cool and frost cake. Let stand overnight in refrigerator before serving. Keep refrigerated.

BISCUIT TORTONI

2 cups heavy cream
⅔ cups sifted vanilla powdered sugar*
¼ cup rum
½ tsp. rum extract
1 cup finely chopped toasted almonds or hazelnuts
2 egg whites, stiffly beaten

Makes 10 to 12

Whip cream until it starts to thicken. Slowly add sugar and beat until stiff. Add rum and rum extract. Fold in ½ cup of the almonds and the beaten egg whites.

Fill 12 to 14 fluted paper cups with flavored cream and sprinkle with remaining almonds. Freeze overnight.

*To make vanilla sugar, see page 85.

BLACK SMITH PIE À LA FORGE

⅓ pkg. (9½ oz.) graham crackers
⅓ pkg. (5¼ oz.) fudge chip cookies
⅓ cup melted butter
5½-oz. pkg. instant vanilla pudding
6 oz. semisweet chocolate
¾ cup heavy cream
1½ envelopes unflavored gelatin
½ cup water
6 egg whites
½ cup sugar
3 cups sweetened whipped cream
Grated chocolate

Serves 10 to 12

Break up crackers and cookies with a rolling pin or mallet to make about 3 cups of crumbs. Mix with butter and press into a 10″ pie pan. Refrigerate for 1 hour.

Prepare instant pudding as directed on package. Melt chocolate over hot water and mix with 1 cup of the pudding. Spread chocolate mixture over the crumb crust.

Whip heavy cream; fold into remaining pudding.

Beat egg whites until foamy. Add sugar and beat until very stiff. Fold into pudding. Spread over chocolate mixture in crumb crust. Refrigerate pie until set.

Cover pie with sweetened whipped cream. Decorate with grated chocolate.

ICE CREAM CAKE

16-oz. candied fruit, chopped
½ cup rum
½ cup pecan halves
2 round 9" sponge cakes

½ pint each chocolate, pistachio, strawberry and vanilla ice cream
1 cup sweetened whipped cream

Serves 8 to 10

In a small saucepan with cover combine candied fruit and rum. Cover and bring to a boil. Remove from heat and stir in pecan halves; cool.

Split each sponge cake in ½. Place 1 sponge layer in a 9" springform pan. Spread with ½ pint softened chocolate ice cream and top with ¾ cup fruit-nut mixture. Repeat layers with sponge cake, pistachio, strawberry and vanilla ice cream and fruit-nut mixture. Garnish top vanilla layer with wreath of fruit and nut mixture. Freeze until firm.

To unmold, remove rim of springform pan. Transfer to a serving platter. Remove bottom of pan. Decorate with sweetened whipped cream before serving.

CASSATA ALLA SICILIANA
(Sicilian Cake with Chocolate Frosting)

5" × 10" sponge or pound cake
6 Tbs. Strega liqueur (or other orange liqueur)
1½ lbs. ricotta cheese
¼ cup heavy cream
1 cup confectioners' sugar
½ tsp. vanilla

1 cup chopped mixed candied fruit
¼ cup pine nuts
3 oz. semisweet chocolate, coarsely chopped
Chocolate Frosting (*below*)
Candied fruit and pine nuts for decoration

Serves 8 to 10

With a very sharp serrated knife, cut ends off the cake and level top if it is rounded. Slice cake horizontally into 3 or 4 even layers, each about ½" thick. Place on a pastry board side by side and sprinkle with 3 Tbs. of the liqueur.

With an egg beater, beat ricotta cheese with cream until very smooth. Add sugar, vanilla and remaining liqueur and beat for about 1 to 2 minutes. Fold in candied fruit, nuts and chocolate.

Place bottom slice of cake onto a serving platter. Spread generously with ricotta cream. Place another slice of cake on top, spread with ricotta. Continue layering, ending with a slice of cake on top.

Lightly press all layers together, then square them neatly. Refrigerate for 3 to 4 hours, or until the cake feels firm to the touch.

Spread Chocolate Frosting on all sides and top of the cake. Decorate with candied fruit and pine nuts. Wrap with wax paper loosely and refrigerate overnight before serving.

Chocolate Frosting

12 oz. semisweet chocolate bits
½ cup very strong coffee

¼ cup heavy cream
12 Tbs. unsalted butter

In a saucepan, combine chocolate bits with coffee and cream. Cook over low heat, stirring constantly, until the chocolate has completely melted. Remove from heat.

Cut butter into small pieces. Add a few pieces at a time to the chocolate, beating with a wooden spoon after each addition until the mixture is very smooth. Refrigerate chocolate cream until it thickens but is still spreadable.

CREMA DI RICOTTA (CHEESE CREAM)

4 egg yolks
1 cup granulated vanilla sugar*
1 lb. ricotta
⅓ cup heavy cream

Grated rind of 1 orange
3 Tbs. Cointreau or brandy
Strawberries or canned peaches
 or pineapple

Serves 4 to 6

Beat egg yolks and sugar until very thick.

Press cheese through a sieve. Add cheese to egg yolks and beat together. Add cream, orange rind and Cointreau; beat for 1 minute.

Pour into serving dish and spread strawberries, peaches or pineapple on top. If using strawberries, sprinkle with powdered sugar. Chill for 2 to 3 hours and serve. If you wish, serve Raspberry Sauce on the side.

Raspberry Sauce

2 pkgs. frozen raspberries in
 heavy syrup

½ cup sugar or more to taste
3 Tbs. Cointreau or brandy.

Defrost raspberries; strain into a bowl and press berries through a sieve. Pour into a saucepan, add sugar and simmer for 5 to 7 minutes, or until slightly thickened. Add Cointreau, stir and chill.

*To make vanilla sugar, see page 85.

CUSTARD CAKE

2½ cups sugar
1 cup water
¼ cup lemon juice
2 tsp. grated lemon rind
½ tsp. cinnamon
¼ cup dark rum

8" sponge cake
10 egg yolks, well beaten
½ tsp. cinnamon
½ tsp. roasted hazelnuts or almonds, coarsely chopped
½ cup raisins

Serves 8

Combine sugar, water and lemon juice. Bring to a boil, stirring constantly. Cover and cook for 5 minutes; remove from heat. Add lemon rind, cinnamon and rum; stir well.

Slice sponge cake into 8 slices. Dip each slice into hot syrup. Place slices side by side on a serving platter or on individual plates.

Strain remaining syrup into a saucepan, cover and cook for 5 minutes. Pour hot syrup in a steady stream onto egg yolks, beating constantly. Pour back into saucepan. Cook over low flame, stirring constantly, until very thick.

Spread egg-yolk mixture over cake slices. Sprinkle with cinnamon, the nuts and raisins. Refrigerate for at least 2 hours before serving.

DOLCE DI MERANO (Chocolate Loaf Merano Style)

12 oz. semisweet chocolate bits
5 Tbs. dark rum
½ lb. unsalted butter, softened
2 Tbs. sugar
2 egg yolks
6 oz. walnuts, grated (about 1½ cups)

2 egg whites
12 Petit Beurre (butter biscuits)
⅓ cup apricot preserves
Powdered sugar
Sweetened whipped cream

Serves 8 to 10

Oil a 5" × 9" loaf pan lightly, invert and let drain.

In a saucepan melt chocolate over low heat, stirring constantly. Add rum gradually; mix well. If the chocolate hardens when you add the rum, add 1 to 2 tsp. boiling water to soften. Set aside to cool.

In a bowl cream butter until very fluffy, add sugar and beat for 1 minute. Add egg yolks one at a time, beating well. Add walnuts and chocolate; blend well.

Beat egg whites until stiff but not dry. Fold into chocolate mixture thoroughly until no white can be seen. Break biscuits into small pieces and fold into chocolate cream.

Pour ½ the chocolate cream into the loaf pan, gently spread the apricot preserves over the cream and then pour the remaining chocolate cream on top. Smooth down the top. Cover with plastic wrap and refrigerate for at least 6 hours or overnight.

To unmold, run a knife around the loaf. Dip bottom of the pan into hot water for about 30 seconds. Cover pan with a serving platter. Invert and shake vigorously until the loaf slides out. If necessary, dip pan in hot water a second time. If loaf does not slide out immediately, smooth down the top. Refrigerate again for 1 hour and repeat procedure.

Before serving sprinkle generously with powdered sugar. Serve topped with sweetened whipped cream.

MOUSSE AU CHOCOLAT (Chocolate Mousse)

5 oz. unsweetened chocolate
5 oz. semisweet chocolate
6 egg yolks
2 cups sugar

4 cups heavy cream
3 Tbs. coffee liqueur or brandy
2 egg whites
Grated chocolate

Serves 12

Place all the chocolate into the top of a double boiler* and melt over simmering water, set aside.

Beat egg yolks until thickened. Add sugar and beat until light in color and very thick. Add melted chocolate and blend well. Cool completely, but do not refrigerate.

Whip cream until stiff. Reserving 1 cup, fold remaining whipped cream into chocolate mixture and blend well with a whisk or beater. Add the liqueur.

Beat egg whites until stiff but not dry. Fold into chocolate mixture gently but thoroughly. Transfer to a large serving bowl or individual serving dishes and refrigerate for at least 3 to 4 hours or until completely set. Decorate with reserved whipped cream and grated chocolate.

*To make double boiler suitable for grill or over-the-fire cookery, use a large and a small cast-iron pot. Half fill the larger pot with water and place the smaller pot into it. Let the water simmer gently for melting chocolate.

MOUSSE ROYAL MOLD

1 pkg. (3½ oz.) raspberry or strawberry gelatin
1 cup hot water
1 cup frozen raspberries or strawberries
1 Tbs. lemon juice
2 egg whites
¼ cup sugar
1 cup whipped cream

Serves 6

Dissolve gelatin in hot water.

Put berries through a fine sieve or purée in a blender. Add berries and lemon juice to gelatin. Refrigerate, stirring occasionally, until consistency of unbeaten egg white.

Beat egg whites until soft peaks are formed, add sugar and beat until very stiff. Fold egg whites and whipped cream into gelatin and mix well. Pour into your favorite mold and refrigerate.

To unmold, invert mold onto a platter and hold hot towel over the mold. Shake from side to side, and lift off the mold. Serve with additional whipped cream or more berries.

ORANGE MOUSSE

9 egg yolks
1½ cups granulated sugar
1 Tbs. finely grated orange rind
1 Tbs. orange flavoring
1 cup orange juice
2 pkgs. unflavored gelatin

⅔ cup orange liqueur
3½ cups heavy cream
½ cup powdered sugar
9 egg whites
1 orange, unpeeled and thinly sliced

Serves 8 to 10

Oil a 1½-quart soufflé dish and sprinkle with sugar. Tie a well-oiled waxed-paper collar around the dish, extending 6" above the dish. Wrap collar snugly around the dish and attach with scotch tape so it holds together securely.

In a large bowl beat together egg yolks and granulated sugar until thick and lemon colored. Add orange rind and flavoring.

Heat orange juice but do not boil. Dissolve gelatin in orange liqueur and mix into hot orange juice. Slowly pour orange juice into egg yolks, beating constantly; cool.

Whip cream until slightly thickened, add powdered sugar and whip until stiff. Reserving 1 cup of the whipped cream for decoration, fold remaining whipped cream into egg-yolk mixture.

Whip egg whites until stiff but not dry. Fold into yolk mixture thoroughly but gently.

Pour mousse into prepared soufflé dish very carefully. Do not bend or disturb the paper collar. Refrigerate for at least 4 to 5 hours or overnight.

Before serving remove paper collar. Leave mousse in soufflé dish—do not unmold. Decorate top with remaining whipped cream and orange slices.

STRAWBERRIES ROMANOFF

1½ quarts strawberries
½ cup vanilla sugar*
½ cup Cointreau

1 pint vanilla ice cream
1½ cups whipped cream
¼ cup sugar

Serves 6

Hull and wash the strawberries. Place into a bowl and sprinkle with vanilla sugar and ¼ cup of the Cointreau. Refrigerate for at least 1 hour.

Just before serving, slightly soften ice cream until it is just the consistency of very thick cream. Fold sugar and remaining Cointreau into the whipped cream; then fold the whipped cream into the ice cream. Fold the strawberries into the cream and serve immediately.

*To make vanilla sugar, see page 85.

STRAWBERRY FLUMMERY

3 cups fresh strawberries, sliced
1 cup sugar
3½-oz. pkg. strawberry-flavored gelatin
1 cup boiling water

3 eggs, separated
¼ cup sugar
2 tsp. lemon juice
Sweetened whipped cream

Serves 6

Place strawberries and sugar in a blender and purée for 30 seconds at high speed. Strain through a sieve to remove seeds.

Dissolve gelatin in boiling water. Beat egg yolks in medium-sized bowl. Gradually beat in softened gelatin. Stir in strained strawberries. Chill mixture until consistency of unbeaten egg whites.

Beat egg whites until foamy. Add sugar, a Tbs. at a time; add lemon juice. Beat until stiff and glossy. Fold meringue into strawberry mixture.

Spoon into 6 dessert dishes and chill until set. Serve with sweetened whipped cream.

6
Holiday Favorites

BAVARIAN CHRISTMAS HAM
(Fireplace)

4- to 5-lb. fully cooked boned ham
½ cup honey
¼ cup Cointreau or brandy
1 tsp. dry mustard

½ tsp. allspice
¼ tsp. ground cloves
1 Tbs. grated orange rind
Topping (*below*)

Serves 8 to 10

Cut off all excess fat from ham. Place ham on double foil. Brush on all sides with honey, Cointreau, seasonings and orange rind. Seal foil, place on an inverted cake pan inside a Dutch oven. Cover and bake over a hot fire for 45 minutes to 1 hour.

Open foil and baste ham with the accumulated juices. Bake for another 10 minutes, basting 3 to 4 times.

Pack Topping on top of ham. Return to Dutch oven. Cover, put hot coals onto Dutch oven lid and cook until slightly browned and bubbly on top, about 15 minutes.

Baste Topping with pan juices. Cool ham completely before serving.

Topping

2 cups walnut halves
¼ cup honey
1 cup brown sugar
½ cup candied orange peel
½ cup orange marmalade or preserves
3 Tbs. Cointreau or brandy

4 tsp. prepared mustard
1 tsp. dry mustard
½ tsp. ginger
½ tsp. allspice
½ tsp. white pepper
¼ tsp. ground cloves
¼ tsp. salt

In a bowl combine all the ingredients and mix well.

CAPON WITH APRICOT STUFFING
(Wood-Burning Stove)

5- to 6-lb. capon
3 Tbs. melted butter
Salt and white pepper
Stuffing (*below*)

¼ cup butter, melted
2 Tbs. flour
Apricot Glaze (*below*)
Brandied Apricots (*below*)

Serves 4 or 5

If frozen, defrost capon as directed on package or in the refrigerator for 24 to 36 hours. Remove package with giblets.

Brush capon inside and outside with melted butter and sprinkle with salt and white pepper. Fill with Stuffing and cover opening with a piece of foil. Tie legs together and tuck in the wings. Place on a well-buttered rack in a large baking pan, breast up.

Blend butter and flour until smooth.

Bake capon in a 350° oven for 2½ to 3 hours, or until the legs move freely, basting frequently with butter and flour mixture. Insert thermometer into the breast without touching the bone. When temperature reaches 185°, capon is done. If you wish, turn the bird over for a few minutes so that the back is also browned. Then place breast up again.

About 15 minutes before serving, glaze capon with Apricot Glaze and continue baking. Cool for 10 minutes before serving. Serve with Brandied Apricots.

Stuffing

1 cup black currants
⅓ cup brandy
12-oz. pkg. dried apricots
1½ cups water
1 cup sugar
4 cups cooked rice

¼ cup melted butter
¼ cup black currant preserves
⅔ cup chopped walnuts
¼ tsp. sage
¼ tsp. allspice
Salt and white pepper to taste

Soak currants in brandy for 1 hour.

While currants are soaking, cook dried apricots in a saucepan in water with sugar for 10 minutes. Drain, cool completely and chop apricots.

Combine apricots, rice, butter and preserves. Add walnuts, seasonings and currants with brandy; blend well.

NOTE: If you have extra stuffing, place into a well-buttered ovenproof dish, cover with foil and bake for 45 minutes in a 350° oven. Or, if you wish, make extra stuffing by doubling the recipe and bake as directed.

Apricot Glaze
> ½ cup apricot preserves
> ¼ cup sherry
> ¼ cup brandy

Press apricot preserves through a sieve into a small saucepan. Add sherry and cook for 5 minutes. Remove from heat and add brandy.

Brandied Apricots
> 15-oz. can whole apricots
> ¾ cup dark brown sugar
> ⅔ cup brandy

Drain apricots well. Sprinkle brown sugar into a baking pan, place apricots over the sugar and pour brandy over the apricots. Bake in a 350° preheated oven for 10 minutes.

Spoon sugar and brandy mixture from bottom of pan over apricots a few times.

ROAST GOOSE WITH CHESTNUT STUFFING
(Wood-Burning Stove)

8- to 10-lb. goose
Salt and coarsely ground black pepper
½ tsp. oregano
½ tsp. thyme
Chestnut Stuffing (*below*)
½ cup pale dry sherry
½ cup orange juice

Serves 5 or 6

If frozen, defrost goose as directed on package or in the refrigerator for 24 to 36 hours. Remove package with giblets.

Sprinkle goose inside and out with salt, pepper, oregano and thyme. Allow 1 cup of stuffing for each pound of goose. Stuff the body cavity and neck of the goose with Chestnut Stuffing.

Tuck in the wings and tie them together under the back of the bird. To close cavity after stuffing, skewer and lace with string, or cover cavity with a piece of foil. Tie legs securely together.

Place the goose on its side on a well-buttered rack in a baking pan. Bake in a preheated 375° oven for 35 minutes. Stab with a fork all over. Turn on the other side and bake for 35 minutes. Stab again all over with a fork to let the fat drip out.

Mix sherry and orange juice.

Turn goose on its back and baste with sherry and orange juice. Baste goose every 15 to 20 minutes.

An 8-lb. goose will take about 3 to 3½ hours to roast, a 10-lb. goose will take about 3½ to 4 hours. Goose is done when leg joints move easily. If you wish to use a meat thermometer, insert it into the thickest part of the thigh. When temperature reaches 180°, the goose is done.

Chestnut Stuffing

2 large onions, minced
2 stalks celery, minced
4 Tbs. butter
10 strips bacon, diced
2 cans whole chestnuts,* chopped (DO NOT use water chestnuts or chestnut purée)
3 cups prepared bread stuffing
1 tsp. salt
½ tsp. poultry seasoning
¼ tsp. pepper
¼ tsp. thyme
¼ tsp. basil
1 cup chicken broth

In a large skillet, sauté onions and celery in butter until just limp. Remove with a slotted spoon and reserve.

Cook bacon in same skillet until golden brown. Drain off ½ the fat. Add chestnuts, bread stuffing, onions and celery and seasonings. Toss together. Add just enough chicken broth to moisten the stuffing.

*You may cook your own fresh chestnuts. Use about 1½ pounds unshelled chestnuts. Cut a gash in the flat part of the skin and cook in 2 quarts of water for 40 minutes. Shell and chop.

GLAZED CRANBERRIES
(Fireplace or Wood-Burning Stove)

2 cups sugar
1½ cups water
⅔ cup slivered orange rind
5 cups fresh cranberries

1 cinnamon stick
⅛ tsp. nutmeg
⅛ tsp. ginger
⅛ tsp. cloves

Serves 5

In a saucepan combine sugar and water. Cook over a low fire or on low heat for 2 minutes. Add orange rind, cranberries, cinnamon stick, nutmeg, ginger and cloves. Cook for 8 to 10 minutes, or until cranberries begin to pop. Remove from heat and cool slightly.

With a slotted spoon, remove orange rind, cinnamon stick and cranberries and place in a bowl. Cook syrup until it is thick. Pour hot syrup over cranberries. Cool and refrigerate.

NUT-CRANBERRY PUDDING
(Wood-Burning Stove)

1½ cups fresh cranberries, washed and drained
½ cup dark brown sugar
½ cup coarsely chopped pecans
2 eggs
½ cup granulated sugar
⅔ cup all-purpose flour
¼ tsp. cinnamon
⅛ tsp. salt
½ cup melted butter
Vanilla ice cream

Serves 6 or 7

Butter well a 9" deep-dish pie pan. Spread cranberries evenly in the bottom of the pan. Sprinkle brown sugar and nuts over cranberries.

In a bowl beat together eggs and sugar until thick and lemon colored. Add flour, cinnamon, salt and butter. Beat well until smooth. Pour over cranberries.

Bake in a preheated 350° oven for 40 to 45 minutes. Cool for about 5 minutes. Slice into wedges and serve with ice cream.

SCANDINAVIAN CARROT PUDDING
(Wood-Burning Stove)

4 cans (15 oz. each) carrots	½ cup honey
1 cup plus 3 Tbs. bread crumbs	¼ tsp. allspice
1 cup evaporated milk	¼ tsp. cinnamon
1 cup sour cream	Salt to taste
4 Tbs. melted butter	5 egg whites
5 egg yolks	⅛ tsp. cream of tartar
1½ cups light brown sugar	

Serves 6 to 8

Drain the carrots well, place in a sieve and press down with a wooden spoon to squeeze out all the water. When carrots are almost dry, press through the sieve into a bowl.

Add 1 cup bread crumbs, the milk, sour cream and butter to carrots. Blend well.

Beat egg yolks with brown sugar until thick and light in color. Add honey, allspice, cinnamon and salt; mix well. Add to carrots and blend.

Beat egg whites with cream of tartar until stiff. Fold into carrot mixture.

Butter well a 2-quart soufflé dish or any other ovenproof dish and sprinkle with 3 Tbs. bread crumbs. Pour pudding into dish and bake in a preheated 350° oven for 40 to 45 minutes, or until a cake tester comes out clean. Serve hot with poultry, meat or ham.

NOTE: If you wish you may fold 1 cup well-drained crushed pineapple into the pudding before the egg whites.

CRANBERRIED SWEET POTATOES
(Wood-Burning Stove)

24-oz. can sweet potatoes
¼ cup melted butter
¼ tsp. cinnamon
⅛ tsp. nutmeg
2 cups light brown sugar
½ cup honey
⅛ tsp. salt

⅛ tsp. white pepper
1 cup water
¼ cup orange juice
1 Tbs. grated orange peel
4 cups fresh cranberries, washed and well drained
Grated rind of 1 orange

Serves 6

Butter well a deep baking dish.

Drain sweet potatoes and cut in half. Place in the buttered baking dish. Pour melted butter over sweet potatoes. Sprinkle with cinnamon and nutmeg; set aside.

In a saucepan combine brown sugar, honey, salt, pepper and water. Cook over low heat, stirring until sugar is dissolved. Add orange juice and peel and simmer for 10 minutes. Add cranberries and stir well. Simmer until cranberries are tender but still whole, about 4 to 5 minutes. Add orange rind and simmer for 2 to 3 minutes.

Pour cranberries over sweet potatoes. Bake uncovered in a 350° oven for 25 minutes. Cool slightly before serving.

YORKSHIRE PUDDING
(Wood-Burning Stove)

2 eggs
1 cup milk
1 cup all-purpose flour
½ tsp. salt
⅛ tsp. pepper

⅛ tsp. nutmeg
½ cup goose drippings (beef or chicken drippings may be used)

Serves 6 to 8

In a bowl beat eggs and milk well with a whisk. Combine flour, salt, pepper and nutmeg. Add to egg mixture. Beat batter until well blended and very smooth.

Heat goose drippings and pour into a preheated 8" × 12" baking dish. Bake in a 425° preheated oven for 30 minutes, or until golden brown and puffy.

Reduce heat to 350°. In a wood-burning stove oven, this is accomplished by opening the oven door just a crack, about 1" to 2". Bake pudding for about 10 minutes. The center may collapse, but this does not detract from the taste. Remove from oven, slice into squares and serve.

To Make Popovers:
Use the same batter as above. Pour 2 Tbs. drippings into 8 or 10 muffin tins; heat. Fill each hot tin ⅓ with batter. Bake in a preheated 425° oven for 35 minutes, or until puffed and golden brown. Serve immediately.

CHRISTMAS KRAPFEN (Filled Christmas Doughnuts)
(Wood-Burning Stove or Electric Deep Fryer)

2 pkgs. granulated yeast
½ cup lukewarm water
3 to 3½ cups all-purpose flour
¾ cup milk
⅓ cup sugar
¾ tsp. salt
5 Tbs. butter or margarine
2 eggs plus 1 egg yolk
Vegetable oil for deep frying

Makes about 24 doughnuts

In a small bowl combine yeast and water.

Measure out 1½ cups of the flour and place into a large bowl. Add yeast and beat well with a wooden spoon for about 30 seconds.

Heat milk to lukewarm; add sugar, salt and butter. Stir until butter is melted and add to flour mixture. Add eggs and yolk; beat well after each addition. If using an electric mixer beat for an extra 2 minutes; with a spoon, beat for an extra 4 minutes.

Add enough of the remaining flour to make a medium-soft dough. Knead by hand or with a bread hook until dough leaves sides of bowl. Turn out onto a floured board and knead for 2 to 3 minutes until very smooth and elastic.

Place dough into a lightly greased bowl. Cover and let rise for about 1 hour, or until doubled in bulk.

Turn out onto a floured board and roll dough to ¼" to ½" thickness. Cut with a 2½" cookie cutter. Cover and let rise for about 30 to 35 minutes.

Heat oil in a stove-top deep fryer or an electric deep fryer at 375°. For stove-top fryer, use a thermometer. Fry in hot deep oil for about 1 minute on each side. Drain on paper towel.

To Fill Doughnuts:
Use 3¾-oz. box instant or cooked vanilla pudding; follow directions on the box. Or use 3¾-oz. box chocolate pudding; follow directions on the box, then add 3 oz. semisweet chocolate melted in ½ cup heavy cream and mix well. Or fill the *Krapfen* with your favorite jam or jelly.

Make a slit in each doughnut and fill using a pastry bag fitted with a tube or a coffee spoon. Dust filled doughnuts generously with powdered sugar.

BOURBON BALLS
(No-Cook)

1 cup sugar
3 Tbs. cocoa
3 cups crushed vanilla wafers
2 cups coarsely chopped pecans

3 Tbs. light corn syrup
¼ cup bourbon, or more to taste
Powdered sugar

Makes about 30 balls

Combine sugar and cocoa with crushed wafers and pecans. Toss well to blend ingredients. Add corn syrup and bourbon and mix thoroughly.

Shape into small balls, about 1" in diameter. Roll in powdered sugar.

CHRISTMAS TRIFLE
(Little-or-No-Cook)

7½-oz. pkg. cherry gelatin
2 cups boiling water
½ cup cherry wine
¼ cup cold water
3 pkgs. lady fingers
¾ cup cherry preserves
¾ cup chopped candied cherries
1 small can dark pitted cherries, drained
½ cup blanched, slivered, toasted almonds
7½-oz. pkg. instant vanilla pudding
Syllabub Sauce (*below*) or sweetened whipped cream
Candied cherries for decoration

Serves 8

Dissolve cherry gelatin in 2 cups boiling water. Add cherry wine and cold water.

Line a large glass bowl with lady fingers. Pour ½ the warm gelatin over the lady fingers. Refrigerate until completely firm.

When lady fingers and gelatin are set, spread ½ cup of the cherry preserves over the gelatin, sprinkle ½ cup of candied cherries, ½ the canned cherries and ¼ cup of the almonds. Cover with another layer of lady fingers and pour remaining gelatin on top. Refrigerate until completely firm.

When gelatin is set, spread with remaining preserves and sprinkle with remaining cherries and almonds.

Prepare vanilla pudding as directed on package. Spread pudding over the trifle; refrigerate. Refrigerate for 2 to 3 hours or overnight before serving.

Before serving, top trifle with Sauce and decorate with cherries.

Syllabub Sauce

2 cups heavy cream
1 tsp. fresh lemon juice
½ tsp. vanilla extract
½ tsp. lemon rind
½ cup powdered sugar
2 egg whites
¼ cup granulated sugar
2 Tbs. sweet sherry or sweet wine

Whip cream until firm. Add fresh lemon juice, vanilla, lemon rind and powdered sugar.

Beat egg whites until stiff. Add granulated sugar and beat until very stiff.

Combine whipped cream and egg whites; fold in sherry.

BRANDY CAKE À LA NORMANDE
(Fireplace or Wood-Burning Stove)

1½ cups candied red cherries, chopped
½ cup maraschino cherries
2 cups raisins, preferably white
2½ cups brandy
¾ lb. butter
2 cups light brown sugar
2 cups dark brown sugar
4 cups flour
6 eggs

2 cups coarsely crushed walnuts
2 cups roasted crushed hazelnuts*
4 tsp. baking powder
½ tsp. allspice
½ tsp. cinnamon
½ tsp. ginger
Powdered vanilla sugar**
Whole walnuts for decoration

Serves 8 to 10

Mix together candied cherries, maraschino cherries, raisins and 2 cups of the brandy; set aside.

Cream butter until fluffy. Add sugars, 1 cup at a time, beating well after each addition. Add 1 cup flour and the eggs, one at a time, beating well after each addition. Add remaining flour, the cherries, raisins and brandy; mix well. Add walnuts, hazelnuts, baking powder, allspice, cinnamon and ginger. Blend well.

Butter well two 6-cup steamed-pudding molds and sprinkle generously with sugar. Fill molds with batter, cover tightly with foil and lid and place each mold into a large pot of hot water. Water should come ⅔ up side of mold. Bring to boil, reduce heat and simmer for 3½ hours.

Cool cakes for 25 minutes, then loosen with a knife and invert onto a platter. Sprinkle with sugar and decorate with cherries and walnuts.

Warm ½ cup brandy slightly in a ladle or a small pot, ignite and pour over the decorated cake just before serving.

You may wrap cooled cake in plastic wrap and foil and refrigerate for 2 to 3 weeks. Before serving, remove foil and plastic, rewrap in foil and warm up in a Dutch oven for 15 minutes over a low fire. Pour ignited brandy on top of cake.

*Hazelnuts are always available in health food stores. To roast, place on a cookie sheet on a grill over a low fire and roast for 10 minutes, until the skins rub off easily. Rub off skins and crush nuts, but do not grind.
**To make vanilla sugar, see page 85.

GLEE WINE, OR GLÜHWEIN
(Fireplace or Wood-Burning Stove)

Juice and rind of 2 lemons
2 cups water
8 whole cloves
½ tsp. nutmeg

2 sticks cinnamon
6 Tbs. sugar
1 quart red Bordeaux wine

Serves 12

Strain lemon juice and cut rind into thin slivers. Place into a pot with water, spices and sugar. Bring slowly to a boil, add wine and heat thoroughly but do not boil. Serve hot in heated punch cups.

Mulled Claret

Serves 12

Follow preceding recipe for Glee Wine substituting oranges for lemons and using only 1½ cups water. Add ¼ cup orange liqueur and ¼ cup brandy to the hot wine before serving.

SWEDISH GLÖGG
(Fireplace or Wood-Burning Stove)

3 bottles red Bordeaux wine
10 orange slices studded with
　5 cloves
15 cardamom seeds

2 bottles aquavit or vodka
30 sugar cubes
2 cups whole blanched almonds
2 cups currants or raisins

Serves 38 to 40

Pour wine into a large pot. Add oranges with cloves and cardamom seeds and simmer for 10 minutes but do not boil.

In a saucepan heat aquavit.

Pour wine into a punch bowl and place a metal grate or rack over bowl. Moisten sugar cubes with a little warm aquavit and place onto the grate. Ignite remaining aquavit and keep pouring over sugar until all sugar has melted into the wine.

Place a few almonds and raisins into each punch cup and pour hot liquid over them.

KRAMBAMBULI
(Fireplace or Wood-Burning Stove)

2 bottles dry white wine
1 cup granulated sugar
1 pound sugar cubes

1 cup dark rum, heated
1 bottle unchilled champagne

Serves 24 to 30

In a pot heat the wine but do not boil. Pour into a thick ceramic bowl and stir in granulated sugar until dissolved.

Put a metal grate or rack over the bowl and place sugar cubes onto the grate. Heat rum until lukewarm, ignite and pour while burning over sugar. When most of the sugar has melted into the wine, add champagne and pour into punch cups.

ICE CREAM EGGNOG
(No-Cook)

12 egg yolks
1 cup sugar
1 cup bourbon whiskey or rum
½ cup brandy

2 cups heavy cream, whipped
1 cup light cream
12 egg whites
1 quart vanilla ice cream

Serves 20

Beat egg yolks with ½ cup of the sugar until thick and light. Slowly add whiskey and brandy, stirring well. Fold in the whipped cream. Gently stir in the light cream. Beat egg whites until stiff with remaining ½ cup sugar; fold into eggnog.

Just before serving, cut ice cream into pieces and add to a well-chilled punch bowl set in a bed of ice. Pour eggnog over the ice cream and stir well.

Appendix
Energy Saver's Directory

Wood-Burning Ranges and Franklin Stoves

The Atlanta Stove Works, Inc.
P. O. Box 5254
Atlanta, Georgia 30307
(404) 524-0881
Fireplaces, Franklin stoves, cooking utensils, grates, accessories, swingout mounting brackets, grills, etc.

"Old Country" Appliances
P. O. Box 330 W
Vacaville, Calif. 95688
(707) 448-4860

W. F. Flanders Co.
P. O. Box 211
Springfield, Mass. 01101
(413) 786-5722

Home & Harvest, Inc.
Dept. 60
2517 Glen Burnie Dr.
Greensboro, N. C. 27406
"Cast-iron ranges which burn wood or coal, feature divided flue construction, oven temperature indicator, front wood loading door, ash pan, adjustable draft, damper control and six 8" stove covers."

Pioneer Lamps & Stoves
71 S. W. Yesler Way
Seattle, Wash. 98104

S/A Import Div.
730 Midtown Plaza
Dept. 74
Syracuse, N. Y. 13210

Contractor Equipment Mfg., Inc.
P. O. Box 290
Ashland, Ohio 44805
(419) 289-2224

Elmira Stove Works
22 Church St., West
Elmira, Ontario, Canada N3B IM3
"Large warming cabinet used for extra storage as well as for warming food, solid copper water tank with tap for easy dispensing, extra large cast-iron and brick-lined firepot, black porcelain on all wear surfaces and highly polished on all heating surfaces."

Portland Franklin Stove Foundry, Inc.
57 Kennebec St.
Portland, Maine 04104
(207) 773-0256

Findlay Foundry Limited
P. O. Box 250, Carleton Pl.
Ontario, Canada K7C 3 P4

Wood Stoves of Southern New York
P. O. Box 27
Thompson Ridge, N. Y. 10985
(914) 361-1566

Hadeler Hardware, Inc.
3 N. Main St.
Pearl River, N. Y. 10965

Stoves & Fireplaces of Bergen County, Inc.
17 Jefferson Ave.
Westwood, N. Y. 07175
(201) 666-0443

R & S Gougelet
350 Wheeler Rd., Rt. 111
Hauppauge, N. Y. 11787

Southport Stoves
Div. of Howell Corp.
1180 Stratford Rd.
Stratford, Conn. 06497
(203) 375-1167

also: 248 Tolland St.
East Hartford, Conn. 06108
(203) 289-6079

Thermo Control Wood Stoves
Cobleskill, N. Y. 12043

National Stove Works, Inc.
Howe Caverns Rd.
Cobleskill, N. Y. 12043
(518) 296-8517

Cumberland General Store
Dept. WBC, Rt. 3
Crossville, Tenn. 38555

Stoves and Fireplaces

Jøtue Fireplaces and Stoves
Krista Associates
Portland, Maine

Timberline Stoves, Limited
110 E. First St.
East Syracuse, N. Y. 13057

Timberline Stoves of N. Y.
1840 Lemoyne Ave.
Syracuse, N. Y. 13208
(315) 454-9201

Fireplaces and Accessories

Superior Fireplace Co.
4325 Artesia Ave.
Fullerton, Calif. 92633
(714) 521-7302

Superior Fireplace Co.
1516 S. Baylis St.
Baltimore, Md. 21224
(301) 342-6500

Superior Fireplace Co.
Dunan Brickyard
1001 S. E. 11th St.
Hialeah, Fla. 33010
(305) 887-1525 and 888-6443
"built-in fireplaces, hoods, chimneys and accessories"

Ye Olde Mantel Shoppe
3800 N. E. 2nd Ave.
Miami, Fla. 33137
(305) 576-0225

TEMCO
P. O. Box 1184
Nashville, Tenn. 37202

TEMCO
Floridale Products, Inc.
205 State Rd. 84
Ft. Lauderdale, Fla. 33315
(305) 523-0551; in Miami, (305) 949-3330
949-3330

TEMTEX Products, Inc.
P. O. Box 1184
Nashville, Tenn. 37202

TEMTEX Products, Inc.
P. O. Box 1148
Perris, Calif. 92370

Malm Fireplaces, Inc.
368 Yolanda Ave.
Santa Rosa, Calif. 95404
(707) 546-8955

Seymour Mfg. Co.
500 N. Broadway
Seymour, Ind. 47274
(812) 522-2900

Brewton Enterprises, Inc.
P. O. Box 872, Dept. W
Brewton, Ala. 36426

Boston Stove Co.
155 John St.
Dept. WB 2
Reading, Mass. 01867
(617) 944-1045

Heritage Fireplace Equipment Co.
1874 Englewood Ave.
Akron, Ohio
(216) 798-9840

Freestanding Fireplaces & Newspaper Log Rollers

Heatery, Inc.
Country Village Shopping Center
11319 Highway 7
Minnetonka, Minn. 55343
(612) 933-4800

Chimney-Cleaners

Jiffy Chimney Cleaner
Dept. WQ
Box 766
Old Saybrook, Conn. 06475

The Chimney Brush
Worcester Brush Co.
Worcester, Mass 01601

Intensi-Fire Grates
Arrowsmith Industries, Inc.
Box 208
Dowington, Penn. 19335

Do-It-Yourself Chimney Kits

Duravent Corp.
P. O. Box 1280
Redwood City, Calif. 94064
(800) 227-7374; (415) 368-2912

Antique Cooking Ranges

Goodtime Stove Co.
P. O. Box 368, Rt. 9
Williamsburg, Mass. 01096
(413) 268-3677

Wood-Burning Stoves, Fireplaces, Barbecues and Accessories

Artfire
230 Creditstone Rd.
Concord, Ontario, Canada L4K 1B1
(416) 669-1356

Wood/Coal Appliances

Monarch Kitchen Appliances
Div. of Malleable Iron Range Co.
Dept. WB96
Beaver Dam, Wis. 53916

Fireview Distributors
P. O. Box 370
Rogue River, Ore. 97537
(503) 582-3351

Barbecues and Equipment

Whittier Steel & Mfg., Inc.
10725 S. Painter Ave.
Sante Fe Springs, Calif. 90670

Evenings Delight
9621 S. Dixie Hwy.
Miami, Fla. 33155
(305) 666-3312

Gas Grills

The Locke Stove Co.
114 W. 11th St.
Kansas City, Mo. 64105

Chemglow Products
Antioch, Ill. 60002

Appliances, Utensils and Accessories

Rival Mfg. Co.
3500 Rival Avenue
Sedalia, Mo. 65301
Crockplate and Slow Cookers

Waring Products
Div. of Dynamics Corp. of America
New Hartford, Conn. 06057
Steam Chef and other small electric appliances; available in most department and specialty stores

Kitchen Bazaar
4455 Conn. Avenue, N. W.
Washington, D. C. 20008

The Wooden Spoon
Mahopac, N. Y. 10541
Crepe makers, pasta makers, cutlery, etc.

The Eli Barry Company
Kearny, N. J.
Pasta machines

Kaleidoscope
2201 Faulkner Road, N. E.
Atlanta, Ga. 30324

Pointe Pedlar
405 Fisher
Grosse Pointe, Mich. 48230
Utensils, accessories, etc.

K & K Marketing
P. O. Box 2740
Grand Central Station
New York, N. Y. 10017
Omelet pans

Nutone Food Center
Madison & Red Bank Roads
Cincinnati, Ohio 45227

The Country Gourmet
512 S. Fulton Avenue
Mt. Vernon, N. Y. 10550
Utensils, accessories, etc.

Gallego
P. O. Box 198
Greenvale, N. Y. 11548
Meat grinders, cookie makers, sausage machines, etc.

Reco International Corp.
138 Haven Avenue
Port Washington, N. Y. 11050

Colonial Gardens Kitchens
270 W. Merrick Road
Valley Stream, N. Y. 11582
Gourmet housewares

Naples Imports
P. O. Box 7533
Naples, Fla 33940
Cooking accessories

Complete Cook
405 Lake Cook Plaza
Deerfield, Ill. 60015
All cooking accessories; pots, pans, etc.

Kitchen Glamour
26770 Grand River
Detroit, Mich. 48240
Tools for cooking, baking and decorating

Vermont Country Store
Weston, Vermont 05161

Iron Craft
Freedom, N. H. 03836

Commercial Aluminum Cookware
P. O. Box 583
Toledo, Ohio 43693
Write for information on Calphalon cookware and other specialties

Utensils and Gourmet Food Sources

Paprikas Weiss Importer
1546 Second Avenue
New York, N. Y. 10028
All imported domestic and imported specialty foods; cooking utensils and accessories

Pampered Chef, Inc.
3145 Commodore Plaza
Miama, Florida 33133
All cooking accessories

Liberty
1513 Wisconsin Avenue
Washington, D. C. 20007
Gourmet, specialty foods and accessories

Bon Appetit Fine Cookware
359 Miracle Mile
Coral Gables, Florida

The Market Place
1445 Larimer Street
Denver, Colorado 80202
Gourmet and specialty foods

Faye & Allen's Foodworks
1241 Third Avenue
New York, New York 10021
A complete gourmet specialty and cooking accessory store

J. A. Demonchaux Co.
827 N. Kansas
Topeka, Kansas 66608
Cooking accessories

The Connoisseur
701 Church Street
Little Silver, N. J. 07739
Gourmet accessories

Epicurean Corner
8460 Higuera Street
Culver City, Ca. 90230

Index

Alaskan beanpot, 60
Alcohol stoves, 203
All-day biscuits, 76
Alsatian-style sauerkraut (choucroute garni); 173
Appetizers:
  banana fritters, 206
  blue cheese and beef canapés, 243
  cheese with mushrooms, 137
  chicken liver pâté, 12
  chicken wings with plum sauce, 140
  coconut cream-cheese balls, 244
  Dutch cheese steaks, 138
  fried cheese, 139
  ham'n cheese sandwich, 207
  litchi nuts stuffed with cream cheese, 245
  orange pickled herring, 246
  pepper, 208
  salmon mousse, 13
  stuffed artichokes, 205
  sweet peppers with garlic and anchovy sauce, 11
  Swiss fondue, 209
Apple(s):
  omelette flambé, 82
  pancakes, layered, 193
  stuffed baked, 236
Appliances, 202–3 (*see also* Crock plates; Deep fryers; Electric skillets; Slow cookers (crock pots); Steamer units; Sterno cookers; Toaster ovens)
Apricot glaze, 273
Armenian kebabs (shish koftesi), 117
Artichokes, stuffed, 205
Asparagus with hot butter and Parmesan cheese, 61
Avgolemono (Greek egg and lemon soup), 141

Avocado:
  and papaya salad, 247
  and tomato salad, 248

Baked beans, old-fashioned, 62
Baking over open fires, 8–9
Banana(s):
  cake, 79–80
  flambé, 195
  fritters, 206
  mafolie, 133
  and prune soufflé (soufflé de Brazil), 194
Barbecues (*see* Grills, outdoor–indoor)
Bavarian Christmas ham, 271
Bavarian cream, mocha, 199
Bayou jambalaya, 52
Bean(s):
  baked, 62
  black, with chicken cassoulet, 172
  hearty soup, 142
  kidney, chili, 51
  pasta e fagioli (pasta and beans), 66
Beanpot, Alaskan, 60
Beef:
  and blue cheese canapés, 243
  blue cheese steak, 114
  cubed steaks, 40
  fondue, 221
  green pepper steak, 41
  grilled filet mignons, 113
  minute steaks, 220
  oyster-stuffed steaks, 115
  pan-cooked steak, 163
  pastel de choclo (Venezuelan meat pie), 170
  picadillo, 44
  roast in foil, 112

(*Beef*, continued)
  rollades, peppery, 42
  shish koftesi (Armenian kebabs), 117
  South American boiled dinner, 171
  steak Diane, 219
Beignets Mamma Jeannette, 237
Belgian endives, braised, 175
Biscuit maxim, 256
Biscuits:
  all-day, 76
  crock plate, 232
  poppy seed, 231
Biscuit tortoni, 257
Black beans with chicken cassoulet, 172
Black smith pie à la forge, 258
Blue cheese:
  and beef canapés, 243
  steak, 114
Boston lettuce salad, 250
Bourbon balls, 282
Bowl braziers, 93
Brandied apricots, 273
Brandy cake à la Normande, 284
Brazier units, 92–93
Brazilian prune and banana soufflé (soufflé de Brazil), 194
Bread pudding, orange, steamed, 86
Breads:
  all-day biscuits, 76
  Cajun corn bread, 73
  currant or raisin muffin, 77
  Dutch oven dill bread, 75
  feather-light bread, 186
  French cheese gannat bread, 187
  honey "dippers," 78
  poppy seed biscuits, 231
  Sally Lunn, 188
  sour cream muffins, 189
  steamed brown bread, 74
  waffles German style, 233
Broccoli:
  and macaroni soup, 14
  salad, 146
Brown bread, steamed, 74
Brussels sprouts salad, 147
Buckwheat groats casserole, 182
Buñuelos, 190

Burrida (Genoese fish stew), 174
Butterflied pork roast, 123

Cabbage:
  and sliced pork with hot sauce, Szechuan style, 47
  stuffed, à la Cevennes, 55
Cacciucco (Italian fish stew), 22
Café au Cointreau, 88
Café Granita, 88
Café Isle Flotante, 88
Café Jamaica, 89
Cajun corn bread, 73
Cakes:
  banana, 79–80
    brandy, à la Normande, 284
  cassata alla Siciliana (Sicilian cake with chocolate frosting), 260
  custard, 262
  ice cream, 259
Calas (rice balls), 191
Candy-coated fritters, 238
Capon with apricot stuffing, 272–73
Carrot(s):
  fritters, 230
  pudding, Scandinavian, 278
  soup, cream of, 143
  spiced, 176
Cassata alla Siciliana (Sicilian cake with chocolate frosting), 260
Casseroles:
  ham and noodle, 181
  kasha (buckwheat groats), 182
Cauliflower, lemony, 126
Celery soup, cream of, 15
Charcoal:
  for fireplaces, 2, 3
  lighting, 95
Charcoal cookery devices:
  indoor, 94–95
  outdoor, 92–94
Chayotes, stuffed (chuchus recheadas), 177
Cheese:
  blue:
    and beef canapés, 243
    steak, 114
  cream (crema di ricotta), 261

INDEX

cream cheese:
  coconut balls, 244
  litchi nuts stuffed with, 245
custard (flan de queso), 85
  fried, 139
  gannat bread, French, 187
  n' ham sandwich, 207
  with mushrooms, 137
  steaks, Dutch, 138
  stuffed (keshy yena), 169
Chestnut:
  refrigerator torte, 234
  stuffing, 274–75
Chicken:
  aspic salad, 252
  baked, 31
    Spanish, 159
  bayou jambalaya, 52
  boned stuffed, 28
  cabbage stuffed, à la Cevennes, 55
  cassoulet, black beans with, 172
  with champagne, 29
  curried barbecued, 106
  East Indian saté, 121
  Ed Dzong, 35
  filé gumbo, 53
  gumbo la belle Marie, 54
  and leeks, 214
  Normandy style, 108
  Orloff, 218
  paella rustica, 49–50
  pineapple, 160
  in the pot, 30
  potted lemon, 213
  Provençale, 33–34
  and rice Español, 215
  saffron, Español, 107
  soup, 16
  in spicy sauce, 216
  from Ticino, 109
  toaster, 217
  à la Viceroy, 32
  walnut, 36
  wings with plum sauce, 140
Chicken liver pâté, 12
Chili, kidney bean, 51
Chimney cleaning, 1, 293

Chimney kits, 293
Chinese fish with pepper sauce, 149
Chinese pork kebabs, 122
Chocolate:
  fondue, 235
  loaf, Merano style (dolce di Merano), 263
  mousse (mousse au chocolat), 264
Choucroute:
  garni (sauerkraut Alsatian style), 173
  with sausage, 56
Christmas krapfen (filled Christmas doughnuts), 281
Christmas trifle, 283
Chuchus recheadas (stuffed chayotes), 177
Cinnamon syrup, 190
Coal-burning ranges (*see* Ranges, wood- or coal-burning)
"Cocambroche Four," 92
Coconut cream-cheese balls, 244
Coconut milk, 151
Coffees, dessert, 88–89
Convection ovens, 202
Cookies, versatile, 192
Cooking kettle, 93
Corn bread, Cajun, 73
Cornmeal dumplings for stews, 69
Cottage cheese pancakes with fruit sauce, 81
Covered barbecues, 93
Crabmeat, fried rice with, 71
Cranberry(ies):
  glazed, 276
  -nut pudding, 277
  with sweet potatoes, 279
Cream cheese:
  coconut balls, 244
  litchi nuts stuffed with, 245
Crema di ricotta (cheese cream), 261
Crêpes Melba, 197–98
Crock plates, 203
  biscuits, 232
  chicken Orloff, 218
  pepper appetizers, 208
Crock pots (*see* Slow cookers)
Cubed steaks, 40
Cucumber and fennel salad, 249
Currant muffins, 77
Curried barbecued chicken, 106

Curried shrimp en brochette, 104
Custard cake, 262

Dan-Bin-Lo, 93–94
Deep fryers:
    fritto misto (fried mixed vegetables), 229
    skin-fried potatoes, 228
Dessert coffees, 88–89
Desserts:
    apple omelette flambé, 82
    apple pancakes, layered, 193
    baked apples, stuffed, 236
    baked fruit Curaçao, 83
    banana cake, 79–80
    bananas flambé, 195
    beignets Mamma Jeannette, 237
    biscuit maxim, 256
    biscuit tortoni, 257
    black smith pie à la forge, 258
    bourbon balls, 282
    brandy cake à la Normande, 284
    buñuelos, 190
    calas (rice balls), 191
    candy-coated fritters, 238
    cassata alla Siciliana (Sicilian cake with chocolate frosting), 260
    chestnut refrigerator torte, 234
    chocolate fondue, 235
    Christmas krapfen (filled Christmas doughnuts), 281
    Christmas trifle, 283
    cold hazelnut soufflé, 84
    cottage cheese pancakes with fruit sauce, 81
    crema di ricotta (cheese cream), 261
    crêpes Melba, 197–98
    custard cake, 262
    dolce di Merano (chocolate loaf, Merano style), 263
    flan de queso (cheese custard), 85
    ice cream cake, 259
    mocha Bavarian cream, 199
    mousse au chocolat (chocolate mousse), 264
    mousse royal mold, 265
    orange mousse, 266
    rice fritters, 239
    soufflé de Brazil (Brazilian prune and banana soufflé), 194
    steamed orange bread pudding, 86
    strawberries Romanoff, 267
    strawberry flummery, 268
    strawberry tart, 196
    versatile cookies, 192
    walnut pudding, 87
"Diffuseur, Le," 203
Dill bread, Dutch oven, 75
Dilled potatoes, 131
Dolce di Merano (chocolate loaf, Merano style), 263
Doughnuts, Christmas (krapfen), 281
Duck:
    with olive sauce, 161
    with oranges, 162
    roast, 37–38
Dumplings for stews, 70
    cornmeal, 69
Dutch cheese steaks, 138
Dutch oven dill bread, 75

East Indian saté, 121
Ecuadorian potato pancakes with poached eggs (llapingachos), 21
Egg and lemon soup, Greek (avgolemono), 41
Eggnog, ice cream, 288
Eggplants, stuffed, 178
Eggs:
    Bercy, 19
    en cocotte, 20
    Florentine, 18
    llapingachos (Ecuadorian potato pancakes with poached eggs), 21
    poached, with potato pancakes, 21
Electric barbecues, 95
Electric skillets, 203
    banana fritters, 206
    chicken in spicy sauce, 216
    desserts:
        beignets Mamma Jeannette, 237
        candy-coated fritters, 238
        rice fritters, 239
    meats:
        Greek meat patties, 222
        piccata di vitello (veal in lemon sauce), 223
        pork chops Melmo, 226
        steak Diane, 219
        veal steak, 224

INDEX

vegetables:
   carrot fritters, 230
   fritto misto (fried mixed vegetables), 229
   skin-fried potatoes, 228
Electric woks, 203
Endives, braised Belgian, 175

Feather-light bread, 186
Fennel:
   and cucumber salad, 249
   vegetables with, 128
Fettucine with nut sauce, 68
Filé gumbo, 53
Filet mignons, grilled, 113
Fire building, 5
Fireplace coffee, basic, 88
Fireplaces, 1–89
  accessories and utensils, 3–4
  appetizers:
    chicken liver pâté, 12
    salmon mousse, 13
    sweet peppers with garlic and anchovy sauce, 11
  breads:
    all-day biscuits, 76
    Cajun corn bread, 73
    currant or raisin muffins, 77
    Dutch oven dill bread, 75
    honey "dippers," 78
    steamed brown bread, 74
  building fires, 5
  buying, 1–2
  chimney cleaning, 1, 293
  cooking over open fires, 7–9
  dessert coffees, 88–89
  desserts:
    apple omelette flambé, 82
    baked fruit Curaçao, 83
    banana cake, 79–80
    brandy cake à la Normande, 284
    cold hazelnut soufflé, 84
    cottage cheese pancakes with fruit sauce, 81
    flan de queso (cheese custard), 85
    steamed orange bread pudding, 86
    walnut pudding, 87
  eggs:
    Bercy, 19
    en cocotte, 20
    Florentine, 18
    llapingachos (Ecuadorian potato pancakes with poached eggs), 21
    potato pancakes with poached eggs, 21
  fish and seafood:
    bayou jambalaya, 52
    cacciucco (Italian fish stew), 22
    deep-fried stuffed shrimp, 27
    filé gumbo, 53
    gumbo la belle Marie, 54
    paella rustica, 49–50
    sautéed fillets of sole, 23
    shad Provençale, 24
    shrimp boiled in beer, 25
    shrimp creole, 26
  fuel, 2–3
  grates, 2
  holiday favorites:
    Bavarian Christmas ham, 271
    brandy cake à la Normande, 284
    glazed cranberries, 276
    glee wine (glühwein), 285
    krambambuli, 287
    Swedish glögg, 286
  installation of, 2
  iron pots, 4–5
  meats:
    cubed steaks, 40
    diced pork and cabbage with hot sauce, Szechuan style, 47
    green pepper steak, 41
    meatballs Götteborg, 43
    peppery beef rollades, 42
    picadillo, 44
    ribs à la Burgundy, 39
    stuffed pork shoulder, 46
    sweet & sour spareribs, 48
    Veona's veal and pineapples, 45
  pasta, grains, and rice:
    fettucine with nut sauce, 68
    fried rice with crabmeat and green peas, 71
    pasta e fagioli (pasta and beans), 66
    risotto with mushrooms, 72
    Roman pasta, 67
    stew dumplings, 69–70
  poultry:
    baked chicken, 31

(*Fireplaces*, continued)
    boned stuffed chicken, 28
    chicken with champagne, 29
    chicken Ed Dzong, 35
    chicken in the pot, 30
    chicken Provençale, 33–34
    chicken à la Viceroy, 32
    roast duckling, 37–38
    walnut chicken, 36
  smoking, control of, 6
  soups:
    broccoli and macaroni, 14
    chicken, 16
    cream of celery, 15
    meatball, with pistou, 17
  sources of, 292–93
  stews:
    Alaskan beanpot, 60
    bayou jambalaya, 52
    cacciucco (Italian fish stew), 22
    choucroute with sausage, 56
    dumplings for, 69, 70
    filé gumbo, 53
    gumbo la belle Marie, 54
    hearty thick, 59
    kidney bean chili, 51
    paella rustica, 49–50
    pork pilau, 58
    pork and vegetables, 57
    stuffed cabbage à la Cevennes, 55
  vegetables:
    asparagus with hot butter and Parmesan cheese, 61
    baked sweet potatoes or yams, 65
    fried potato cake, 63
    hash brown potatoes, 64
    old-fashioned baked beans, 62
Fish:
  baked, in coconut sauce, 151
  burrida (Genoese fish stew), 174
  cacciucco (Italian fish stew), 22
  Chinese, with pepper sauce, 149
  fillets of sole:
    Burgundy style, 152
    à la crème, 154
    sautéed, 23
    in white wine, 153
  fish foil packages, 100
  grilled, 97
  Peruvian medley, 156
  red snapper:
    spit-roasted, 90
    tropical, 150
  shad Provençale, 24
  steamed, with seafood and vegetables, 210
  stuffed flounder, 99
  stuffed yellowtail, 211
  trout amandine, 155
Flan de queso (cheese custard), 85
Flounder, stuffed, 99
Fondues:
  beef, 221
  chocolate, 235
  seafood, 212
  Swiss, 209
Franklin stoves, 6–7, 8
  recipes (*see* Fireplaces)
  sources of, 291–92
Freestanding fireplaces, 293
French cheese gannat bread, 187
Fritters:
  banana, 206
  candy-coated, 238
  carrot, 230
  rice, 239
Fritto misto (fried mixed vegetables), 229
Fruit Curaçao, baked, 83

Garden salad mold, 254
Gas barbecues, 95
Genoese fish stew (burrida), 174
German-style waffles, 233
Glee wine (glühwein), 285
Glögg, Swedish, 286
Goose, roast, with chestnut stuffing, 274–75
Greek egg and lemon soup (avgolemono), 141
Greek meat patties, 222
Green peas, fried rice with, 71
Green pepper(s):
  with garlic and anchovy sauce, 11
  steak, 41
Griddles, 202–3
Grills, outdoor-indoor, 91–133
  care of, 96
  charcoal cookery devices:
    indoor, 94–95
    outdoor, 92–94

INDEX

desserts: bananas mafolie, 133
fish and seafood:
  curried shrimp en brochettes, 104
  fish foil packages, 100
  grilled fish, 97
  grilled shrimp, 101
  Mongolian hot pot, 105
  shrimp Italiano, 102
  shrimp Pierre, 103
  spit-roasted red snapper, 98
  stuffed flounder, 99
meats:
  blue cheese steak, 114
  butterflied pork roast, 123
  Chinese pork kebabs, 122
  East Indian saté, 121
  grilled filet mignons, 113
  grilled lamb roast, 118
  ham steak barbecue, 125
  Hawaiian meatballs on skewers, 116
  lamb shish kebabs, 119
  Macedonian shish kebabs, 120
  maple-flavored barbecue spareribs, 124
  oyster-stuffed steaks, 115
  roast in foil, 112
  shish koftesi (Armenian kebabs), 117
poultry:
  barbecued turkey thighs, 111
  chicken Normandy style, 108
  chicken from Ticino, 109
  curried barbecued chicken, 106
  grilled turkey, 110
  saffron chicken Español, 107
preparation for cooking, 95–96
sources of, 293–94
vegetables:
  baked potatoes with bacon and cheese, 130
  baked sweet potatoes or yams, 132
  deep-fried zucchini, 129
  dilled potatoes, 131
  with fennel, 128
  herbed, 127
  lemony cauliflower, 126
Gumbo:
  filé, 53
  la belle Marie, 54

Ham:
  Bavarian Christmas, 271
  n' cheese sandwich, 207
  and noodle casserole, 181
  steak barbecue, 125
Hash brown potatoes, 64
Hawaiian meatballs on skewers, 116
Hazelnut soufflé, cold, 84
Hearty bean soup, 142
Hearty Italian soup (minestrone), 144
Herbed vegetables, 127
Herring, orange pickled, 246
Hibachis, 91, 94, 95
Holiday favorites, 269–88
  Bavarian Christmas ham, 271
  bourbon balls, 282
  brandy cake à la Normande, 284
  capon with apricot stuffing, 272–73
  Christmas krapfen (filled Christmas doughnuts), 281
  Christmas trifle, 283
  cranberried sweet potatoes, 279
  glazed cranberries, 276
  glee wine (glühwein), 285
  ice cream eggnog, 288
  krambambuli, 287
  nut-cranberry pudding, 277
  roast goose with chestnut stuffing, 274–75
  Scandinavian carrot pudding, 278
  Swedish glögg, 286
  Yorkshire pudding, 280
Honey "dippers," 78

Ice cream:
  cake, 259
  eggnog, 288
Insalata broccoli (broccoli salad), 146
Iron pots, 4–5
Italian fish stew (cacciucco), 22
Italian soup, hearty (minestrone), 144

Japanese cooking equipment, 94

Kasha casserole (buckwheat groats casserole), 182
Kerosene stoves, 203
Keshy yena (stuffed cheese), 169
Kidney bean chili, 51
Krambambuli, 287
Krapfen, Christmas (filled doughnuts), 281

Lamb:
  East Indian saté, 121
  roast, grilled, 118
  shanks, 225
  shish kebab, 119
    Macedonian, 120
Leeks and chicken, 214
Lemon chicken, potted, 213
Litchi nuts stuffed with cream cheese, 245
Little-or-no-cook recipes, 241–68
  appetizers:
    blue cheese and beef canapés, 243
    coconut cream-cheese balls, 244
    litchi nuts stuffed with cream cheese, 245
    orange pickled herring, 246
  desserts:
    biscuit maxim, 256
    biscuit tortoni, 257
    black smith pie à la forge, 238
    bourbon balls, 282
    cassata alla Siciliana (Sicilian cake with chocolate frosting), 260
    Christmas trifle, 283
    crema di ricotta (cheese cream), 261
    custard cake, 262
    dolce di Merano (chocolate loaf, Merano style), 263
    ice cream cake, 259
    mousse au chocolat (chocolate mousse), 264
    mousse royal mold, 265
    orange mousse, 266
    strawberries Romanoff, 267
    strawberry flummery, 268
  salads and vegetables:
    avocado and papaya, 247
    avocado and tomato, 248
    Boston lettuce, 250
    chicken aspic, 252
    fennel and cucumber, 249
    garden salad mold, 254
    salad Español, 251
    turkey with pineapple–horseradish sauce, 253
  special minute rice, 255
Llapingachos (Ecuadorian potato pancakes with poached eggs), 21
Lobsters, scampi fra Vintone, 157

Macaroni and broccoli soup, 14
Maple-flavored barbecue spareribs, 124
Meatball(s):
  Götteborg, 43
  Hawaiian, on skewers, 116
  soup with pistou, 17
Meat patties, Greek, 222
Meat pie, Venezuelan (pastel de choclo), 170
Microwave ovens, 202
Minestrone (hearty Italian soup), 144
Minute steaks, 220
Mocha Bavarian cream, 199
Mongolian hot pot (device), 93–94
Mongolian hot pot (recipe), 105
Mousse:
  au chocolat (chocolate mousse), 264
  orange, 266
  royal mold, 265
  salmon, 13
Muffins:
  currant or raisin, 77
  sour cream, 189
Mushrooms:
  with cheese, 137
  with risotto, 72

Neapolitan bean bake, 227
Newspaper log rollers, 293
No-cook recipes (see Little-or-no-cook recipes)
Noodle casserole with ham, 181
Nut–cranberry pudding, 277

Old-fashioned baked beans, 62
Open-fire cooking, 7–9 (see also Fireplaces)
Orange:
  bread pudding, steamed, 86
  mousse, 266
  pickled herring, 246
Oyster-stuffed steaks, 115

Paella rustica, 49–50
Pancakes:
  cottage cheese, with fruit sauce, 81
  layered apple, 193
Papaya and avocado salad, 247
Pasta:
  fettucine with nut sauce, 68
  ham and noodle casserole, 181
  pasta e fagioli (pasta and beans), 66
  Roman, 67

INDEX

Pastel de choclo (Venezuelan meat pie), 170
Pâté, chicken liver, 12
Pepper(s):
  appetizers, 208
  steak, 41
  stuffed, 164
  sweet, with garlic and anchovy sauce, 11
Peppery beef rollades, 42
Peruvian fish medley, 156
Picadillo, 44
Piccata di vitello (veal in lemon sauce), 223
Pilaf, fast, 184
Pineapple(s):
  chicken, 160
  –horseradish sauce, 253
  Veona's veal and, 45
Pistou, 17
Plum sauce, 140
Poppy seed biscuits, 231
Pork:
  chops:
    Margarita, 167
    Melmo, 226
  East Indian saté, 121
  hearty thick stew, 59
  kebabs, Chinese, 122
  Neapolitan bean bake, 227
  pilau, 58
  roast, butterflied, 123
  sausage with choucroute, 56
  shoulder, stuffed, 46
  sliced, and cabbage with hot sauce, Szechuan style, 47
  spareribs (*see* Spareribs)
  stuffed scallopini of, Marengo, 166
  and vegetables, 57
Portable ovens, 203
Potato(es):
  baked, with bacon and cheese, 130
  cake, fried, 63
  dilled, 131
  hash brown, 64
  llapingachos (Ecuadorian potato pancakes with poached eggs), 21
  skin-fried, 228
  sweet:
    baked, 65, 132

    cranberried, 279
    orange, 180
Pots, iron, 4–5
Poultry:
  capon with apricot stuffing, 272–73
  roast goose with chestnut stuffing, 274–75
  (*see also* Chicken; Duck; Turkey)
Primus stoves, 203
Prune and banana soufflé (Soufflé de Brazil), 194
Puddings:
  bread, steamed orange, 86
  nut–cranberry, 277
  Scandinavian carrot, 278
  walnut, 87
  Yorkshire, 280

Radar ovens, 202
Raisin muffins, 77
Ranges, wood or coal-burning, 135–99
  appetizers:
    cheese with mushrooms, 137
    chicken wings with plum sauce, 140
    Dutch cheese steaks, 138
    fried cheese, 139
  breads:
    feather-light, 186
    French cheese gannat, 187
    Sally Lunn, 188
    sour cream muffins, 189
  desserts:
    bananas flambé, 195
    brandy cake à la Normande, 284
    buñuelos, 190
    calas (rice balls), 191
    crepes Melba, 197–98
    layered apple pancakes, 193
    mocha Bavarian cream, 199
    soufflé de Brazil (Brazilian prune and banana soufflé), 194
    strawberry tart, 196
    versatile cookies, 192
  fish and seafood:
    baked fish in coconut sauce, 151
    burrida (Genoese fish stew), 174
    Chinese fish with pepper sauce, 149
    fillets of sole Burgundy style, 152
    fillets of sole à la crème, 154
    fillets of sole in white wine, 153

(*Ranges*, continued)
    Peruvian fish medley, 156
    red snapper tropical, 149, 150
    scampi fra Vintone, 157
    shrimp risotto with curry, 185
    shrimp Tolliver, 158
    trout amandine, 155
  holiday favorites:
    brandy cake à la Normande, 284
    Christmas krapfen (filled Christmas doughnuts), 281
    cranberried sweet potatoes, 279
    cranberry–nut pudding, 277
    glazed cranberries, 276
    glee wine (glühwein), 285
    krambambuli, 287
    Scandinavian carrot pudding, 278
    Swedish glögg, 286
    Yorkshire pudding, 280
  meats:
    pan-cooked steak, 163
    pork chops Margarita, 167
    scallopini of veal with Marsala, 165
    stuffed peppers, 164
    stuffed scallopini of pork Marengo, 166
    sweet and sour spareribs, 168
  pasta, grains, and rice:
    fast rice pilaf, 184
    ham and noodle casserole, 181
    kasha casserole (buckwheat groats casserole), 182
    rice Venetian style, 183
    shrimp risotto with curry, 185
  poultry:
    baked Spanish chicken, 159
    duck with olive sauce, 161
    duck with oranges, 162
    pineapple chicken, 160
  salads:
    Brussels sprouts, 147
    insalata di broccoli (broccoli salad), 146
    Russian, 148
  soups:
    avgolemono (Greek egg and lemon), 141
    cream of carrot, 143
    hearty bean, 142
    minestrone (hearty Italian), 144
    sour and hot, 145
  sources of, 291–92, 293
  stews:
    black beans with chicken cassoulet, 172
    burrida (Genoese fish stew), 174
    choucroute garni (sauerkraut Alsatian style), 173
    keshy yena (stuffed cheese), 169
    pastel de choclo (Venezuelan meat pie), 170
    South American boiled dinner, 171
  temperature determination, 135–36
  vegetables:
    braised Belgian endives, 175
    chuchus recheadas (stuffed chayotes), 177
    spiced carrots, 176
    spinach soufflé, 179
    stuffed eggplants, 178
    sweet potatoes orangé, 180
Red currant glaze, 196
Red snapper:
  spit roasted, 98
  tropical, 150
Rice:
  balls (calas), 191
  and chicken Español, 215
  fast pilaf, 184
  fried, with crabmeat and green peas, 71
  fritters, 239
  minute, 255
  with mushrooms, 72
  shrimp risotto with curry, 185
  Venetian style, 183
Risotto with mushrooms, 72
Roman pasta, 67
Russian salad, 148

Saffron chicken Español, 107
Salad Español, 251
Salads:
  avocado and papaya, 247
  avocado and tomato, 248
  Boston lettuce, 250
  Brussels sprouts, 147
  chicken aspic, 252
  fennel and cucumber, 249
  garden salad mold, 254
  insalata di broccoli, 146
  Russian, 148
  salad Español, 251
  turkey with pineapple–horseradish sauce, 253

INDEX

Sally Lunn, 188
Salmon mousse, 13
Sauerkraut:
    Alsatian style (choucroute garni), 173
    with sausage, 56
Sausage with sauerkraut, 56
Scampi fra Vintone, 157
Scandinavian carrot pudding, 278
Seafood:
    filé gumbo, 53
    fondue, 212
    gumbo la belle Marie, 54
    paella rustica, 49–50
    steamed, with fish and vegetables, 210
    (*see also* Fish; Shrimp)
Shad Provençale, 24
Shish kebabs, 119
    Macedonian, 120
Shish koftesi (Armenian kebabs), 117
Shrimp:
    boiled in beer, 25
    creole, 26
    curried, en brochette, 104
    deep-fried stuffed, 27
    grilled, 101
    Italiano, 102
    Pierre, 103
    risotto with curry, 185
    Tolliver, 158
Sicilian cake with chocolate frosting (cassata alla Siciliana), 260
Skillets (*see* Electric skillets)
Skin-fried potatoes, 228
Slow cookers (crock pots), 203
    chicken:
        and leeks, 214
        potted lemon, 213
    meats:
        lamb shanks, 225
        Neopolitan bean bake, 227
Sole, fillets of:
    Burgundy style, 152
    à la crème, 154
    sautéed, 23
    in white wine, 153
Soufflés:
    de Brazil (Brazilian prune and banana), 194
    hazelnut, cold, 84
    spinach, 179

Soups:
    avgolemono (Greek egg and lemon), 141
    broccoli and macaroni, 14
    chicken, 16
    cream of carrot, 143
    cream of celery, 15
    hearty bean, 142
    meatball, with pistou, 17
    minestrone (hearty Italian), 144
    sour and hot, 145
Sour and hot soup, 145
Sour cream muffins, 189
South American boiled dinner, 171
Spanish chicken, baked, 159
Spareribs:
    à la Burgundy, 39
    maple-flavored, 124
    sweet & sour, 48, 168
Spinach soufflé, 179
Spit roasting (*see* Grills, outdoor–indoor)
Steak:
    blue cheese, 114
    cubed, 40
    Diane, 219
    green pepper, 41
    grilled filet mignons, 113
    minute, 220
    oyster-stuffed, 115
    pan-cooked, 163
Steamer units, 203
    chicken and rice Español, 215
    steamed fish, seafood and vegetables, 216
Sterno cookers, 203
    beef fondue, 221
    chocolate fondue, 235
    seafood fondue, 212
    Swiss fondue, 209
Stews:
    Alaskan beanpot, 60
    bayou jambalaya, 52
    black beans with chicken cassoulet, 172
    burrida (Genoese style stew), 174
    cacciucco (Italian fish stew), 22
    choucroute garni (sauerkraut, Alsatian style), 173
    choucroute with sausage, 56
    dumplings for, 69, 70
    filé gumbo, 53
    gumbo la belle Marie, 54

(*Stews*, continued)
  hearty thick, 59
  keshy yena (stuffed cheese), 169
  kidney bean chili, 51
  paella rustica, 49–50
  pastel de choclo (Venezuelan meat pie), 170
  pork pilau, 58
  pork and vegetables, 57
  South American boiled dinner, 171
  stuffed cabbage à la Cevennes, 55
Stoves, conventional, 201–2
  beef fondue, 221
  chicken and leeks, 214
  desserts:
    beignets Mamma Jeannette, 237
    candy-coated fritters, 238
    chestnut refrigerator torte, 234
    chocolate fondue, 235
    rice fritters, 239
  lamb shanks, 225
  Neapolitan bean bake, 227
  seafood fondue, 212
  Swiss fondue, 209
Stoves, wood- or coal-burning (*see* Ranges, wood- or coal-burning)
Stove-top ovenette, 203
Strawberry(ies):
  flummery, 268
  Romanoff, 267
  tart, 196
Stuffing:
  apricot, 272–73
  chestnut, 274–75
Swedish glögg, 286
Sweet & sour spareribs, 48, 168
Sweet peppers with garlic and anchovy sauce, 11
Sweet potatoes:
  baked, 65, 132
  cranberried, 279
  orangé, 180
Swiss fondue, 209
Szechuan-style sliced pork and cabbage with hot sauce, 47

Table-top braziers, 93
Toaster ovens:
  ham 'n cheese sandwich, 207

minute steaks, 220
poppy seed biscuits, 231
stuffed artichokes, 205
stuffed baked apples, 236
stuffed yellowtail, 217
toaster chicken, 217
waffles German style, 233
Tomato and avocado salad, 248
Torte, chestnut refrigerator, 234
Trifle, Christmas, 283
Trout amandine, 155
Turkey:
  barbecued thighs, 111
  grilled, 110
  salad with pineapple–horseradish sauce, 253

Veal:
  piccata di vitello (veal in lemon sauce), 223
  scallopini of, with Marsala, 165
  steak, 224
  Veona's, with pineapples, 45
Vegetables:
  asparagus with hot butter and Parmesan cheese, 61
  baked potatoes with bacon and cheese, 130
  baked sweet potatoes or yams, 65, 132
  braised Belgian endives, 175
  carrot fritters, 230
  chuchus recheadas (stuffed chayotes), 177
  deep-fried zucchini, 129
  dilled potatoes, 131
  with fennel, 128
  fried potato cake, 63
  fritto misto (fried mixed vegetables), 229
  hash brown potatoes, 64
  herbed, 127
  lemony cauliflower, 126
  old-fashioned baked beans, 62
  skin-fried potatoes, 228
  spiced carrots, 176
  spinach soufflé, 179
  stuffed eggplants, 178
  sweet potatoes orangé, 180
Venezuelan meat pie (pastel de choclo), 170
Veona's veal and pineapples, 45
Versatile cookies, 192
Viennese Cappuccino, 88

INDEX

Waffles German style, 233
Walnut:
  chicken, 36
  pudding, 87
Woks, 203
Wood for fireplaces and Franklin stoves, 2–3
Wood-burning ranges (*see* Ranges, wood- or coal-burning)

Yams, baked, 65, 132
Yellowtail, stuffed, 211
Yorkshire pudding, 280

Zucchini, deep-fried, 129